THE VIEW
BENEATH

THE VIEW
BENEATH

MISHEL MCCUMBER

The View Beneath
Copyright © Michelle McCumber 2016
All rights reserved
Published by: Mighty Roar Books, 2016, Canada.

ISBN: 978-0-9950607-08

Mishel McCumber has asserted her right to identify as the author of this work. This book is a work of non-fiction. The conversations in this book come from the author's recollections and are not written to represent word-for-word transcripts. Rather, the author has retold them in a way that evokes the feeling and meaning of what was said and in all instances, the essence of the dialogue is accurate. The events are portrayed to the best of the author's memory. While all the stories in this book are true, some names have been changed to protect the privacy of the people involved.

Cover and Interior Design: Mishel McCumber

Printed in the United States of America

To Donna: You are the best, best-friend ever. Here's to long talks and large phone bills. You are awesome.

To Mom: You grab each day and live it to the fullest. Here's to ziplining and rollercoasters. You inspire me!

CONTENTS

ONE
THE VIEW BENEATH

I don't remember much about my grandfather, only that the family whispered in their talk of him. How odd that this dark, enigmatic figure, a man I now barely recall, could have affected my life so. Now deceased, he is still imprisoned in my mind, frozen in time by the memory of an incident long ago.

My grandfather and I are in a canoe. I stare into the murky water, fascinated by the weeds waving like ghosts in the darkness. As we glide toward the center of the lake, the water blackens beneath us. An eerie quietness creeps across the boat. I peer into the water, straining to see into the darkness below. I am frightened.

My grandfather shifts his weight causing the boat to bounce from side to side. The water swells outward into dark rolling rings. He smiles, "It's bottomless," he whispers.

I am frantic now. I begin to cry. I look back toward the shore anxiously, "Grandpa, please!" My grandfather laughs, then placing his calloused hands on either side of the boat, begins to rock it back and forth. The canoe tumbles awkwardly from side to side—slowly at first, then faster and faster. I scream. Agitated water pours over the sides of the boat sloshing noisily across its steel belly.

My mother is on the shore now, screaming at her father, pleading with him to bring me back. He stops. The boat bobs on the surface for a minute then settles quietly. My screaming dwindles to a whimper. I look up at my grandfather, my eyes full of tears, nose running. There is no remorse.

I have no other recollection of my grandfather—well, perhaps a glimpse here or there. I remember he always wore dark clothes—and a hat. I remember a hat. I have never actually been sure if I recall his features or merely remember seeing his picture. He died when I was six.

The house felt peculiar after my grandfather's death. Strangers came and went, whispering and wagging their heads. I recall women, hair pulled into buns under church hats with veils—bushy-browed faces, ashen and sour, whispering, "Terrible, terrible, terrible." I was well accustomed to plainness. God demanded it. Our religion was a dark, colorless world—bland as egg whites, humorless.

It was an odd world that my grandfather had ordered for his children —a world in which sinless perfection was both strived for and expected. He called his quest for perfection, the "second blessing." His family called it madness.

It had started innocently enough with the gift of some books given to him by a misguided, but presumably well-meaning, minister. They were authored by the late R.C. Horner. If only someone had warned my grandfather that the words he was about to consume would later consume him.

R.C. Horner was a third-generation farmer from the Quebec side of the Ottawa Valley. He was converted in a Methodist Camp Meeting in 1872 and subsequently became a minister in the Methodist Church.[1] At that time, the Methodist Church was the largest Protestant denomination in Canada, and internal dissension began to fester concerning R.C. Horner.

Horner's career with the Methodist Church was as turbulent as it was short-lived. Criticism of his methods, teachings, and doctrines led to him being unceremoniously ousted and his later refusal to submit to church discipline only served to increase the schism between himself and the Methodists. Instead of submitting to discipline, Horner thumbed his nose at them and in 1895 formed his own denomination. He called it the Holiness Movement. Its membership was sparse at best and was mostly confined to rural Ontario, upstate New York and parts of the Canadian Prairies. When Horner's leadership of this fledgling movement was challenged a mere five years later, he formed yet *another* church—the

---

1. "The Origins in Revival"

Standard Church of America.[2] It was into the Standard Church that my grandfather and his family would eventually tumble.

Horner believed in a second work of Grace in which one could be cleansed of the carnal nature entirely. He exhorted his followers to strive continually for sinless perfection.[3] To achieve and stay in this blessed state required intense, sustained effort, and constant self-repudiation. Of course, striving for perfection in our own flesh can never end well. My grandfather was no exception.

In the days before his death, my grandfather's religious fervor intensified. Everything became a sin. He required perfection from himself and demanded it from others. It was as if his striving would somehow win God's favor, make him more acceptable, more needed—loved. He needed a simplified world, a predictable world, a world of black and white. He needed to rid himself of the tyranny of color.

When his family recoiled from his excessive demands for outward holiness and inward perfection, he tried harder. When he perceived they had fallen into sin, he felt he had failed. He needed to control his world—he needed to conform it to *his* image and to *his* standards. His world and *all* those in it had to fit within the confines of his narrow ideal. It was a very tight fit.

Unable to cope with the world he had created, he readied his affairs, quit his job and sold the family farm. Without my grandmother's knowledge, he purchased a house and placed the remaining money in an account in her name.

My grandmother, sensing impending tragedy, was frantic. She pleaded for help from the church but was brushed aside like a bothersome fly. She watched my grandfather day after day, never leaving him alone until convinced the danger had passed. He seemed more relaxed, more at peace. When he asked her one day to make the trek up the laneway to retrieve the mail, she did so without hesitation.

She was returning from the mailbox when she heard the shotgun blast. She ran toward the farmhouse scattering mail across the laneway. Desperately, she ran through the house racing through the rooms in her frantic search—nothing. She ran from the house to the barn. When she opened the door, she stopped, unable to move in the horror of it all.

---

2. Sturgeon, B. 2008
3. Synan, V. 1997

Her beloved husband lay dead, twisted in the hay—his hunting rifle by his side.

Sometimes I think about my grandfather; about the black rings of water rolling outward from the jostled canoe. I think about my fear of being swallowed by the dark water— consumed and forgotten.

In many ways, my sojourn was similar to my grandfather's, although it certainly *ended* quite differently. Regardless, it was a descent into religious deception that took years to unravel. We called it the River of God. It wasn't. It was more a foul mixture of prophecy, mysticism, Gnosticism, and Neo-Pentecostal Dominionism. Once submerged, I was conditioned to accept the distorted world I saw looking up through these squalid waters. This is the story of the view from beneath. This is *my* story.

TWO
THE WANDERER

In the years following my grandfather's death, the vestiges of his fanaticism clung like grave clothes to the lives of those who had loved him. When truth and error are entwined, it is often hard to tell one from the other. While my mother rejected conspicuous extremes, she still felt that adherence to outward holiness would win her favor with God and man—mostly man.

Keeping outwardly holy was a very fine line to her. One button on a blouse could mean the difference between holiness and whoredom. Small earrings might be okay, maybe, but larger ones would *certainly* evoke the wrath of God.

My mother described herself as plain, and while I loved her fiercely, we often clashed. Her feet were firmly planted. She was down-to-earth and full of common sense—driven by a sense of duty. I was an idealistic dreamer, creative and easily distracted. If my mother was the salt of the earth, then I was the clouds in the sky—open and expansive, with incurable wanderlust.

From the time of my birth, my family attended the Free Methodist Church in our small, sleepy town. My father liked to boast that the beams for our church were hewn from the trees felled at his father's farm.

My mother was a teacher. She had explained to me the history of the Free Methodist Church and how it was formed as a protest against the lax morals of the church hierarchy in the Methodist Episcopal Church. They wanted a return to the strict morals central to the roots of

Methodism. The word, "free" had been adopted to denounce the practice of allowing wealthy congregants to purchase or rent pews for congregational worship.[1]

Our universe revolved around this church. The members grew up and raised their families together, bound by a sense of honor, and commitment. In times of sickness the front door would open to arms bearing casseroles, and there were always hands to help if the roof needed mending or the house needed repairs. In the summer, the church would have bonfires and corn roasts, and in the winter, we would toboggan on snow laden hills and skate on home-made ice-rinks. It was the church of storybooks and postcards, but *something* was missing for me.

Most did not enjoy church. They were like conch shells washed up on sun-bleached beaches, the creature within having long since died. I hated the staunch and starchy atmosphere of people who smiled stiffly—who slid into pews with a scowl and folded arms. There they would sit, sighing, crossing and uncrossing their legs until the closing hymn was sung. Then, like seeds in the spring that had weathered the winter, they would magically spring to life.

Church seemed like a curious ritual, and its real meaning was lost on me. My faith didn't appear to be a real *relationship*, but something I had to earn. If I did *this*, I would win the love of God and the acceptance of my peers. If I did *that*, I would be punished by the wrath of God and shunned by all I held dear. God seemed only available to me at select times and in select places. It seemed to me that we went to church to meet with God, but when the church service was over, we turned the lights out, locked the doors and left Him there. I felt sorry for Him, alone in that darkened church.

As a young child, a portion of my summer was always spent at Orland Church Camp. On the first night, we would have a campfire, sing songs, and roast hot dogs. As the evening progressed, our songs would become sillier and sillier, and we would shriek and giggle as the fire snapped, sending showers of sparks flying upward to Heaven.

In the mornings, we would wake, sun pouring through the windows in our musty cottages. After trips to the bathrooms, where our teeth were brushed and faces washed, we would clump together on the grass outside the dining hall and wait for the ringing of the breakfast bell.

---

1. Howland, C.L. 1953

In the afternoons, we would rush to the swimming hole, a cold, muddy creek full of tadpoles, weeds, and leeches. It was far too small for the clotting of camp kids that would throng there on August afternoons, but it never seemed to bother us. We would have gladly swum in a paper cup if we had fit.

The tabernacle was the focus and rallying point for the camp. It was a long, primitive wooden structure flanked by banks of windows with heavy shutters that could be lifted and propped open with a stick. I can remember smelling wood chip floors and wearing light cotton dresses that clung to the hard wooden benches in the summer's heat.

The edges of my memory have frayed, but I remember one night walking down the dirt pathway to the Tabernacle, pine needles crunching underfoot. It was late and the lights streaming from the Tabernacle into the darkness beyond cast an ethereal glow. It made the tired wooden structure look like the pictures of Noah's Ark I'd seen in my Bible story books.

As I got closer, I could hear the wailing and sobbing of children. I pulled open the heavy wooden door, and there was my older brother along with several other children, weeping. They were crying out in repentance, some walking and praying, others prostrate before the altar. I stopped and stood for a moment, a sudden and peculiar sweetness spreading over me. It was in that small fragment of time that I was unmistakably *sure* of being wholly and completely loved by God.

I don't know how long I was there, but I do remember the pastor giving me tissues, which I drenched with my tears. It was there, in that old Tabernacle, nestled among pine trees and clouds of black flies that I experienced the God I would later long to find.

It was the 70's and the clash between rigid social norms, and extreme liberalism was in full swing. It was the era of hippies, LSD, women's liberation and the sexual revolution. I was protected here— too young to understand how the world was changing or to realize that things would not always be as they were now.

THREE
PINNING PAPER LEAVES

I am alone in my college dorm room in Toronto when the call comes.

"Mishel?"

"Yes," I answer hesitantly, trying to place the voice.

"Uh, this is Raegan, from school, high-school, do you remember?"[1] I pause, knowing the name but not recalling her face. "From Mr. Ingram's Communication class," she adds, "remember?"

"Uh, oh, yes! I *do* remember. How *are* you?"

"Umm … I'm fine, I'm all right. I bet you are wondering why I'm calling you. Well, I've been going to church—I got saved!"

"You got saved?" I ask incredulously, suddenly fearing that I am about to be proselytized.

"Yeah, I wanted to talk to you about that."

"You wanted to talk to me about *that?*" I stall for time to think before answering. "Look, I'm not into Jesus, I grew up in church, okay? I've been there, done that, and I'm *really* not interested."

"That's all right," she insists, "could I come see you anyway? I don't have a car, but if I take the bus, maybe you could meet me at the Scarborough bus station? I could be there by two o'clock tomorrow afternoon."

Suddenly I'm fearful. "Well yes, I could meet you, but you are not coming here to try to convert me are you? I don't *want* Jesus, and I don't want to talk about any of that stuff! Really, I *mean* it!"

---

1. Not her real name

"No, no, I just want to come see you. Is that okay?"

"Well yeah ... I guess. So, I am meeting you at two tomorrow afternoon?"

"Yeah."

"And you won't talk to me about Jesus?"

"Not a word."

Of course, she *was* there to talk to me about Jesus. She visited me that week and almost every week after that. She left witnessing tracks on my bed and little Bible verses on my mirrors that I had to squint to read. I got letters, too; letters with Scripture, letters of encouragement, letters telling me she was praying—that her entire youth group was praying. I'm not sure why, but somehow it enraged me. I told her so, too. How dare her youth group pray for me without my permission!

I am sitting in a restaurant eating dessert. Raegan eyes me sympathetically. "Are you *happy?*" she asks."

"Sure, ecstatic," I grin, sliding a bite of cheesecake off my fork with my teeth.

"No, I mean, you know, with life in general."

"Oh *well*, look at you waxing philosophical. Yes, I'm happy."

"You don't *seem* happy," she says, looking over her glasses in a way that makes her look far too old for her age.

"How can you *say* that?" I react, wounded. "I have a good job. I'm managing over two hundred people! Oh, and I'm putting myself through school!"

"And you drink too much." She looks around cautiously to be sure no one can hear. "Who knows what *else* you do."

I smile stiffly, letting it fade slowly from my face before finding her eyes and locking her gaze. "Let me make one thing clear. I do not *ever* want to have this conversation again. I do not *want* Jesus! If you wish to continue to visit me, you can't bring your Bible, mention anything religious *or* listen to Christian music in my presence. *Nor* can you stick

Bible verses to my mirrors, to the dash of my car, or to anything else you might find to stick them to!"

She looks down for a moment, tears misting her eyes. "Are you *really* my friend? I know I've made you angry with all this, but do you really care about me as a person and how I *feel?*"

"Yes, of course!" I insist, feeling a slight stab of guilt. "The Jesus stuff annoys me, but I still consider you a good friend."

"Can I ask you something then?"

"Oh no, *here* it comes," I moan, rolling my eyes.

"Listen, if you would just do one thing for me, just one, I will never bother you again about any of this! Surely if you were *really* my friend, you would do this one small thing."

"What is it?" I ask cautiously, hating myself for taking the bait.

"Come to church with me!" she blurts out excitedly. I push back from the table with an exasperated gasp. "Once, just once," she continues. I will *never* ask again. We will sit in the back, the very *very* back—please! We can even leave if you get uncomfortable. I promise! Surely if you were my friend, you would not deny me this one tiny favor."

"First, let me ask you something. Why is it so important to you *what* I think about Jesus?"

"Mishel, if you knew Him, if you really *knew* Him, you would *want* to serve Him."

"Alright," I say, consigning myself to the fact I have lost this round. "I will go, *once*, that's it—then no more of this, okay? It's *upsetting* me."

I am lying on the cold linoleum floor in my college dorm staring out the window at the small pinpricks of light piercing the night sky. It is mid-winter and bitter cold. I begin to wonder if God is out there—if He sees me—if He knows my thoughts. Oh certainly, He exists. Who else could have flung those stars in place—but a God I can actually *know?* No.

I reach for the radio to tether my thoughts to earth. As the music floods the room, I lay back down on the floor, staring again at the distant stars. I listen for a moment then realize I'm listening to a Christian song. Anger rushes to the surface. I begin to curse. *Why am I so angry?* I reach for the knob but can't bring myself to turn it. *What is wrong with me?* I don't want to listen to this!

No, no, no! I'm not giving into this—this feeling, whatever it is. Whoever it is! I want to live *my* life, *my* way, and I don't want God or anyone else, for that matter, telling me what to do! *You can't have my life, God, do you hear me? Where were you when I needed you—when I called to you for help? Didn't you see Lord, didn't you care? You are too late!*

I begin to cry, overcome with the emotions rushing to the surface. I jump up, grab my towel and soap and head for the showers. Surely God can not—*will not*—speak to me there. I open the door to the dorm showers and slowly peek around, relieved to find them empty.

I stand like a statue, face turned toward the warm stream of water, not wanting to move, not wanting to breathe. I feel outside of time and space, frozen in a moment that has somehow been selected and elevated above all other moments. *Please go away God, I can't follow you. I won't.*

I feel a sense of urgency now. I am struggling for control. I must hurry and finish and get back to my room. Perhaps I can reason with God—maybe He will accept a bargain. I finish my shower, wrapping and tying my robe before running down the hall, wet feet sliding on the polished linoleum. I close my door and hurl myself on my bed. "Okay, God, if you leave me alone for now, I will serve you later. I just need to finish school and have a career and, and ..." My voice trails off leaving me with nothing left to say. Even as I'm speaking, I can hear how ridiculous I sound. *This is crazy. I'm crazy! This is all in my head.*

Then I hear it; a voice, hushed and gentle—inaudible, yet so conspicuously clear. *What is keeping you from me, Mishel? I have pursued you without ceasing, but I will not always strive with you. What is so important that it keeps you from Me?*

"Lord," I cry, "You have *not* pursued me; you left me—abandoned me! Where have you *been? Where?* There are things that I can't forgive now—people I can't forgive. If I give you my life, you will *make* me forgive and I can't—I just can't!"

When He speaks again, His tenderness and gentle affection undo me. *Mishel, are you willing for me to make you willing to forgive?*

I think for a moment, the idea seems foreign—so simple, yet so utterly profound. *Am I willing for God to make me willing to forgive?* I pause, reflecting for a long time before answering thoughtfully. "If you could change my heart to the point that I would be *willing* to forgive, then yes, I suppose I *would* forgive."

Then that is all I require. I will not demand what you don't yet have to give.

Suddenly, my reasons and excuses seem foolish—my resentment toward God, my feelings of abandonment, it all seems stupid and trivial. I begin to pray. "Lord, if *this* is who you are, if *this* is how you love me, if *this* is the passion by which you have pursued me, then yes, I will follow you! I give you my life, and I give you permission to change the things that need to be changed. I am *willing* for you to make me willing to forgive. Make me more like you. Jesus, come and be the Lord of my life. I recognize you as the one true God, and I ask you to forgive my sins. Cleanse me and make me right before you."

Before I have even finished praying, I can feel that something in the core of my being has changed. I begin to smile. In fact, I smile so long and so hard that my face starts to hurt. *How long has it been?* Suddenly, I start to laugh. Raegan is *never* going to believe this!

It's Saturday, and I'm waiting anxiously for Raegan to arrive for her visit. The Greyhound bus pulls in and begins to unload. Where is she, I think, impatiently searching the faces as they exit the bus. Hurry, hurry, where *is* she? Finally, I see her and begin to jump up and down, waving my arms madly in the air. As she steps off the last step of the bus, I run to her and throw my arms around her with reckless abandon.

"What are you doing!" she says, "what is *wrong* with you?"

"What do you mean?" I retort, suddenly wounded.

"You have never *hugged* me before." Her eyes narrow suspiciously, "And what is with that stupid grin?"

"What grin?" I ask, putting a hand over my mouth to conceal it.

"That grin—that grin you have! Stop it! What is *wrong* with you? You're not *yourself!*"

"I know!" I shriek excitedly. She ignores the comment then begins to eye me as one would a moldy sandwich. "You haven't *taken* anything have you?"

"What do you *mean?*"

"Drugs, you haven't taken any drugs, have you? I don't want to drive with you if you have, or if you've been drinking, either!"

I laugh and shake my head vigorously. "No, of course not, but let's go get some coffee. We *have* to talk!"

As we sit down, she inquires again, "Really, Mishel, what's *up* with you? You're scaring me!"

When I can stand it no longer, I blurt out "I got saved!" She stares at me blinking several times. She looks hurt.

"I don't think that's *funny* Mishel. You're making fun of me, and it's not funny—it's cruel."

"No! I'm not making fun of you. Honestly!" I stammer, suddenly thinking that this is not going at all as I had planned.

"Yes, you are! I know you don't want to be a Christian, but you don't have to mock me!"

"But I *did* get saved. I really did!"

"I don't believe you."

"But I did! I'm not lying to you. I *honestly* did!"

"Who prayed for you?" she asks suspiciously.

"No one prayed for me. I prayed for myself!"

"Now I *know* you're lying. How would you even know what to pray?"

"I grew up in the church. I *know* how to get saved!"

"Tell me what you prayed?" she asks, in a mocking sing-song voice.

"I told Him I was sorry and asked Him for forgiveness. I told Him I wanted Him to be the Lord of my life."

"Yeah, then what happened?"

"Then I felt peace, *incredible* peace. Oh, and I got this grin—this stupid grin, that I can't get rid of!" She laughs but keeps eyeing me for a moment to be sure.

"Did you bring your Bible?" I inquire, ignoring her obvious skepticism.

"No! Of *course*, I didn't bring my Bible. You told me I couldn't."

"But you never listened to me before. Are you sure you didn't sneak one in—not even one of those itty bitty New Testaments?"

"No! I didn't. I was respecting your wishes."

"Oh great," I joke, "now that I *really* need a Bible you decide to respect my wishes." I stand up suddenly. "Well, if we're done here, let's go see if we can find a Bible at the mall!'"

Raegan looks at me for a moment, shaking her head and smiling. "I think you actually *did* get saved. If the Lord can get through to you, he can get through to *anyone*. "Hey!" I interject, pretending to be wounded. "I am not so sure you mean that as a compliment!"

"Oh, I *do* mean it as a compliment!" Raegan grins, "Just not for you."

Of course, my other friends were not so thrilled about my conversion, and I was soon ostracized. Friends became scarce and depression set in as I struggled to adjust to the rejection of those I had run wild with such a short while ago.

The youth in Raegan's church became my lifeline, and I was only too eager to make the two-hour trek on weekends to be with them. I grew exponentially and spent every minute I could reading the Word and praying. I poured over commentaries and pestered Raegan's pastor who seemed only too willing to answer the hundreds of questions that tumbled out of me one after another. I was so spiritually hungry. I wanted to know Him more, know His Word more, and experience more of Him.

Eventually, the focus of my life shifted more toward this little country church and away from the city. I quit my job, said my goodbyes and came back to the rural area I had grown up in.

Little did I realize, that like my grandfather, I too, had fallen into a sect started by R.C. Horner. The Holiness Movement believed that a Christian could achieve a state of holiness in which they could be entirely free from original sin and depravity. Like Horner, they thought they could achieve the pre-fall Adamic sinlessness. In other words, every lust and passion could be rooted out to leave one's soul in pre-fall sinlessness. They thought they could reach full sanctification in which all desire toward sin would be utterly vanquished. Many tried, and struggled year after year to obtain a level of perfection that could *never* be obtained. Some realized the utter absurdity of their striving. They grew cold and cynical and fell away. Others languished for years before succumbing to abject despair—or madness.

Yes, our God is a Holy God, but trying to live up to an impossible standard of perfection gives the enemy a place to take up residency in our lives. Repeatedly failing to meet impossibly high standards can only result in self-recrimination. This was an easy trap for me—it was so *familiar*.

Certainly, I am not talking about willful sin! Willful sin should *never* be a part of *any* Christian's life. We are not new creatures in Christ if we remain the same—period. If we claim to be saved and to belong to Him yet fail to exhibit the marks of a regenerated life, then we are liars. However, sinless perfection can *never* be attained. If it could, then the sacrifice of Christ would have been in vain! Scripture plainly tells us that, "If we claim to be without sin, we are deceiving ourselves, and the truth is not in us." (1 John 1:8)

The problem with this doctrine, as preached by Horner's sects, is that it took the emphasis off of the progressive nature of sanctification, as accomplished through the Holy Spirit, and instead placed emphasis on *man's* ability to perform. Striving in the flesh for absolute perfection can only end one of two ways. Either you will become ensnared in a dangerous delusion of your own earned righteousness, or the dawning realization that perfection is beyond your grasp will pull you under and drown you in despair.

For me, the constant striving was like trying to reach a cookie on the very top shelf. I could stand and stretch, shift my weight and stretch again. I could even stand on the very tips of my tippy toes, but I *still* fell short every time. My fingers could touch the edge of the cookie, but the harder I struggled, the more it would be pushed beyond my grasp. It wasn't long before I turned my vexation inward and cursed myself for falling short.

It always seemed that there was one more mountain to scale, one more obstacle to overcome. Maybe then God would love me. Maybe then He would be pleased with me. Just one more hurdle, just one more hill, just one more besetting sin to conquer. There was always that nagging feeling of not *doing* enough, not *being* enough, not *trying* enough. It was never, *ever* enough!

My life now seemed wrapped in a damp and pervasive darkness, a vague sense of God's condemnation and disapproval. It bathed me in anxiety and guilt. I could never be satisfied with myself or my accomplishments; therefore, I reasoned that God must not be pleased with me, either. In my mind, my first love had transformed Himself into a harsh and punitive God, waiting for mistakes so he could beat and berate me. I never stopped to ask myself where the God had gone who had pursued me with such reckless abandon; the God, who had spoken so tenderly and wooed me so completely. Where was *that* God? Was God schizophrenic or was this *another* god? I never asked those questions. I should have.

Slowly, anger took root, and bitter resentment toward God began to grow. If only I had known then that I was not angry with the real God. I was angry with the god I had fashioned with my *own* hands! Every sermon I heard that stressed perfection provided more gold for the forging of my idol. This replacement god was cruel and demanding, never satisfied or pleased with anything I did or how hard I tried.

I didn't want others to see the bitter resentment I was harboring toward God, so I began to build a wall of denial, and every day I added more bricks. I needed to remain separate and aloof to keep up the façade of holiness. Surely if others truly knew me, they would reject me as I believed God had. When the burden became too heavy to bear, despair set in. If God had rejected me, surely the rejection of others would not be far behind. Finally, I could bear the striving no longer. I gave up and walked away.

I was so tired of the masks, the charades, the striving for perfection, the never measuring up. It was like pinning paper leaves on a dying tree. If you were skilled enough, you could fool some, but it would never change the tree itself or stop its decay. I had been pinning paper leaves for a very long time while I rotted from the inside. Sure, you can pin leaves on a dying tree for a while. You can even prop up the rotting wood for a season—but sooner or later, when the storms come, and the winds blow hard, you will fall to the ground with a terrible crashing.

FOUR
A TERRIBLE CRASHING

I awaken, skin yellow from jaundice, cold gray machines hissing from behind my bed. I stare at a bag of liquid, drip, drip, dripping into my arm. The sheets are tightly tucked, and my feet are imprisoned. I want to kick at the sheets to loosen them, but my legs will not obey.

I don't know how long I've been here, only that a pink sliver of light is glowing through the crack in the curtains and falling across the sterile white sheets. Is it morning or evening? I cannot tell.

My mind races desperately. What happened? Why am I here? The sickening realization washes over me like raw sewage. What a loser— I can't even kill myself properly!

A doctor comes. She stands over me. She checks the tubes and shakes her head. "You are dying," she says, in a detached voice. I say nothing. She speaks to me again. My eyes follow her around the room, but I say nothing. "I *know* you hear me," she grunts. She stares, pausing for a moment before shaking her head again. "What a waste," she mutters, "what a *tragic* waste." I want to respond. I want to tell her that I have been dying for a very long time.

A man comes, a kind man with vivid blue eyes. His presence fills the room. He is paralyzed from the waist down and walks with leg braces and crutches. He sits by my bed and studies me. I wonder who he is, but I dare not ask. He tenderly takes my hand, which arouses a knot of emotion I cannot untangle. There is a nurse present to draw blood. He asks her to leave, and she hurriedly obeys. His eyes are moist and empathetic. "I can help you," he whispers. He has a high-bred English lilt that is strangely soothing. I struggle to stay aloof. "If I were a betting man I wouldn't have put money on you pulling through," he muses. I am silent. He pauses, studies me for a moment and continues. "On some level, you must have wanted to live to have survived those odds. Maybe you just wanted the pain to stop." I lay unmoving, staring at the ceiling, his empathy suddenly making me aware of a crushing need to be understood. *Why is he so kind to me? He must want something.* Inside I want to rage against him; I want to tell him to leave and never come back, that his mere presence causes pain—but I can't. I am unable to arrange my thoughts into words, so I say nothing. "I will see you tomorrow," he says. As he leaves, there is a flurry of activity around him. He orders the nurses and gives instruction to the doctors. "She is to be treated well," he says to the nurses, "treat her as if she were my daughter."

He comes back the next day, and the next, and the next day after that. I find out he is the head of Psychiatry at the Hospital and a professor at the University. The nurses tell me I am very fortunate to have someone of his stature take such a personal interest in my well-being. They tell me there have only been a handful of patients he has ever worked this closely with. They say I should be grateful for the time he invests in me, but most of the time I am too angry to be grateful. My anger does not intimidate or dissuade him, and he tells me so. He tells me I am to call him David, but the intimacy of that small act unravels me so I avoid his name altogether. I feel safer at a distance. Trust is hard won in my world, and he is still a long way from earning mine.

They transfer me out of intensive care. The nurses busy themselves removing things from my room. I don't question them. I let them go through my personal belongings and purse. I am too weak to put up much resistance. They remove the laces from my shoes and take away my jewelry. They shake their heads and cluck their tongues. I don't want to watch them so I stare at the floor. I notice their shoes—they have ugly shoes.

"We can't leave anything that will be a temptation to you," they announce. I look at them incredulously.

"I could still remove the curtains and strangle myself, or I could drown myself in the tub."

They do not see the humor in this and tell David. When he comes to see me, he smiles. "You mustn't tease the nurses," he says grinning. I am pleased that he understands. He gives me back my belongings, and that angers the nurses. I flash them a sarcastic smile the next time I see them.

It is morning, and I am in David's office.

"Pull your chair closer."

"I'm close enough."

"Please, I want to see your eyes. Pull your chair closer."

I sigh. The chair is heavy, and the task seems difficult.

"My interns were here for a meeting this morning, and they moved the furniture. Please, Mishel, pull it closer!"

I rise, stand behind the chair and push, and then fold myself back into it trying to take up as little space as possible. David reaches for a small lamp and positions it so the light falls across my face. His office is always dim except for this small light.

"You are still in a lot of pain," he says flatly. I say nothing. His secretary comes with hot tea, and he pauses, taking a long sip before placing it on the table beside him. "Would you like me to have her bring you some?" I shake my head, somehow thinking that accepting this small token might make me indebted to him.

My eyes travel the room, studying his oil paintings and roaming over his books from Oxford. "I went to school at Oxford," he offers, somehow extracting the question from me before it has been asked.

My interest is piqued. "That is where C.S. Lewis taught. Did you know him?"

"Do you like C.S. Lewis?" he asks.

"Did you know him?" I repeat.

"Yes, I knew him."

"Really, you *knew* him?"

"We weren't personal friends if that is what you are asking, but yes, I knew him."

My eyes travel the room, finally locking on a picture of a ship on rough seas.

"Do you like that picture?" he asks.

"Huh?"

"The one you are staring at. Are you looking at it or just staring?"
I shrug.

"You must feel very much like that ship, tossed and buffeted—torn by the tempest."

I smile and turn to find his eyes. "Yes," I whisper, "that is *exactly* how I feel."

"You have a fascination with water, don't you Mishel?"

I look away, my eyes traveling to the window and outside to the blue-gray sky. A light snow has begun to fall.

"Did you know that I sail?" he continues.

"Yes, I think you told me, or maybe I read it in the paper."

"It makes me feel free with the water beneath me. I can almost forget that my legs are paralyzed. I have a boat with special riggings I can control with my hands." He pauses for a moment and studies me. "How does water make you feel?"

It is an odd question, and I reflect for a moment before answering. "Nervous," I say faintly, "you can never really know what is down there."

"It frightens you?" I shrug again and look away.

"I didn't say that it *frightened* me."

"Then what? Are you afraid you will drown?"

"No no, it's not that. I'm a very strong swimmer."

"Then what?"

"I don't know, maybe I'm afraid of being pulled under."

"Ahaa," he says smugly as if somehow he was expecting this enigmatic answer.

"I had a dream a few years back." I hesitate and look away, wondering why I've brought it up.

"Yes, go on, I'm listening."

"I was in the river by my childhood home. The river has a swift current, and the water is carried over dams that power the hydroelectric plant. The people from the Holiness Church were there. They were running and laughing and playing catch on the shore. I was in the water and being carried by the current, which was pulling at me from underneath. I was crying out, but no one heard me. The pastor was there. He was a kind enough man and very sincere, but in my dream he was just staring at me, clutching a life vest tightly against his chest. He wouldn't throw it to me. He kept it there against his chest, blankly staring, watching the current pull me under."

"How did that make you feel?"

"How do you *think* it made me feel? Desperate, I suppose, maybe even angry or betrayed."

"Can I ask what you were doing in the water in the first place?" He looks at me quizzically, then nods slightly and purses his lips as if he already has the answer.

"Uh, I don't know! What kind of question is that? I was in the water when the dream started. I must have been pushed in or … or maybe I fell in. I don't know!"

"Or, maybe you just got in willingly," he adds. He smiles, taking a sip of tea and holding it to his lips for a moment as he studies me from above the rim.

"No, I did *not* get in willingly! Only an idiot would get into the middle of that river with such a strong under-tow. Why on earth would I have done that?"

"Well, isn't it obvious?"

"No! It's not obvious at all."

"You thought you were safe."

I look at him, mouth ajar, not wanting to believe but suddenly realizing it's too late. The truth has found its mark and penetrated like an arrow.

"You were being pulled under the water by deception and lies; the belief that you had to be perfect for God or anyone else to love and accept you. You looked to your pastor to save you, but he couldn't. He either didn't know he had a life vest or he didn't know how to use it. This is precisely why I think you got into the water willingly. You would have had no reason to fear the water because you thought you were safe."

I look away, unable and unwilling to look him in the eyes. "I don't know," I whisper, "I think you are reading too much into it. It was just a stupid dream."

"I don't think it was such a stupid dream, Mishel, and I don't believe *you* do, either. After all, it was *you* who brought it up."

My eyes travel to the window again. The snow is collecting in the corners of the sill, and the sky is darkening. My mind begins to wander.

"Mishel, Mishel!" My eyes catch David's hand waving in my peripheral vision. "Where are you? What are you thinking?"

"I don't know," I shrug.

"Yes, you do know. You must tell me!"

"I don't know. Honestly, I wasn't thinking anything. I mean nothing related, just thinking."

"You were lost for a moment, where did you go?"

"Nowhere, I was just thinking thoughts, you know, blank thoughts, random thoughts … stuff like that."

"Mishel, you mustn't lie to me. Avoiding your pain will only make things worse. You can't be whole until you face this. Do you understand?"

I nod and look away then cross my legs away from him and stare at his paintings.

"Mishel, what are you feeling right now?"

"I don't know!"

"You *do* know, tell me!"

"I feel frustrated, I'm trying so very, hard, but I'm lost. It's dark and cold, and I'm all alone. No one will show me the way out. I feel abandoned and rejected, like nothing I ever do will be good enough. All I can see is darkness, heavy darkness, around me, in me; it's *everywhere*, and it's just sucking me further and further under. It's drowning me!" I pause, trying to gain composure, terrified that the tears filling my eyes will spill down my cheeks as a testament to my pain. I take a deep breath and continue.

"Sometimes I wake up in the night, and I feel I can't go on, that it's all too much for me." I shake my head wiping at my tears with my sleeve. "Then I think, maybe if I can hold on through the night, morning will come … and … and the darkness will go." My voice trails off. I look above his eyes and stare at the ceiling trying to quell the rush of tears.

"Yes," he whispers, "that's exactly right. The morning *will* come, and the darkness will leave, but you must endure until then." He smiles, searches my eyes and continues. "By replacing the lies you have believed with the truth, you will find your way out. I can't walk it for you, but God is with you, of that I am sure."

I squeeze my eyes shut trying more than anything to stop the sobs rising up from somewhere deep within. "Oh Mishel," he whispers, leaning toward me and pressing a tissue into the palm of my hand. "You have believed so many lies. There will be a new beginning for you— there *will* be, you'll see.

FIVE
A NEW BEGINNING

I t's New Year's Eve, and I am sitting in a downtown bar sipping wine. My boyfriend is chatting with friends, laughing, gesturing. He speaks to me once, twice, maybe more. I turn my head in his direction but look straight through him.

"You have had too much to drink," he says, flatly.

"It is only my first," I reply, turning to look at the others. I study their faces, trying to appear interested when clearly I am not. I lean toward my boyfriend not wanting the others to hear. "I don't want to be here," I whisper. He leans back, shakes his head and knits his brows together in a puzzled frown.

"I didn't force you to come tonight, you wanted to come. Do you have another pressing engagement I don't know about?"

"No, but I *do* think I'm supposed to *be* somewhere." I look past him not wanting to look him in the eyes.

"I don't understand," he says, concern registering in his eyes. He gestures to the waitress to bring me another before turning to look at me again.

"No, I don't want any more! I want to go. *Please* come with me." There is a note of urgency in my voice that surprises me.

"You are not making sense, Mishel. Go with you *where?*"

I am embarrassed now; the others are looking at me. I pause, afraid to say what I need to say, but unable to keep from saying it. "I need to go to church," I stammer. "I need to be right with God." The others are laughing now. My boyfriend is staring not knowing what to say.

"Are you serious? You are actually going to leave me here on New Year's Eve and go to church?"

"There are no churches open on New Year's Eve," the others chide. They look at each other and laugh loudly; a boisterous laugh that has no doubt come from too much beer. I stand up quickly, my mind is made up. I take my black wool coat from the back of the chair and heave it around my shoulders, slipping my arms into it and buttoning quickly. I snatch my scarf and hurriedly wrap it around my neck, then sling my purse over my shoulder and turn to leave.

"She's probably going to meet a man," one of them says in a hushed voice.

"No," my boyfriend interjects, "I think she may actually be going to—um, to church."

I push the heavy wooden door open and step out into the frigid winter night. Without looking back, I walk to my car, bracing myself against the sting of cold. *What did I just do? This makes no sense! Why am I so sure there is a church open?*

I begin to drive. There is a large Pentecostal church on the edge of town. There must be people there. As I make the approach up the hill, I can see a sprinkling of cars in the church parking lot. A feeling of relief washes over me. I pull in, park and exit the car striding quickly to the entrance door. *What am I doing here? I don't know these people! What will I say to them?* I take a deep breath, open the door as quietly as possible and step inside. *Maybe no one will notice me, and I will be able to slip in the back unnoticed.*

As the door shuts behind me, I suddenly realize that going unnoticed will not be an option. An usher strides toward me with his hand outstretched, "Welcome, welcome!" I nod and swallow not knowing what to say, or if indeed, I should say anything.

"You missed most of the service," he says, almost apologetically. "They're praying now, getting ready for communion." He leads me in quietly, but even so, heads rise and turn in unison staring for a moment before turning back to pray. I slowly slip off my coat and scarf, desperately fearful that the pew will creak. I sit looking forward with a wide-eyed stare, transfixed by the silver communion cups gleaming in the lights. *I want to take communion,* I think. *I want so badly to be right with God.*

The pastor is a tall, clean-cut man, stylish without being overdressed. His eyes scan the congregation and lock on mine. I look away. When he stops speaking, I stand to my feet and start toward the altar before my mind has even registered what I am doing. There is an Associate Pastor at the front facing the congregation, and he holds out a hand toward me. I smile awkwardly as I come to a stop before him.

"What is your name?" he asks, taking both my hands in his.

"My name is Mishel and … I can't stand it anymore, I want to be right with God. I used to be a Christian, but I messed up. I want to try again."

The Associate Pastor shakes his head. "*No one* can reach God's standard on their own, Mishel!" He reaches for a Bible on the altar, flips through the pages quickly, nodding when he's found his mark. "Look here … here in Romans 10:3–4. *'For they being ignorant of God's righteousness, and seeking to establish their own righteousness, have not submitted to the righteousness of God. For Christ is the end of the law for righteousness to everyone who believes.'* The Scribes and Pharisees with their hundreds of laws trusted in what they *did* to be righteous, and they failed! We are justified by our faith in Jesus Christ, not by trying to be good!

Let's look at Galatians 2:16. *'Knowing that a man is not justified by the works of the law, but by the faith of Jesus Christ, even we have believed in Jesus Christ, that we might be justified by the faith of Christ, and not by the works of the law: for by the works of the law shall no flesh be justified.'* You see! *No one* can be justified just by trying to be good, Mishel. The law was meant to show us what sin is. If there was no law saying it's wrong to covet, then how would man have ever known it was wrong?

He pauses for a moment and smiles before continuing. Look, over here in Romans 7:7. It tells us this very thing! *'What shall we say then? Is the law sin? God forbid! Nay, I had not known sin, but by the law: for I had not known lust, except the law had said, Thou shalt not covet.'* You can't be good enough! That is why you need a Savior. You need to submit to Him and allow Him to do the work *in* you. He will *transform* you through the *renewing* of your mind, not through you *trying* to be good. Confess your sin, pray, read your Bible and then get with other believers who can encourage you and help you grow!"

"But—do you really think He will give me a *second* chance?"

"Of course! He is the God of second chances—and third and fourth and fifth chances, too! I can assure you, He has been waiting for His prodigal daughter to come home. He loves you!"

"Do you really think so?" I ask, suddenly hopeful.

He smiles, his eyes are kind and understanding. "Of course—you need only to return and ask His forgiveness." I nod, biting my lip to stop the tears. His wife grabs a box of tissues from behind the altar and presses one into the palm of my hand before drawing me in for a long hug. When we separate, her husband continues. "Mishel, do you believe that Jesus is the Son of God?"

"Yes," I nod.

"Do you believe that He died for your sins and on the third day rose from the dead?

"Yes."

"Do you believe that if you confess your sins, He is faithful and just to forgive those sins and cleanse you from all unrighteousness?"

"Yes."

"Can you ask him to forgive you, out loud? We will agree with you in prayer."

I nod and softly begin to pray. "I'm sorry, Lord, I'm so sorry. I want you to forgive me and be the Lord and ruler of my life again."

My life changed radically and rapidly once I had rededicated my life to the Lord. I immersed myself in this church. Finally, I felt fulfilled and part of a church family that loved and supported me. I finished university, then spent a brief span of time in the Central American rain forest doing missions.

I am in Palacios, a small isolated village on the Northeastern coast of Honduras. It is a bucolic place hewn from the rainforest and accessible only by water or small plane. The area is populated with Garifuna and Miskito Indians and has no running water, electricity, or phone lines. It is a place that appeals to the spirit—but definitely not the flesh.

I have met up with American missionaries here and have busied myself with teaching their children. On this particular day, the children skip across the well-worn path to my tiny hut. It is more like a dollhouse than a proper dwelling, and there is barely room to move inside. It overlooks one of the marshy inland waterways which snake through the thick jungle terrain. Today is exceptionally hot. The oldest of the children calls to me. "Miss Mishel, the men are going swimming, and we are going, too! Please, please come with us!"

I scrunch my face up and shake my head. "That water is not safe to swim in."

"Sure, it is! We swim there all the time, please come."

The idea of cooling off and ridding myself of the dust stuck to my sweating skin is more than I can resist. "Yeah, hang on!" I yell. "Let me change and grab a towel. I'll be right out."

"She's coming, she's coming!" they holler across to their mother who is hanging over the gate of the missionary compound across the way. I walk out to join the children who can barely stand still for excitement.

"Mishel, don't swallow any water!" their mother yells. "It could make you terribly ill. Keep your head above water. Oh, and don't go out in the middle, the current is too swift—stay close to the shore! Oh, and whatever you do, don't go near the marshy part, there are crocodiles in there!"

"I'm an excellent swimmer!" I yell back before turning away from her and knitting my brows together in a worried frown. Did she say *crocodiles?*

"No, no!" she shakes her head vigorously. "It doesn't matter how well you swim. Please stay near the shore where your feet can touch the bottom!"

I tramp down the well-worn path laughing with the children as they sing songs in Spanish. The trees are a canopy overhead, and the sounds of exotic birds and howler monkeys echo through the dense branches. I love it here.

When we get to the river, the men are already chest-deep in the middle of the waterway. I watch for a few moments, then climb in at the shallow sandy area where the kids are playing. The water is divine. I wade out a bit from the edge.

"Don't go past the sandy area," the children warn. "It isn't safe!"

The men are standing in a clump, talking and laughing in the middle of the waterway. "Hey!" I call to them, "I thought the middle was too deep to stand."

"It is!" they shout back, "There's a small sand bar we're standing on. Come on out!"

"Can I walk straight out to it from here?"

"No, there is a deep spot in between you and us. When you get to the end of the sandy area where you are now, push off with your feet.

Swim hard and we will catch you and pull you up. You should be able to stand here—it's not that deep."

"What if I miss the sand bar?"

"No, no," they say shaking their heads vigorously, "you don't want to miss the sand bar. The current will carry you into the marshy area—there are crocodiles in there."

"Oh, come on," I scoff, "for real?"

The men laugh. "It'll be alright, we'll catch you. You'll be safe."

As promised, they grab me and pull me to the sandbar, but I immediately know I'm in trouble. I am far shorter than the shortest man making the water far too high for me to stand against the current. Within seconds, I have slipped beyond their grasp. I fight and thrash, exhausting myself with my flailing as I'm sucked beneath the water. I fight to quell the rising panic. *I'm a good swimmer, stay calm.* When my head bobs above the surface, I hear the shouts.

"Keep pushing toward the shore! Don't fight the current. Push toward the shore!" I am nearing the marshy section, and their shouts are getting louder. The men and children are on the shore now, running alongside me. When they see me getting closer to the shore, they run and get into the water near the shore, ahead of me. As I pass, one of the men grabs my outstretched hand and pulls me into safety.

I am too weak to climb out. My legs are sinking deeply into the black mud of the marsh. Two of the men on shore grab each arm and pull me out of the mud with a terrible sucking noise. Then I lay where I've fallen, covered in filth, heaving and coughing up water.

"You shouldn't have followed us out to the sandbar," one of the men says sheepishly."

"I *didn't* follow you out there, you *called* me out!"

"Well, why on earth would you listen to us?" they question, apologetically.

I wait for a moment, chest heaving, before adding in measured breaths. "You *said* I would be safe."

It seems unthinkable that soon I would willingly dive headlong into a dangerous river of *another* kind. Not content with the shallows I would be lured straightway into unsafe depths. There I would be swept unwittingly into the river's cryptic tide. This time it would not be so easy to escape—there would be no one there to pull me out. There would be no one *left* to pull me out.

SIX
THE RIVER PEOPLE

My return home was not a happy one. A widening void seemed to yawn across the chasm of my unfulfilled life. I began to despair. I wanted so desperately to be used of God and returning to the dreariness of schedules and time constraints seemed very unlike the exploits I felt that I had been called to. I continued to sing on the worship team at my home church and also for a small start Vineyard church in the same city. However, serving in this manner did little to appease me.

There were whisperings at that time of a movement in Toronto; a revival, or *blessing*, of unprecedented proportions. The church was called the Toronto Vineyard Church but later changed its name to the Toronto Airport Christian Fellowship after a split with the Vineyard movement. The revival began as a small church in a strip mall near the Pearson International Airport in Mississauga, a bedroom community of Toronto, Ontario.

Oddly enough, this warehouse-type church acted as ground zero for the *new thing*, which emanated like rings of water across the ocean to churches around the globe. Of course, there *was* no "new thing," the *new* thing was *old* paganism cloaked in Christian-sounding doublespeak and attractively repackaged to Christians. This was a *new* gospel that relied on feelings and experiences. For a girl desperate to feel loved and accepted by God, I was soon deceived.

The Vineyard movement was a neo-charismatic, evangelical association of churches started in part by John Wimber in the early 1980's. By the late 1980's, Wimber had begun to form relationships with Bob Jones, Paul Cain, and Mike Bickle. They, along with a handful of others, collectively came to be known as the Kansas City Prophets. Bickle pastored a church in Kansas City. This church would eventually be absorbed into the Vineyard movement and become the Metro Vineyard.[1] The Kansas City Prophets initially wielded an enormous amount of influence over Wimber, however, by 1991, Wimber was growing disillusioned with these so-called prophets and began to cut ties.

The infamous revival at the Toronto Vineyard Church was touched off by Randy Clark. Clark was a St. Louis Vineyard pastor who had been strongly influenced by a series of Rodney Howard-Browne meetings in Tulsa in the latter half of 1993.[2] Rodney Howard-Browne, a South African-born Pentecostal preacher, was the primary impetus behind the Holy Laugher phenomenon that invaded the Toronto Revival and the churches it subsequently spread to.[3]

Browne blasphemously referred to himself as "God's Bartender."[4] He was called such because he believed he could actually dispense the Holy Spirit allowing others to drink and be drunk in it. Evidently, Browne felt he had power and control over whatever "spirit" he was dispensing. Randy Clarke received "it" from Rodney Howard-Browne and then took what he had received to the Toronto Vineyard Church when he arrived for a series of meetings scheduled to take place January 20–24, 1994. These meetings continued nightly for months without ceasing, and by the spring of that year, news of the revival had spread, and international visitors began arriving en masse.

The term, "Toronto Blessing" was actually first coined by the British Press, but the movement was known by other names. [5] We called it *The River of God*. Christians, mainly of the Pentecostal or Charismatic persuasion, flocked there from all over the world to receive an impartation and carry "it" back to their respective churches. The fact that this church was so close to the Toronto Pearson International Airport made it accessible for visitors from abroad to gather there—and they did, by the thousands. In a matter of months, the movement had raced around

1. Bickle, M. 1996.
2. "Catch the Fire: History." 1995.
3. Bearden, M. 1999.
4. "God's Bartender in Good Spirits." Guardian & Mail. 2012
5. Poloma, M. 1998 and Poloma, 1996(a) and 1996(b).

the globe like a virulent contagion, leaving very few denominations unscathed.

Oddly enough, this movement had a strange way of bridging gaps between diverse faiths, uniting them through an exchange of sound doctrine for extra-Biblical, experiential-type faith. It was a Biblically illiterate movement, not dependent on proper Scriptural exegesis, but rather on the progressive revelation and aggrandizing prognostications of its self-proclaimed prophets.

In this world, roaring, barking, hopping, crowing, slithering, shaking, vibrating, and uncontrollable fits of laughter became typical manifestations of being *touched* by the Holy Spirit. It was not uncommon for recipients of the *blessing* to be pinned to the floor by an unseen hand. Neither was it uncommon to see them lying on the carpet giving birth *in the spirit*, legs spread apart, panting and pushing while others coached them on. Then there were the infamous trite phrases like, "Have another drink," "Belly up to the bar," and "More Lord."[6]

In this movement, the Holy Spirit was reduced to an alcoholic beverage that could entertain our senses and make us drunk. He became a commodity that could be poured out, passed around, transferred, imparted, and consumed. He became nothing more than an electrical current or an impersonal force that could be called down and directed to do man's bidding. In retrospect, this movement denied both His personhood and His holiness. He became the organ grinder's monkey, tethered by a chain and commanded to perform. It was blasphemous.

*The Toronto Vineyard Drinking Song was particularly irreverent
and sacrilegious. It went like this:
Now I'm just a party animal, grazing at God's trough.
I'm a Jesus junkie, and I can't get enough!
I'm an alcoholic for that great New Wine.*

*'Cause the Holy Ghost is pouring, and I'm drinking all the time.
Now I laugh like an idiot and bark like a dog.
If I don't sober up, I'll likely hop like a frog!
And I'll crow like a rooster, 'til the break of day,
'Cause the Holy Ghost is moving, and I can't stay away!*

---

6. Taken from my own first person observations of this movement

Now I roar like a lioness who's on the prowl.
I laugh and I shake, maybe hoot like an owl!
Since God's holy river started bubbling up in me,
It spills outside, and it's setting me free!

So, I'll crunch and I'll dip and I'll dance round and round,
'Cause the pew was fine, but it's more fun on the ground!
So I'll jump like a pogo stick, then fall on the floor,
'Cause the Holy Ghost is moving, and I just want more.[7]

Many still ask me how I could have been so blind, so stupid, so naïve. I wish I could answer that. I just don't know. However, what I *do* know is that once you were steeped in this atmosphere for a while, it was like taking a hit of spiritual heroin—you wanted more. There was something so persuasive, so enticing, so utterly addicting about it. It pulled you in and seduced your soul despite your questioning mind.

Had I researched these experiences before allowing myself to be absorbed by them, I would have found that the Holy Spirit cannot be transmitted or transferred like an electrical current or mystical force. In fact nowhere in the Bible is He referred to as an impersonal *force*. He is a Person! Nowhere in Scripture does God equate the Holy Spirit with staggering, loss of control, disrupted motor function, slurred speech, confusion, disorientation, or animal sounds. If I had taken the time to research, I would have found that Scripture teaches the exact *opposite* by admonishing us to stay sober and vigilant! Perhaps if I had searched hard enough, I would have actually found that many of these wild manifestations were, in fact, characteristic of Eastern religions and the occult, *not* Christianity.

However, I didn't research. I simply trusted. It didn't occur to me that those who led this movement might have been deceived themselves, or that worse yet, they might be *trying* to deceive others. I was

7. Brother Greg, 2006

too attracted to this new world with its new gospel to question my involvement.

There was something so anesthetizing, so profoundly persuasive about it. This god was unlike the one I had forged in my earlier holiness days. He was not cruel, demanding, or punitive. The rigid works based doctrine, so much a part of my early years, was quickly being replaced by a theatrical and experiential-type gospel. The services seemed more for the purpose of personal enjoyment and empowerment than for real teaching, or holiness. This was a fun god, a playful god, a non-demanding god. There was never a message of sin or condemnation, nor was there anything controversial or confrontational. In my spiritual life, the pendulum had swung from one extreme to the other with only a few short years of balance in between.

Many drawn to this movement, were experiential thrill seekers who were Biblically and doctrinally illiterate. They wanted to *feel* God—but not actually *know* Him. They claimed to want the *Holy* Spirit, yet they didn't want to be *Holy*. Some, like myself, had been wounded by performance-based churches that stressed doctrine over relationship. Others came from churches with tepid services they'd grown grievously bored with—and rightfully so. They wanted fire and passion. They wanted to *feel* something, *anything*—and they felt it in Toronto.

The entire movement discouraged the use of Scripture and exchanged it instead for *new* revelation. Questions were never welcomed. We needed to be open to these new revelations and manifestations. After all, God was doing a *new thing* and to refuse these experiences would be akin to denying God Himself! Those who *did* question were told they had a religious spirit. Questioning a man of God or any of the strange manifestations that followed him, showed a lack of faith. How dare we question a man of God. How dare we *touch* the Lord's anointed!

Questions were carefully managed by those in charge. Leadership seemed to anticipate what queries might arise and head them off at the pass. To be considered spiritual one had to shut both their mind *and* their mouth. The idea was to blindly receive whatever they dispensed and let *it* take control; whatever *"it"* was.

John Arnott, the pastor of the Toronto Vineyard Church, articulated quite plainly what one had to do to receive this so-called blessing—accept *it*, relinquish control to *it*, and not question, analyze or pray about *it*!

Another thing that hinders is people pray all the time. Praying in English or even praying in tongues. Mention the Holy Spirit and they start praying in tongues, you know. Our experience is that that will hinder substantially your ability to receive. And so I say to people, 'Look don't pray' it's hard to pour out and to pour in at the same time. Pray on the way out, you can pray later. Don't take control, you can take control later. The whole deal is, you lose control. He takes control. He gets you out of your comfort zone, makes you feel vulnerable, right? You can analyze it later can't you?
—John Arnott[8]

Why would the God of the Bible tell us not to question, analyze or pray? He wouldn't! However, we weren't dealing with the God of the Bible. This was *another* Jesus and *another* gospel.

Leadership assured those hesitant to embrace the manifestations that these experiences were no different than those described in the book of Acts.

But Peter, standing up with the eleven, raised his voice and said to them, "Men of Judea and all who dwell in Jerusalem, let this be known to you, and heed my words. "For these are not drunk, as you suppose, since it is [only] the third hour of the day. —Act 2:14–15

In retrospect, their defense of these manifestations was really just the opposite. Accusations of drunkenness were leveled against Peter and the eleven other disciples because they were speaking in other tongues, *not* because they were laughing, falling, slurring their speech, or losing control of their own bodies! These Judean bystanders had nothing in their past experiences to explain this strange phenomenon and naturally thought that the disciples must be drunk.

However, Peter clearly articulated that they *were not* drunk. He then went on to preach a clear and convincing message that the multitudes were able to hear, understand and respond to. Does that sound like a man who was drunk in the same manner as those under the power of the

---

8. John Arnott, speaking at Holy Trinity in Brompton England, February 14, 1995

Toronto Blessing? Peter very easily could have said, we are drunk but not of wine, but he didn't. He denied being drunk *at all!*

In the meetings I attended at Arnott's church, the speaker was *never* able to bring a message without shuffling, lurching, floundering, falling, laughing, slurring words or making strange vocalizations. When they did compose themselves enough to begin their message, the animal sounds, screeching laughter and raucous shouts rising from the congregation would inevitably drown them out. If, as the leaders of this movement claimed, these verses in Acts were referring to the *same* manifestations then why were the Toronto Pastors unable to deliver a clear message? If it was the Lord bringing the Word and also the Lord eliciting the manifestations, why did He keep interrupting Himself?

However, these were not the only verses this movement used to convince the skeptics. They were also quick to point out Paul's admonition to be filled with the Spirit.

> And do not be drunk with wine, in which is dissipation; but be filled with the Spirit. —Eph 5:18

Interestingly enough, those in this movement still claim that being filled with the Holy Spirit results in drunkenness. I didn't question this twisting of Scripture then, but its falsehood is certainly evident to me now. Paul was not *comparing* the two, he was *contrasting* them! In *contrast* to wine, which leads to debauchery, the apostle Paul was admonishing us to be filled with the Sprit, which leads to soberness and self-control! The later explanation should have *immediately* been evident to me just by examining what the Bible lists as the Fruit of the Spirit!

> But the fruit of the Spirit is love, joy, peace, longsuffering, kindness, goodness, faithfulness, gentleness, self-control. Against such there is no law. —Gal 5:22–23

What was occurring at this so-called revival was the work of the flesh—the *opposite* of the fruit of the Spirit!

> Now the works of the flesh are evident, which are: adultery, fornication, uncleanness, lewdness, idolatry, sorcery, hatred, contentions, jealousies, outbursts of wrath, selfish ambitions,

dissensions, heresies, envy, murders, drunkenness, revelries, and the like; of which I tell you beforehand, just as I also told [you] in time past, that those who practice such things will not inherit the kingdom of God. —Gal 5:19–21

According to Scripture, it is the work of the *flesh* that produces drunkenness and revelry, and it is the Holy Spirit that produces self-control, order, and sobriety. Therefore, spiritual drunkenness, staggering, and slurred speech cannot be the work of God's Holy Spirit as it would be inconsistent with His nature according to scripture.

If I had looked to the Word for my answers, I would have realized that we are continually admonished to remain *sober* and vigilant. Consider the following Scriptures.

> Be sober, be vigilant; because your adversary the devil, as a roaring lion, walketh about, seeking whom he may devour. —1 Pe 5:8

> But the end of all things is at hand; therefore be serious [sober] and watchful in your prayers. —1 Pe 4:7

> Likewise, exhort the young men to be sober-minded. —Ti 2:6

> Therefore gird up the loins of your mind, be sober, and rest [your] hope fully upon the grace that is to be brought to you at the revelation of Jesus Christ.— 1 Pe 1:13

Scripture does in fact, have a great deal to say about drunkenness. It is forbidden and considered a work of darkness—those who practice it will not inherit the Kingdom of God.

> Therefore let us cast off the works of darkness, and let us put on the armor of light. Let us walk properly, as in the day, not in revelry and drunkenness, not in lewdness and lust, not in strife and envy. But put on the Lord Jesus Christ, and make no provision for the flesh, to fulfill its lusts. —Rom 13:12–14

> Do not be deceived. Neither fornicators, nor idolaters, nor adulterers, nor homosexuals, nor sodomites, nor thieves, nor

covetous, nor drunkards, nor revilers, nor extortioners will inherit the kingdom of God. And such were some of you. But you were washed. —1 Cor 6:9–11

For those who sleep, sleep at night, and those who get drunk are drunk at night. —1 Th 5:7

Since God *forbids* drunkenness and calls it a work of darkness does it make any sense that he would manifest Himself in it? Does it make sense that he would tell us that drunkards will not inherit the Kingdom of Heaven but then cause us to imitate the very drunkenness He condemns? If you search Scripture, you will soon find that God sending drunkenness is a curse and not a blessing!

Pause and wonder! Blind yourselves and be blind! They are drunk, but not with wine; They stagger, but not with intoxicating drink. For the LORD has poured out on you The spirit of deep sleep, And has closed your eyes, namely, the prophets; And He has covered your heads, [namely], the seers. —Isa 29:9–10

Make him drunk, Because he exalted [himself] against the LORD. Moab shall wallow in his vomit, And he shall also be in derision. —Jer 48:26

He takes away the understanding of the chiefs of the people of the earth, and makes them wander in a pathless wilderness. They grope in the dark without light, and He makes them stagger like a drunken man. —Job 12:24–25

Thus says the Lord: "Behold, I will fill all the inhabitants of this land—even the kings who sit on David's throne, the priests, the prophets, and all the inhabitants of Jerusalem with drunkenness! I will not pity nor spare nor have mercy, but will destroy them." —Jer 13:13–14

The Holy Spirit causes us to be *Holy* and to exhibit the fruit of the Spirit not mimic the unfruitful works of darkness. If you do a Biblical word search for the word drunkenness you will soon come to the realization, as I did, that drunkenness is *always* associated with a curse and not a blessing.

Another hallmark of those who embraced this movement was spiritual elitism. We honestly believed that God had given us a special anointing and deeper revelation. We felt we were God's chosen, His elite, His enlightened ones. "Get into the River," was our mantra and our manifesto and we were hopelessly immersed.

I am in Toronto, seated in the service. There is a lady behind me with a peasant skirt and scruffy blond hair. She is beside herself. She is looking straight ahead in a mindless stare. With the precision of a cuckoo clock, she doubles over every few minutes, hands flying out to her sides, head shaking. "Hoooooooo!" she yells, then "Shoo Shoo Shoo" in shorter gasps. I turn around and stare at her, but she is blissfully unaware.

Others sit, peppered throughout the church on folding chairs set row upon row upon row. Some are quietly giggling while others are shrieking with laughter and holding their sides. Some fall to the floor between rows of chairs thrashing drunkenly while others fall sloppily across the laps of strangers.

There is a nicely dressed man in a business suit, hands on his hips, palms outward. He is strutting like a rooster head jutting forward and back as he goose-steps down the aisle. "Errrr er errrrrrrrrrrr," he crows, cocking his head to the side, eyes blinking strangely, "Errrrr er errrrrrrrrr!"

There are taped lines on the carpet to show us where to queue for ministry. Most everyone gets ministered to—a special impartation of *it*. On this particular evening, I have stood in line for hours waiting for ministry. A member of the worship team, a woman, suddenly runs toward me and places one hand on my stomach and the other on my back. I'm thrown to the floor in the blink of an eye.

"Get her up!" I hear her say. Two ushers are with her. They have been tasked with catching those who fall under the power of *it*. I stand to my feet dazed and wobbly. She lays hands on me again, and I am suddenly slammed to the ground by an unseen force. It happens far too quickly for the men to break my fall.

I hear my name and open my eyes.

"Mishel, are you ready? We are leaving. You need to get up and come on. You've been lying there forever!" I open my eyes, staring straight up as the ceiling slowly comes into focus. Like an angelic vision, my friend looks down at me from above. "Look, we are almost the last ones to leave. Get a hold of yourself and come on! We have to get moving, we have a long drive, and we need to stop and get something to eat."

"Oh—yeah, yeah."

"Mishel, hurry!" Her voice is jarring.

"I'm *coming*," I say, perturbed.

"You are not coming! You are just lying there on the floor and ..." she starts to giggle, "your hair is sticking up everywhere."

"Oh, really?" I mutter, as I smooth my hair down with my hands and prop myself up on an elbow to look around. The building is nearly empty. I struggle to my feet groggily and look around for my purse.

"I have it," my friend says, "someone could have robbed you blind, and you never would've known."

I take my purse from her and sling it over my shoulder. "I need to use the restroom before we leave."

My friend sighs in exasperation and rolls her eyes. "Can't you wait till we get to the restaurant?"

"No!"

I am in the stall. "Hey, are you out there?" I call to my friend.

"Yes, now *please* hurry up!"

"Did you get anything tonight?" I holler.

"No, not really," she replies obviously agitated.

"Hey" I continue, "are we alone in here?"

"Yes! Hurry up!"

"Okay already, stop rushing me." As my hand touches the latch to exit the stall, I start to laugh.

"What's so funny? What are you laughing at?" I'm gasping for air now, laughing and snorting as my legs buckle beneath me. I can't answer my friend for the laughter that has seized me. "What are you doing? What is so funny?" she asks.

The laughter is coming in spasms now that have left me completely out of control of my own body. I am trapped, my feet splayed into the stalls on either side of me. I work at the latch struggling to gain control of my legs and catch my breath. The spasms of laughter have contracted my stomach muscles so violently that I feel faint and dizzy. I pour out of the stall and fall on the bathroom floor in a messy heap. I am still convulsing with laughter.

"Mishel, they are shutting off the lights, COME ON!"

The seriousness of the situation makes me laugh harder. I am crying and unable to get enough air. I hear myself laughing in a high-pitched hysterical voice, but inside I'm frightened and confused. For a moment, I wonder if it is actually possible to die laughing.

My friend has now brought others to help. They lift me from the floor supporting me on either side to get me to the car. My legs refuse to work. They drag me out and across the carpet toward the door. I gather my feet beneath me as we exit the church and then stagger and fall. I struggle to stand again then careen to the ground once again. Determined, I struggle to stand wobbling wildly for a few seconds before lurching into the traffic and falling to the pavement. I am looking up at the night sky and convulsing with laughter in the roadway. I can't get control.

This was one of my first experiences with *it*. Looking back, it was anything but a *blessing*, but I saw it as such then. In my mind, the Holy Spirit had poured Himself out on me, and I was giddy with His drunkenness. In retrospect, there is no doubt I was filled with *something*, but it was definitely *not* the Holy Spirit. The indwelling of the Holy Spirit leads to holiness, but this spirit led me away from the Word of God and away from Biblical Christianity.

Toronto was only a few hours' drive from my home church in Kingston, Ontario and we piled into cars like hungry pilgrims to make the frequent trek. In the winter, we would brace against the cold in our thick coats uttering no complaints about waiting outside in long lines to get a seat. We wanted our fix. It was junk food. It fed our flesh and dulled our senses. We needed *it!*

Returning back at our home church, the pilgrims would laugh and whoop, jerking and convulsing, limbs trembling violently. We were only too eager to impart *it* to anyone who would stand still long enough to have hands laid on them. Those who didn't understand we scoffed at. "Religious bigots," we would sneer. They clearly did not understand the things of God as *we* did. *We* were *special*.

Things began to change in our home church, and a split began to form. Those who opposed the movement mocked us by calling us the *River People*, and we retaliated by calling them legalistic Pharisees who refused to let loose of the old wine skins. Like Toronto, there were now long *ministry* times in every service complete with strange guttural sounds and odd contortions. Our services also included extended periods of *soaking* in the presence of *it*. This was fondly referred to as *carpet time*.

As unbelievable as it seems to me now, it was not uncommon for some to lay on the floor of the church giving *birth* in the *Spirit*, uttering deep groans of labor while others walked about dipping and shaking yelling "Shooooooo!"

The old wineskins in my home church did not like this new and constant emphasis on the supernatural, but we River People felt above reproach. We didn't seem to notice that sin was now running unchecked through the church. We were too drunk in the spirit of *it* to notice much of anything. "It's a revival," we would coo, "come join us in the River!" In retrospect we were right, it *was* a revival—a revival of Gnostic Mysticism and outright occultism.

One of the signs of a *genuine* revival is an overwhelming awareness of our own sinfulness in light of the holiness of God. There is a sincere sorrow for sin and a longing to return to His Word. There is a breaking and molding, a shaping and forging, that *humbles* us. This revival did none of those things. It brought a haughty pride that reveled in the flesh and brought an atmosphere more akin to a local bar than a house of prayer. It seemed that wherever the *River* flowed, it brought a carnival-like presence and a tide of lewdness and sexual impurity. It also split churches by the thousands.

I noticed the lewd behavior first in Toronto. People gyrated obscenely in abandoned bliss as if in the throes of sexual ecstasy. It soon spread to the other churches who had taken *it* back to their home bases.

Our church was no different. Some openly claimed they were being *taken* (sexually) by the Holy Spirit. This was blasphemy, and I knew it.

I will never forget a close friend who described a prayer meeting she attended with several members of our home church. One young lady lay on the floor ecstatically moaning while she pleaded with *it* to take her sexually and consummate the marriage.

Understandably, it was not long before a scandal ensued in our church. A close friend of the senior pastor, a board member, deacon and fellow River person, decided to bed a young teenage girl a third of his age. We all knew it was happening, although it was vehemently denied. He continued to minister as a deacon, and she continued to minister in song. It was not long before her tiny frame showed the tell-tale bulge and a marriage hastily ensued. The church was already fractured, but this ratcheted up the schism. Not even the River People could justify this kind of behavior. One woman, who openly rebuked the deacon, found a stone in a small box sitting on her car hood. It was a reference to the Scripture, "Let he who is without sin cast the first stone." Soon it was not just the River People against the old wineskins. It was the River People against other River People.

Not long after being immersed in the River, I was introduced to the teachings of Rick Joyner. Joyner was considered one of the Kansas City Prophets (although he denies this claim) and instrumental in formulating and steering the Apostolic and Prophetic Movement in America, as well as the Dominionist Movement at large. He headed a ministry called MorningStar, which he founded with his wife Julie in 1985. Most River people considered Rick to be a true prophet of God.

I remember the first time I heard his name. My associate pastor's wife had handed me a dog-eared, photocopied chapter from his article entitled, *The Hordes of Hell are Marching*. It was written in February of 1995, roughly a year after the start of the Toronto Blessing. He published it first in his ministry newsletter, *The MorningStar Journal*. According to Joyner, it was the first in a series of prophetic experiences he had in a cabin in Moravian Falls, North Carolina. He later expanded these experiences into a book entitled, *The Final Quest*.

The associate pastor's wife was clearly enchanted. "It's the most beautiful, most anointed, most inspired thing you will ever read," she gushed. It was far from anointed in my mind. I regarded it as the incoherent ramblings of a hyper-charismatic lunatic. To say I was unimpressed would be a gross understatement. In my opinion, it was nothing but a disjointed and mystical tale that bordered on the bizarre. However, it didn't take long before this dog-eared copy had circulated the church, winning the hearts and imprisoning the minds of those I deeply loved and respected. They thought this man was a true prophet. Thus, in time, my misgivings dissolved and he became one to me, as well.

The chaotic crumbling of my home church disturbed me. Church became a battlefield, and no one was left unwounded. Clearly, the church was now in her death throes and the sounds of her slow and arduous death rattle had replaced the raucous party atmosphere we had grown dependent on.

I began to look outside of my church. Joyner seemed to be the prophetic voice for this movement, and I felt unexplainably drawn to his ministry. Apparently, I was now in the River deep enough to be pulled by its current. *It* was directing my path, and I was compelled to go where *it* was flowing.

I packed a small suitcase and hitched a ride with a friend who happened to be moving to Charlotte, North Carolina for a nursing job. I had known my friend Macey from my days in the Holiness Church.[9] We had each learned that the other was moving to Charlotte only after our individual plans had been made. It was an odd turn of events, and the coincidence was not lost on either of us. We decided to make the journey together, both for convenience and for moral support. For me, this was to begin a dizzying spiral descent into darkness and deception. A deception so sly and insidious that it would take almost twenty years to find the truth and several more to recover.

---

9. Not her real name

SEVEN
THE EMERALD CITY

The day has dimmed, and Macey and I are in the car watching the cows, pastures, and little towns zip past us in the dying light. As the North Carolina border sign appears in the headlights, silence creeps across the car. The lights of the car hit the sign like the flash of a camera imprinting the image on the film in our minds. It is a momentary burst of significance in a journey full of road signs and sleepy towns we would never visit. With the state welcome sign retreating quickly in the rear view mirror, the silence is broken by our snorts and giggles. We are *very* tired.

We begin to see billboards for a giant outlet store and decide to read them aloud. *JR's, Biggest Cigar Store in the World*, followed by, *JR's, Biggest Selection in the World*; followed by, *JR's Lowest Prices in the World*. The constant signage seems buffoonish, and every passing sign is met with a loud eruption of raucous laughter. Macey shakes her head. "How many signs do they need for that place?"

"Only one," I reply, "but you know how Americans like to brag." More giggles.

As the Charlotte skyline creeps closer, the well-lit Bank of America Tower looms in the distance. I stare, lost for a moment, wondering why it somehow feels familiar. Even in the gray of the night, the headlights reveal bright wildflowers carpeting the grass in the median. My eyes travel past them to the tower beyond. I am mesmerized. I am like Dorothy in the Wizard of Oz, following the yellow brick road, past the field of flowers to the Emerald City.

Like Dorothy, I too, would encounter a wizard—a pretender who would set himself up as powerful god-like being; projecting authority, possessing none. He would order a world so convincing, I would swear that it was real. At the end, when the curtains were drawn and the illusion dispelled, my disappointment would be complete.

However this night, with the twinkling Charlotte skyline hurtling toward me like a shooting star, it seemed an adventure God had planned and ordained. Nothing could dissuade me. I didn't worry about how I would support myself, where I would live, or how I would work here as a Canadian. These things didn't concern me. I was fearless and literally felt carried by an unseen hand. I trusted that I was in God's will.

It would be years before I would finally understand why God allowed it, and the deeper purpose my time here played in God's will for my life.

It is days after my arrival in Charlotte, and I am at MorningStar. The service is being held in an old warehouse in a business park off Pressley Road. A staff member has graciously agreed to pick me up and accompany me to my first meeting.

I am standing at the door, visibly shaking. I feel fearful, lightheaded and unsteady. A greeter asks me if I'm alright, and I nod feeling confused and disoriented. I open my mouth, but no words come. "It's the Glory!" she coos as she gently pushes me through the door. I look down at my trembling hands and fight the advancing confusion. I'm just excited, I reason. Who wouldn't be? How many people get to experience this? I guess it's nothing to fret over, but—but it feels so dark here, so ... so evil.

I look around, stunned. Whatever I had been expecting, it wasn't this! There are chairs set up facing the front and round tables lining the walls to the left. People are milling around in the back drinking coffee and browsing the bookstore—a small partitioned area at the back of the church. The noise and confusion are piercing. It is half an hour before service, and the place is in an uproar. People rush to and fro, running, throwing things and laughing. Some sit at the tables trying desperately to talk above the din while others have food spread out enjoying a meal before service.

The room is filled with mostly young people in wrinkled, unkempt clothing. It's evident that many of them have not washed for the occasion, or for any occasion in a long while. There are barely-sober, homeless people lolling around on the floor in the back drinking coffee. They seem to homogenize with the surroundings. Their presence *almost* feels normal, like what I would expect to find here.

The commotion and carnival-like atmosphere is trance inducing, and I am both appalled and intrigued. I feel somehow changed on a cellular level for even *being* here. It is as though I have entered through the looking glass and nothing would ever be the same, nor indeed, could it *ever* be the same.

The staff member approaches. She touches my arm and leans toward me. "We are sitting over there." She points to one of the round tables near the front, on the left-hand side. "You need to save yourself a seat at the table, or you may not get one!" I nod politely. "Go sit down and introduce yourself to the others at our table, tell them you're with me." I nod again and head toward the table obediently. I still feel disoriented, like I'm trying to read a book upside down. Oh sure, the letters are all there, but they refuse to arrange themselves into words and sentences to make themselves understood. The harder I struggle, the more perplexed I feel.

I sit down at the table and introduce myself. I'm cordial but distant. The staff member joins us a few minutes later and asks the others at the table if they have met me. They nod in unison and smile. "Mishel is Canadian," she offers. "She's going to be attending the ministry school." I nod and smile politely, not really wanting to discuss my plans with strangers.

The music starts. It feels like an outdoor rock concert. Many have their arms raised, hands snaking through the air like Indian belly dancers, eyes closed in abandoned ecstasy. I am uncomfortable. Surely it must be me, I reason. I mean, after all, what makes me think that all of these people are wrong. That would make my pastor and friends and everyone I love and respect wrong, too. No, it *has* to be me! Maybe these people are just on a higher spiritual level than I am. Maybe this is so high-level that I just don't understand it. Maybe there is sin in my life, or maybe I'm just too carnally minded. Is it possible for something to be so high level that it feels evil? Maybe it is my flesh reacting to the anointing. What's *wrong* with me?

Sensing my inner struggle, a woman near me leans toward me. "You will get used to it," she yells above the pulsating music. "You are not used to being in this level of anointing," I tell her it feels foreign to me—maybe even wrong, but she admonishes me and tells me to relax into it.

As I listen to the music, my discomfort grows. I begin to study the faces of those around me. Nearly everyone now has their eyes closed, some with mouths open as if asleep standing up, others swaying gently, wearing oddly plastic smiles. It is almost creepy. They look as if they have gone somewhere and their bodies have been left to mark their spot.

I see Rick Joyner through the sea of abandoned bodies. It's a curious sight. He is stone-faced and unmoving, evidently unaffected by the music that others have so willingly vacated their bodies for. I study him intently for several minutes. I wait for some indication that he is actually worshiping, but there is none—not a flicker of a smile nor the twitch of muscle.

When the preaching starts, I listen with rapt attention, expecting something deep. Surely this great prophet of the Lord will bring forth a critical message. I wait past the preliminary statements for the preaching to start. It doesn't. No Bible, no Scripture—nothing but the mystical dreams, strange visions and disjointed observations of Rick Joyner.

When the service ends, I feel strangely seduced—almost hypnotized. It is an odd feeling, and I search through my mind's catalog of experiences to assign it a place. I can't. The staff member stands to her feet. She stretches and then looks down at me, smiling benevolently as one would a child. "So, what did you think?"

"I don't know," I reply haltingly, "I just don't know *what* to think."

"It wasn't what you were expecting was it?"

"No, no it wasn't—but then again, I'm not sure exactly what I *was* expecting." She laughs almost nervously.

"Everyone feels that way at first—the way you are feeling. They question it. It seems different because it's on such a higher level than most will ever, or *can* ever, experience."

"I just don't know." I look around anxiously, "I mean, I thought I had a very close relationship with God, and yet all these people are so *into it*—you know?"

"Of course, they are *into it*, the Spirit is very powerful here—can't you feel it?"

"Well, I do feel *something*, but the praise and worship—it felt wrong to me—it felt *off*." She laughs almost mockingly.

"Girl, you need to get out of your mind and into the spirit! You can't hope to understand this sort of thing. All this analyzing is holding you back from the things of the Lord. You are called. There are so few who get to be here and experience this. Let all the other stuff go!"

"Maybe," I say, suddenly questioning my own judgment "but it just feels *wrong*."

She shakes her head perturbed, "Well it seems wrong because you are trying to filter the things of the Spirit through your mind. You know Rick prophesied there is going to be a civil war in the church. "You don't want to wind up on the wrong side."

"Hey, I don't want you to think that I'm against what God is doing here," I interject, suddenly fearful that I have upset her with my questions. "I came here to seek God. I wanted to be where He is and where He is moving!"

"Look, why don't you just go on up for prophetic ministry—hear what the Lord is speaking to you. It might put a stop to your doubts. It is an enormous waste of time, all these questions—it'll only make you miserable." She motions toward the front of the church with her chin, and I watch as people scurry around setting up booths with soundboards as dividers at the front of the church.

There is a woman with numbers on laminated cardboard squares handing them to those who ask. I am so engrossed in the scene before me that I jump when the staff member speaks again.

"Go! Go-on."

"What do the numbers mean?" I ask mindlessly, as I continue to stare wide-eyed at the booths.

"Each booth has a number associated with it. Get your number and stand in front of the corresponding booth number. There will be three people in there who will prophesy to you. You need to hurry, though! They only hand out a certain amount of numbers!" I hesitate, looking anxiously at the booths. "Go!" she urges.

When I get my number, I stare at the small, laminated, square of poster board with a big number four, in my hand. It feels like the key to an unknown world; the gateway to some strange mystical adventure. I am fearful, yet it seems a process I am now fully committed to. Like a small stone kicked from the top of a cliff, I am careening down the mountain unimpeded. Who would stop me now? Who *could* stop me?

I don't recall precisely what was spoken over me that evening, but I do remember that it convinced me and I so desperately *wanted* to be convinced. In fact, entering the prophetic booth became a powerful addiction. A spiritual crack pipe I could not put down. I was ruined. I needed it! Tell me again, how special I am, how chosen, how blessed, how anointed, how called. Tell me again how I will stand before kings and influence nations, tell me, tell me, TELL ME!

In time, I became a member of the prophetic team myself. We were instructed to keep all prophecies positive and never to address a person's sin, even if we plainly saw it. In fact, we didn't even ask if a person was a believer before prophesying over them. It seemed odd to me even back then, how some, through prophecy, could receive glowing commendations from "God" yet still be living lifestyles contrary to His Word. If God was actually speaking to these people through the prophets, don't you think He would address their sin?

Think about it, even King David, a man after God's own heart, was rebuked by Nathan the prophet when he sinned with Bathsheba. Where was *that* kind of prophet? Where was *that* kind of prophecy—the kind that confronted sin and tore down the high places of idolatry and wickedness? Surely a *real* prophet would never flatter men with meaningless platitudes. Surely a *real* prophet would reveal and confront the sin that one had hidden in their heart!

In retrospect, most of these prophecies were nothing but soul reading and fortune telling. However, the accuracy was often chilling. It is, quite frankly, one of the reasons I remained ensnared in this movement for so long. I reasoned that by virtue of their accuracy, these prophecies *had* to be from God. I didn't stop to think about the fact that Satan can also prophesy. While only God knows the future for certain, Satan is quite gifted at forecasting. He also has the ability to make his own predictions come true through manipulating people and events (self-fulfilling prophecy).

Many, including leadership, prophesied things that at times contradicted the Word of God altogether. It seemed to me that great pains were taken to redefine biblical prophecy as something other than that defined by Scripture. Most of these so-called "personal prophecies" were nothing more than vague exhortations and flatteries of a kind not mentioned in Scripture at all. The prophecies given by leadership were difficult, if not impossible, to quantify or prove—prophecies such as *this is a break-through year* or *many entrepreneurs will come into the body of Christ this year.* Since many entrepreneurs come into the body of Christ *every* year, and *every* year is a break-through year for *someone*, these prophecies were impossible to prove or disprove.

The people at MorningStar and the throngs of people who streamed to their conferences depended on prophecy. They gushed and cooed over it, always quick to tell others what had been spoken over them. Rick became a type of Moses to us, and we listened intently to what God was saying through him. The words, "Rick said," were uttered in almost every conversation.

Even though I had concerns, the prophecy booths made my difficult life, endurable. It was a constant stream of encouragement and reassurance. It was very beguiling to be told you would one day stand before kings and influence nations when you currently felt insignificant, impoverished, and dispossessed. After all, life was difficult. It would have been easier to plant flowers in concrete than establish myself in the Emerald City.

I was a Canadian with no legal right to work in the United States and as such, I could only lawfully remain for six months as a tourist. With my Canadian degree, I knew I would be eligible for a NAFTA work visa, but there were tremendous hurdles to overcome. First, I would have to secure a job that fit within the stringent NAFTA guidelines. Then, I would need a letter of intent-to-hire from a would-be employer. With that in hand, I would be required to return to Canada because the actual work visa had to be requested while physically in my country of origin. If the visa was approved, I would have to return to the States to obtain my social security number. It should have been relatively straightforward. It wasn't. I soon became disheartened because interested employers invariably told me to come back when I had a social security number. However, the social security number required the work visa, and the work visa required the offer-of-employment letter and the offer-of-employment letter required the social security number. It was an endless cycle of frustration, and it did not take long for despair to set in.

However, the work visa situation was not my only source of consternation. While I had previously traveled extensively in the United States, living in a foreign country with few personal resources soon tried my patience. It seemed to me that I was surrounded by people living the American dream while I struggled for the basics. Unemployment was extremely low in Charlotte at that time, but it seemed no one wanted to take a chance on a foreigner and endure the immigration hassle that would ensue.

Macey and I had come to the States with only a small suitcase each. She had obtained a job relatively quickly as a nurse, but our apartment was still bare of any furniture. She slept on the floor in the bedroom, and I slept on the hardwood floor in the living room. For weeks, we shared the only towel having to let it dry out before the other one could take a shower. While our apartment building was upscale, we failed to realize we were residing in a dangerous part of town. We heard gunshots late into the evenings and heard horrific screams the night our upstairs neighbor's throat was slit.

It is understandable why MorningStar was a reprieve for me. The atmosphere there was more like a crack house than a house of prayer. It was a church of the living dead with stupefied, trance-like zombies, bouncing to the beat. I was becoming one as well. It felt good. It made me spiritually high and anesthetized me to the pain of all that was unpleasant. In this world, I was special, anointed, called and chosen.

By the end of my first summer in Charlotte, I was completely immersed in MorningStar's culture. I had also stopped reading my Bible. Why would I have *needed* to read it? I was always *told* what God was saying. Why spend hours in prayer agonizing and seeking the Lord, when one of His so-called prophets could just *tell* me what God wanted me to know?

It seemed no one talked about the Bible much, and precious few brought one to service. In all my time at MorningStar I *never* saw anyone preach from one. I remember the time a visitor brought a Bible to service. He was a small-framed, nicely dressed man, who had looked rather harmless and gentle. He had his Bible open on his lap and was reading it silently in his seat before service. Suddenly, two ushers came rushing down the aisle and standing one on each side, strong-armed the man brusquely out the door. He had asked them what he had done, but his pleas were to no avail. The incident had left me unsettled, but eventually, I reasoned it away. After all, he *must* have done *something* wrong.

In retrospect, it is curious to me that no one had ever addressed the problem of homeless drunks drinking coffee and lolling around on the floors in the back during service. Nor had anyone addressed the witches that were somehow magnetically drawn there. A man reading a Bible, however, was a monstrous threat that had to be dealt with right away.

In contrast, Rick Joyner seemed actually *pleased* that the witches were there. We were told to make them feel welcome. The witches needed to hear about Jesus. While this was certainly true, looking back, it is clear that the real Gospel was not being presented to them. If it was, I doubt they would have been comfortable enough to return week after week with no conversion. In fact, in all my time at MorningStar I never heard an actual salvation message.

In hindsight, the witches *should* have felt welcome. Joyner made it very plain to us that he was not in the business of casting out demons. In fact, in one service he told us he didn't want us going to him for prayer. "It is not my job to cast out your demons," he had said to an incredulous audience. "In fact, I like to keep a few demons in there to keep things interesting."

Years later I asked a friend of mine who made it out of MorningStar if he remembered Rick saying that to us. "Yes," he said, "I remember it well." He paused, then pensively added, "What was *wrong* with us?"

Of course, looking back, there is little wonder why so few of us questioned or confronted leadership. Steve Thompson, Joyner's second in command liked to brag that he was gifted with the "spirit of rude." He was! I remember a very unsettling incident at the weekly School of the Spirit meeting. It was commonplace during these meetings for someone in leadership to call a student forward without warning, to preach. In this particular service, Steve Thompson had called a girl's name as the speaker for that evening. He had scanned the congregation, his eyes coming to rest on a young girl desperately trying to hide. Her boyfriend, at least I assume he was her boyfriend, was pointing to her and pushing her forward. She was terrified and looked to be on the verge of tears. Steve kept admonishing her to come forward, and her boyfriend kept insisting that she *had* to go. Finally, resigned to the fact that she had no choice, she skulked to the front with her head down, embarrassed. Steve then held up a wallet and asked her if it was hers. She looked relieved, smiled wide and nodded that it was. He then explained to her that some-one had found the wallet and brought it to him. Steve was smirking and trying not to laugh. He then handed her the wallet and told her she could take her seat. She returned to her seat with the sounds of raucous laughter exploding around her. It was cruel. The young girl had gone to the front petrified, thinking she would be forced to speak. She was not a student, and no one seemed to know her. He had purposely *chosen* to embarrass her, and he evidently found her embarrassment hilarious.

After my first summer at MorningStar, I enrolled in MorningStar's ministry school. As Joyner was quick to point out, this was not a Bible school. The emphasis was not on the Word of God but on prophecy, dreams, visions, and the supernatural. Most of the curriculum consisted of Joyner's books. We were being trained for the coming Harvest and prepared to fulfill Joyner's prophecy of a coming civil war in the church. Psychologists call this a self-fulfilling prophecy. He prophesied about the very thing he was working to bring about. A "redefining of Christianity" he had called it. It was like prophesying that a house would catch fire and then lighting the match that would set it ablaze.

In the American Civil War, the Northerners wore blue uniforms and the Confederates—the so-called rebels, wore gray. Likewise in Joyner's civil war, a battle would be waged between the Blue's and Gray's. We were the Blues. Like the ocean and the sky, blue stood for revelation, expanse, spiritual enlightenment, and openness of spirit. We were special—a new breed. We were Joel's Army, who would go forth victoriously to build the kingdom of Heaven on earth.

The Grays were spoken of by Joyner with disdain and derision. Gray represented the brain—logical reasoning. If there was one thing this movement *didn't* want, it was logical reasoning! The Grays were beneath us; they lived in their mind without regard to the higher work-ings of the spirit. They were the old wineskins—the legalists. They clung to doctrine and Scripture rather than to progressive revelation. They were portrayed as the staunch and sterile church that had long since faded into antiquity and outlived its usefulness. With this type of con-stant indoctrination I grew to distrust anyone from a traditional Chris-tian background, and although it grieves me to admit it, I came to view them as either lost or spiritually beneath me.

Looking back, *anyone* who opposed Joyner and his teachings was considered a Gray and not open to the moving of the spirit. The Grays,

Joyner stated, would be overcome and destroyed in the fight for the *true* church to evolve to the next level. Of course, in his estimation, the Grays would not go quietly into that good night. It might be necessary for us to assist God in finishing up the job. Let me put that in plain English—the Blues were going to help God kill them.

I can't begin to tell you how many people have challenged me on this point. I understand. After all, their plan is wrapped in a cloak of religiosity and hidden in double speak. However, I assure you it *is* there, hidden in plain sight for any that care to examine the matter closely enough.

I suppose it made sense in a twisted sort of way. After all, Joyner wanted a *redefinition* of Christianity and redefining Christianity it hard to do with all of those pesky Bible-readers hanging on. Of course, Joyner was not the first to think that way, and I am quite certain he will not be the last.

> All we lack is a religious genius capable of uprooting outmoded religious practices and putting new ones in their place. —Joseph Goebbels, Adolf Hitler's Propaganda Minister[1]

For *his* generation, Rick Joyner *was* such a genius—uprooting what he considered outmoded religious practices—like repentance, and the study of Scripture and putting new ones in their place—like conversing with angels, mystical experiences and progressive revelation.

By the time I started ministry school, I had been in the United States almost six months, living from a suitcase and sleeping on the floor. I began to despair as I questioned why God was not providing. I had all but given up hope when a job offer came. The catch—I only had a small window of time to get back to Canada and apply for my work visa. Macey agreed to accompany me and share the driving.

---

1. Hachmeister & Kloft. "The Man behind Hitler (Transcript) Diary Entry"

We are riding through downtown Charlotte toward the interstate when it happens. My car loses power, smoke rolling from under the hood in thick gray clouds. *No! No! Not now!* I quickly pull the vehicle over to the curb, but I am still blocking traffic. There are honks, beeps and animated gestures from passing motorists. Stress is mounting by the minute.

After what seems like an eternity, a flash of blue light pulses behind me in my rear-view mirror. The policeman exits his vehicle and saunters up to the driver side window. "There is something wrong with my car!" I blurt out anxiously before he has a chance to speak.

"Evidently," he says rolling his eyes. "And what were you planning on doing with your disabled vehicle ma'am?"

"Uh—I don't know."

"Will the car start?"

"Yes, it will start, but it won't go forward—the gears won't work—except the reverse."

"It sounds like your engine's gone. Do you need a tow truck?"

"No, I can't pay for a tow truck!" By this time, another officer is there. They seem amused. They look at each other and snicker.

"So what do you plan on doing—backing your car home?"

I look at them, tears filling my eyes, "I need to get to Canada."

"Sweetheart, this car ain't gonna get you to Canada, and it, sure enough, can't stay here in the road blocking traffic."

"But I have no money for a tow truck and ... "

"Look, there is a garage right around the corner." He looks at Macey. "You get out and let her stay in the car to steer. Shift it into neutral." By now a couple more men have joined the officers, and they push the car to the garage and leave. Macey gets in, and we sit there in the parking lot of the garage for several minutes saying nothing. I can't hold the tears any longer. I put my head in my hands and begin to cry.

"Macey, I'm sorry, I don't know how we are going to get back to the apartment. I just don't know what I am going to do. They are not going to hold my job—I'm out of time. It's all over for me. I can't stay here without a job."

"Dan[2] is coming," Macey says matter-of-factly.

"What?"

"Dan. You know him, right?"

"Well, yeah. I sort of know him. I know *of* him. You mean Dan the MorningStar student?"

"Yeah, him. I called him when the men were pushing you. He's coming to pick us up."

I say nothing. While the immediate problem of how to get home has been solved, my mind races ahead wondering what I am going to do with the car and how I can pay to fix it, and whether or not it *can* be fixed and how I will finance a new one and who will give me a loan without a job and ...

After several minutes, Dan pulls in beside us in his gleaming white truck. He winks at us, smiling broadly. "This isn't good!" he grins.

"What are you grinning about? My whole life is over!"

"Your whole life? Seriously? You are going to let this ruin your *whole* life? Wow. It's worse than I thought."

"Dan! My car just blew up, and I have no money to fix it. Heck, I have no money *period*. That's because I need a job. Oh wait, I *have* a job, but I can't *take* that job because I have no car to get to Canada to get the paperwork for that job. I can't fix my car because I have no money, and no one is going to give me a loan for another car because I don't have a job! Do you get the picture?"

"Your car didn't actually blow-up, Mishel."

"Dan. You're *not* helping!"

"Well let's just tackle one thing at a time. First, you need to get back to your apartment. That is where I come in." He looks at us both his eyes moving from one to the other. "You know my truck only fits two. Y'all are going to have to decide who sits on who." Macey giggles and I gasp audibly.

"Just when I thought things couldn't get worse."

Dan laughs and Macey scrambles into the truck. He walks around and climbs in on the driver's side. I climb into the truck and sit on Macey's lap. "You know," he says dimples flashing. "I think the Lord might be telling me something."

"I think He might be telling you to shut up," I quip sarcastically.

---

2. Not his real name

He chuckles, "I think He might want me to take you to Canada."

"What?" I ask incredulously, "You don't even *know* me!"

"Well, you don't know *me* either."

"Precisely! You could be a serial killer.

"Well, I'm not."

"That's what *all* serial killers say."

"I guess you will have to take your chances."

"It's a long way to Canada, Dan."

"Are you trying to talk me out of it?"

"No, I just don't understand why you would do that for a stranger."

"Look, I feel like the Lord *wants* me to do this. I can't explain it because if you ask me, it's insane. I can't take you both, though. I think it might be uncomfortable riding all the way to Canada like that." He looks at us and laughs.

"I'm *already* uncomfortable!" I moan.

"What are you complaining about," Macey yelps, "*you're* sitting on *me*. I can't feel my legs!"

"Oh stop, I'm not hurting you."

"Says you!"

"I can't feel my legs," Macey insists.

"Well, what do you want me to do about it—levitate?"

"Okay, here's the plan. Dan says ignoring our quibbling. "I will drive Macey back and drop her off at the apartment. We'll leave from there and drive straight through."

I somehow feel comfortable with Dan, safe. Though I do not really know him, he feels familiar, like a comfortable pair of shoes that are worn in just the right places. We chatter non-stop as if we have known each other forever.

My short time back in Canada is riddled with anxiety. I fear being turned down for my work visa and being denied entry back into the United States. When the time comes to return, and the border inches closer, I feel sick to my stomach. I go inside to talk to the border agents and tell them I need to apply for a TN1 NAFTA Visa to enter the United States as a legal alien. I stand at the desk waiting with trepidation for an immigration officer to see me. He takes my papers, shuffles through them, then looks at my University degree.

"Hmm," he mumbles, shaking his head.

"What? What's wrong?"

"Your degree."

"What about it?"

"It's written in Latin."

"So?"

"We don't speak Latin here in America."

"Sir, *no one* speaks Latin. So, I'm not sure I understand what you mean."

"What I *mean* is, I can't *understand* what your degree says. That is an important detail if you want this kind of visa. You are entering our country on your professional qualifications, but I can't tell from this *what* your qualifications *are*."

"Can't you call the university?"

"No, we don't do that."

"So, what are you saying?"

"I'm saying that you will need to get your degree translated."

"Why can't I just tell you what it says?

He laughs sarcastically, "Uh no, we need an *official* translator. You will need to have it translated at your university, and that translation will need to be notarized."

"We have an officer here who will escort you back to the Canadian side. When you have the proper paperwork, you can come back and see us."

I walk out to where Dan is waiting. He sees my expression and his smile fades.

"What is happening?" he asks anxiously.

"I have to have my degree translated. We have to turn around and go back."

The next time through, I stand at the counter while the immigration officer shuffles through my papers once again. He scowls, pursing his lips, shaking his head slowly.

"What?" I ask anxiously. "I had my degree translated and notarized by my university. That is what I was told to do! Everything else should be in order!"

"Yes, yes, what you have looks to be in order, but you are missing something."

Fear seizes me. "What? What could possibly be missing? I provided everything that was asked for!"

"There is no immunization record here."

"What? That was not on the list! Nobody told me it was needed. No!"

I hear someone in the back laughing and the officer grins and starts to snicker. "I'm kidding, just kidding … relax. I'm going to approve it." Relief washes over me. "It's just a little joke I like to play."

"Well, it's not funny!" I say perturbed. "This process is stressful enough."

"I know," he says, looking penitent for a moment before lowering his head and chuckling again. He finally looks up, trying not to laugh.

"When you get to Charlotte you will need to take this to the local Social Security Office. They will give you your social security number." He hands me my papers and smiles broadly. "Welcome to the United States!"

"Thanks," I say sarcastically. "You've been a regular riot."

On the drive back to Charlotte, Dan and I chat incessantly as the miles fly by. As Charlotte comes into view, I look ahead in the distance, past the flowers, to the tower beyond and start to smile. Dan looks over at me and gives me a nod of understanding. "It's a beautiful city isn't it?"

"It's like a jewel. I can't believe that it's really my city now—that I can stay here, legally. I feel like I am dreaming—that it can't actually be happening."

"It *is* happening," Dan says reassuringly, "you *are* here, and you are *legal*, and I am happy to have played a part in that."

I notice a rainbow off in the distance and stare for a moment. The rainbow is *crooked*.

"Hey, do you see that?" I ask, pointing with my index finger to show Dan where to look. Dan's eyes follow my finger's trajectory. He searches the sky for a moment before knitting his brows together in a puzzled frown.

"Huh!" he interjects, hunching over the steering wheel to get a better look. He pauses for several minutes, shaking his head perplexed. "What *is* that?" he gasps.

"I don't know. I don't know *what* it is!"

As we pull into the house he shares with several other students, he shifts his truck into park and steps out to look. "It's still there. What *is* it?

"Is it even possible? I muse aloud, "for a rainbow to be crooked?"

"No, it's *not* possible," Dan insists, shaking his head.

"Then what are we looking at?"

"I—don't—know," he says hesitantly.

We stand there transfixed, staring at the sky, saying nothing. "Huh!" Dan suddenly grunts, shaking his head, bewildered. "I'm going to go in and get the guys and have *them* look."

So he did get them, and they did come and look, and we all stood in the driveway intermittently saying, "Huh!"

Years later, Dan and I called to mind the day we saw the crooked rainbow and how it almost seemed to portend the broken dreams and coming desecration of all that we held sacred.

EIGHT
ANOTHER GOSPEL

The theology Joyner embraced was multi-faceted. It was not readily discernible and often cloaked in double-speak. This made it difficult, for those entrapped in his mind-numbing labyrinth of complicated ideas to pinpoint *exactly* what it was that he *did* believe. Joyner was a Dominionist; however, he was more than that. He was a modern day Gnostic, and much of his teaching was steeped in Kabbalistic mysticism.

Inarguably, his teachings were part of a larger agenda that was well hidden behind Christian-sounding words and phrases to quell the fears and suspicions of discerning sheep. It was part of a greater plan to open up unsuspecting Christians to spirit guides, mystical experiences, and hidden wisdom, in preparation for the coming false Christ.

Joyner didn't believe that Christ was coming *for* the church. He believed that a New-Age Corporate Christ was coming *in* the church. Oh sure, he hid it well. After all, he didn't want to spook the Bible-believers. He merely wanted to placate them for a while with familiar Christian terms until their spiritual senses had been dulled enough to accept the lie. Perhaps, *he* even believed the lie. I don't know.

Joyner and the other leaders in this movement sought to pave the way for a New Breed—a new generation of believers who would discard the old and violently lay hold of the New Order Kingdom. In *this* kingdom, the church would rule the inhabitants of the earth with a rod of iron—whether they liked it or not! Not an ounce of this was Scriptural, but how would any of us have known? We had long ago exchanged our Bibles for the progressive revelation of an experience-based gospel.

It is critical to understand the doctrinal error of Dominionism if one has any hope of understanding the danger inherent in the movements who embrace it. Dominionism is a broad term, and many movements and sub-movements embrace its theology. All Dominionists believe that Christians should seek to influence and ultimately control secular civil governments and institutions. One of the best descriptions of Dominionism comes from Christian Apologist, Sarah Leslie. In her article, *Dominionism and the Rise of Christian Imperialism*, she explains what Dominionism teaches.

> **Dominionism Teaches:**
> The Gospel of Salvation is achieved by setting up the "Kingdom of God" as a literal and physical kingdom to be "advanced" on Earth in the present age. Some Dominionists liken the New Testament Kingdom to the Old Testament Israel in ways that justify taking up the sword, or other methods of punitive judgment, to war against enemies of their kingdom. Dominionists teach that men can be coerced or compelled to enter the kingdom. They assign to the Church duties and rights that belong Scripturally only to Jesus Christ. This includes the esoteric belief that believers can "incarnate" Christ and function as His body on Earth to establish His kingdom rule. An inordinate emphasis is placed on man's efforts; the doctrine of the sovereignty of God is diminished.—Sarah Leslie.[1]

While this is an excellent overall description of what they believe, let's break it down a bit further.

- Dominionists believe *they* are mandated by God to establish the Kingdom of God on earth in the here and now. Hence, this belief is often called Kingdom Now Theology.

- Dominionists believe Adam and Eve forfeited their dominion over the earth, through sin, and it is now *their*

---

1. Leslie, S. "Dominionism and the Rise of Christian Imperialism."

responsibility, (not Christ's) to win it back. Emphasis is placed on *them*—their exploits, their warfare, to overcome the enemy so that God's Kingdom can be established.

- They believe *they* will restore paradise by progressively capturing and restoring the seven societal "mountains" of business, government, media, arts, education, family, and religion. They aim for *complete* takeover and control of these seven areas.

- They believe that all people, nations, and governments will eventually be subjugated to *their* rule and that all enemies of Christ (people that oppose *them*) will be overcome (slaughtered). This belief, however, will be well masked in Christian doublespeak. Please note that while all Dominionists do not hold this particular view. The ones discussed in this book, do.

- Dominionists believe that Christ *cannot* return until *they* have taken control of the earth's governments and all civil institutions.

- They believe *they* will hand over the Kingdoms of this world to Christ after *they* have successfully conquered, (killed) or subdued, (imprisoned) all enemies of God, (those who do not hold their views including other Christians).

- They believe *they* will be the ones to conquer death, and that the government will be upon *their* shoulders.

- Radical Dominionists wish to abolish the separation between Church and State and establish the United States as a theocracy (with themselves standing in for Christ) under Mosaic Law. With this aim, many have sought and successfully attained key positions in government.

- Radical Dominionists ultimately strive to take over all world governments and civil institutions and place them under Mosaic Law to establish a global theocracy.

- Dominionists believe that all prophecy concerning the end times was fulfilled in 70 AD.

Those who hold Dominionist views believe scripture *compels* them to dominate, subdue, rule over, tear down, and unite, all in the name of the Lord. The question is, *which* Lord? They transmute the concept of an invisible, spiritual Kingdom of God into a global mandate to establish an earthly *political* kingdom in the here and now. They conveniently discard the fact that Jesus told us in His Word that His Kingdom is *not* of this world. Ostentatiously, they believe that it is only after *they* have conquered and subdued the nations that Christ can return.

Dominionists blasphemously claim that Jesus' hands are tied until we take our rightful place as rulers of the kingdoms of the world. How ludicrous to think that the Lord of the universe, the one who hung the stars and moon in place, who divided the day from the night and gave man life, needs *man* to subdue His enemies! No wonder God sits in the Heavens and laughs.[2] Rest assured my friends, our Lord can raise up an army from a box of corn flakes if He so desires. He does not *need* us.

While Dominionists have bent the Word of God to fit their agenda, they *are* right about one thing. There *will* be a worldwide unified church at the end of the age. Unfortunately, according to Scripture, it will be a *harlot* church and certainly *not* the Bride of Christ! Whether they are aware of it or not, they are building their kingdom for the New Age Christ—the Anti-Christ!

Aside from being scripturally inaccurate, Dominionism defies all logic and reason. Think about the implications of such a doctrine. It requires Christians to govern non-Christians and achieve complete subjugation, by force if necessary, of the entire world to their rule. Anyone who has ever been subjected to the abuse, scandal, and politics present in some churches knows that the last thing on earth we need is politically motivated, power hungry "Christians" ruling over us with a rod of iron.

But here is where it gets really scary. Since Dominionists regard the Kingdom of God as a literal *earthly* kingdom to be advanced in the here and now, they believe, as Israel of old, they are commissioned to literally take up their swords against their enemies. Their literature, songs, and sermons are rife with battle rhetoric. In fact, many Charismatic Dominionists, such as those of the Apostolic and Prophetic Movement, tend to justify, and even glorify, the killing of their enemies and romanticize the military-industrial complex. It goes beyond mere saber-rattling and

---

2. Psalm 2: 4

spiritual allegory. Radical Dominionists plan to take the battle against their flesh and blood enemies far beyond the spiritual realm. In other words, their doctrine includes a plan to kill those who oppose their agenda. I will look at this particular point more in depth in coming chapters.

Certainly, one would have to discard large portions of Scripture and suspend all logic and discernment to accept Dominionism as truth. The apostles, who felt the return of the Lord was imminent in their day, didn't attempt to build an earthly kingdom after Christ's crucifixion! Think about it—they were the ones *closest* to Jesus, and they knew him best. If the Lord's plan had been for the church to overthrow governments and establish an earthly rule, do you not think the Apostles would have been taking steps toward that aim?

The Apostles knew their task was to preach the Gospel—period. Neither Paul nor any of the other apostles *ever* instructed Christians in the New Testament church to seek political office or establish earthly governance. In fact, Jesus told the disciples to simply shake the dust off their feet if they were not received—which, need I say, a far cry from killing them!

> And whosoever shall not receive you, nor hear your words, when you depart from that house or city, shake off the dust from your feet. —Mat 10:14 KJV

> Never once were they instructed to kill those who refused to convert to Christ, nor were they told to subjugate them to their governance.

Dominion theology is primarily based on a misapplication of Genesis 1:26.

> And God said, Let us make man in our image, after our likeness: and let them have dominion over the fish of the sea, and over the fowl of the air, and over the cattle, and over all the earth, and over every creeping thing that creepeth upon the earth. —Gen 1:26

While God *did* instruct Adam to take dominion over the fish, fowl, cattle, and creeping things, He did *not* instruct him to dominate other men, or subdue secular governments, institutions or nations! In fact, Jesus plainly tells us *not* to exercise authority over one another.

> But Jesus called unto them and said 'Ye know the princes of the Gentiles exercise dominion over them, and they that are great exercise authority over them. But it shall not be so among you; but whosoever will be great among you, let him be your minister, and whosoever will be chief among you, let him be your servant; Even as the Son of Man came not to be ministered unto, but to minister, and to give his life as a ransom for many.' —Mat 20:25–27

Christ clearly told the disciples they were *not* to be like the Gentiles whose rulers and civil authorities subjugated and exercised ascendancy over them. In contrast, they were to be servants. Think about it! Why would Jesus forbid the disciples from exercising authority over one another if He *really* meant for them to subdue all world governments under their leadership? Would that make any sense?

So, how exactly do Dominionists plan on conquering the nations? After all, it goes without saying that overthrowing governments and subduing nations can't be accomplished without significant bloodshed. After all, people don't take kindly to being conquered and subdued. They are going to need an army for that. In fact, they are going to need a supernaturally (demonically) endowed army. It will need to be an altogether *different* kind of army. A *new breed* of army—an army of elite overcomers to strike terror into the hearts of their enemies. Enter Joel's Army.

Oh I know, if you are anything like I was, you think they are talking about a *spiritual* or allegorical army, right? Oh, how I wish that were true. However, their *own* literature refutes that interpretation. Oh certainly, they camouflage it by wrapping it in double-speak, but it is there—hidden in plain sight. After spending almost twenty years in this movement, I can assure you that radical Dominionists such as Joyner believe in a *literal* army who will slaughter their *human* enemies to establish an *earthly* rule. They firmly believe that the governance of the entire world will be upon *their* shoulders, and insist *they* will rule with a rod of iron for a thousand years. Amazingly, they maintain that at the conclusion of *their* thousand-year reign, *they* will hand over the keys of the kingdom to Jesus. Isn't that nice of them? What a swell bunch of guys.

This blasphemously places Christ in the position of an impotent cosmic wimp, relegated to the wringing of His hands as He anxiously awaits Dominionist rule. After all, according to them, this is the only way Jesus can receive the keys to His own kingdom!

Rest assured, the *real* Christ is both sovereign and omniscient. The time of His coming is appointed by God the Father and is not mandated by man. Revelation, chapter 20, tells us that Jesus Christ will come to earth *personally* and *physically* to overthrow the wicked nations of the earth *prior* to the establishment of His millennial reign. The government will be on *His* shoulders, not the churches.

> Then comes the end, when *He* [Jesus] delivers the Kingdom to God the Father when *He* puts an end to all rule and all authority and power. For *He* must reign till *He* has put all enemies under *His* feet. The last enemy that will be destroyed is death."—1 Cor 15:24–26

Furthermore, the book of Isaiah states that the government will rest on *His* shoulders, not ours.

> For unto us a child is born, unto us a son is given: and the government shall be upon *his* shoulder: and his name shall be called Wonderful, Counsellor, The mighty God, The everlasting Father, The Prince of Peace. —Isa 9:6

So, why do you suppose the Dominionists insist on impersonating Christ by claiming the government will be on *their* shoulders? Why do they insist *they* will rule with a rod of iron? Why do they maintain it will be *them* who place death beneath their feet before handing over the keys of the kingdom? After all, wouldn't that make *them* Christ? Precisely! Dominionists, such as Joyner believe the church will actually *become* Christ—that Christ will come *in* His church and not *for* them. Therefore, they feel entirely comfortable with replacing Christ with themselves since they are convinced they will actually *be* Christ. In other words, they believe they will evolve to Godhood.

This concept of becoming God is the very core of occult doctrine!

They actually assume that once everything is under *their* control, and their enemies have been conquered, then Christ will come *in* them, and they will attain godhood and immortality.

Make no mistake about it my friend, Jesus is coming back *bodily*, and He is not feeble. He is coming back as a conquering lion this time, not as a lamb, and He does not need *us* to subdue His enemies for Him. He is *more* than capable of doing that for himself. Revelation, Chapter 7 states that He is coming with the clouds, and every *eye* will see him.

> Behold, He is coming with clouds, and every eye will see
> Him, even they who pierced Him. And all the tribes of the
> earth will mourn because of Him. Even so, Amen.
> — Rev 1:7

Incidentally, Scripture does *not* teach that Christ is returning to a peacefully conquered earth to receive His Kingdom from an elite breed of ruling Christians. The Book of Zechariah describes the Lord coming back to a world that has gathered together to war against Israel. Additionally, at the time of Christ's return, according to the Book of Revelation, there will be unprecedented evil, apostasy, upheaval and bloodshed.

> For then shall be great tribulation, such as has not been since
> the beginning of the world to this time, no, nor ever shall
> be. And unless those days were shortened, no flesh would be
> saved, but for the elect's sake, those days will be shortened.
> —Mat 24:21–22

The earth will, in fact, be as it was before the great flood—wicked, vile and corrupt.

> But as the days of Noah were, so also will the coming of the
> Son of Man be. —Mat 24:37

Additionally, Scripture states that Christians will be hated by *all* nations and will be delivered up to be afflicted and killed!

> Then they will deliver you up to tribulation and kill you, and
> you will be hated by all nations for My name's sake. And then

many will be offended, will betray one another, and will hate one another. And because lawlessness will abound, the love of many will grow cold. —Mat 24:9–12

Forgive my sarcasm, but if the Dominionists are actually in charge before the Lord's return, they will be doing a very bad job! How utterly absurd to think that the modern church with its hordes of power hungry, Biblically illiterate, pleasure-seekers will usher in justice, peace and stability for all nations! Seriously, one would have to be either profoundly deceived or mentally ill to even entertain that thought.

It gets worse. You see, to institute a global law for all nations, there will have to be a world government as a framework for those laws to operate within. These laws, the Dominionists insist, will be based on Old Testament Mosaic law. Think about it! Does this make any sense? If the enforcement of Mosaic Law could have saved souls and transformed the nations, then why would we have *needed* a Savior, to begin with? The Law in and of itself cannot save, change or transform *anyone*, let alone a whole nation! The Old Testament account of Israel's ongoing rebellion and apostasy should be proof enough of this fact.

Joyner was and still is, one of the staunchest supporters and propagators of Dominionism. I too, operated for years within the borders of this doctrine, although I would have been loath to admit it. The truth is, I actually didn't *know* I was a Dominionist or what a Dominionist even *was*. I most certainly didn't understand, at that time, what the leaders were *actually* teaching. For the most part, I took what was given me and didn't question or analyze it. The movement was designed that way. We were not to question! Blind faith was encouraged and openly applauded. Inquisitive thought was said to be an affront to God and openly discouraged.

Dominionism is essentially no different than what the New-Age and other esoteric religions teach. However, in my opinion, it is far more dangerous and deceptive because it is white-washed with Christian-sounding terms and phrases. Deception is inevitable when a movement uses equivocal or ambiguous terms *intended* to mislead.

It is imperative to understand that double-meaning, ambiguous words are scattered like buried landmines in the language of this movement, and they will quickly take you down if you are not aware that they are hidden there. When a leader uses the term "Christ," are you *sure* they mean Jesus or are they referring to the Christ Spirit? They are *not* the same thing! This is equivocation or double-speak and this movement is notorious for it. When they talk about Shekinah are talking about the Glory of God or are they actually talking about Sophia and the divine feminine.

Although this aberrant doctrine of Dominionism was certainly present centuries earlier in Christian mystics and heretical movements, much of modern day Dominionism can be traced back to the Latter Rain Movement. Latter Rain was a Dominionist movement that came to popularity in the early part of the 20th century. This movement brought the heresy of a world church reigning in dominion and unity over the kingdoms of this world. The Latter Rain Movement was largely responsible for fueling the Healing Movement, the Charismatic Movement, the Prophetic Movement, and the New Apostolic Reformation. Latter Rain was denounced as heresy by the Assemblies of God in 1949, but this certainly did nothing to stop it from spreading into their churches through subsequent movements.

Although the term "Latter Rain" is no longer used much, its toxic influence certainly has not diminished—in particular among the self-styled prophets and apostles of the Prophetic Movement and the New Apostolic Reformation. MorningStar was a seething caldron of Latter Rain Dominionism and one of its chief disseminators. I didn't understand the significance of that when I was submerged in the movement and only fully understood all the connections years after I was free of it.

The Lord brought me out in stages. As He peeled off one layer of deception, I would discover several more. I had been so deeply immersed in this movement that it had literally altered who I was. Had I not decompressed in stages, I would not have survived—emotionally or spiritually.

NINE
LATTER RAIN

Inarguably, the bulk of Joyner's heretical beliefs were gleaned from the teachings of the Latter Rain Movement. While Latter Rain doctrine was heavily Dominionist, it was also infused with Gnosticism. Gnostic and Kabalistic "Christianity," is not predicated on the worship of Jesus Christ, but rather on the evolution toward a deified superhuman state. Certainly, it would be difficult to draw a dividing line between Kabbalistic thought and Gnosticism as they are so intricately entwined philosophically.

Modern Gnostics believe they are a spiritually elite group who hold hidden knowledge revealed only to them. This knowledge or *gnosis* is acquired through direct contact with the spirit world. They receive their extra-Biblical revelations through dreams, visions, and angelic (demonic) encounters. To the Gnostics, these mystical experiences trump Scripture because they believe God is continually adding to Scripture through progressive revelation. However, we *know*, according to Scripture, that demons are agents of deception who masquerade as ministers of righteousness. They lead people *away* from God's Truth and *away* from salvation and holiness by presenting themselves as God's agents with direct messages and revelation from Heaven. We are warned about this throughout Scripture!

> For such [are] false apostles, deceitful workers, transforming themselves into apostles of Christ. And no wonder! For Satan himself transforms himself into an angel of light. Therefore

> [it is] no great thing if his ministers also transform themselves into ministers of righteousness, whose end will be according to their works. —2 Cor 11:13–15

The Apostle Paul actually warned us about those who worship angels and deceive people by placing emphasis on mystical experiences.

> Let no one cheat you of your reward, taking delight in [false] humility and worship of angels, intruding into those things which he has not seen, vainly puffed up by his fleshly mind. —Col 2:18

The Gnostics believed that salvation could only be obtained by the elite few—the *enlightened* or *illuminated* ones who held secret knowledge. They denied the deity of Christ and believed instead that Jesus was merely a man who achieved divinity through *gnosis,* or knowing. They saw Jesus as more of a pattern to follow—an archetype or blueprint to lead them to the Cosmic Christ Consciousness and their *own* deification. To them, salvation was dependent on *knowledge* and not on the shedding of Christ's blood for the remission of sin!

Gnostics sought to perfect the world by creating the conditions necessary for the second-coming of Christ. They believed the second coming was not to be a literal bodily return, but rather a silent indwelling of them *corporately* through the advent of the Christ Consciousness or Christ Spirit. Thus, they didn't look for a literal bodily return of Christ because they believed they would *become* Christ! This is fundamentally no different than what the Dominionists, the Kabbalists, and the New-Age Movement teach. It's all the same occult doctrine!

As I have stated before, you cannot take ultimate dominion over the kingdoms of the world without unity. So naturally, all threats to said unity will have to be eliminated. Those unwilling to evolve to the next *"level"* through the acceptance of the Christ Consciousness or the Christ Spirit, will be killed.[1] In this regard, what the Dominionists believe is at least similar in content, if not syntax, to the teachings of the New Age Movement and Gnosticism. Alice Bailey, the well-known occult prophetess who first coined the term, "New Age," put it this way.

---

1. Woer, S. 2013

All who wish to enter the New Age on the physical plane must undergo an energy activation or *rebirth*—usually marked by a subjective *trance-induced light experience* where one meets either a *spirit guide* or one's higher self. This *altered state of consciousness* will eventually lead to a *Luciferic initiation* into the *new humanity* or a *vow of allegiance to Lucifer as god*. Those who cannot or will not (not sufficiently developed in their spiritual journey) *will be sent on to their next life in a global cleansing action*.
—Alice Bailey [emphasis mine][2]

The phrase, *"race within a race"* is coming out in the open now. This quote by Bailey, although written in 1972 is referencing this very thing. This *new race* consists of those who have been deceived into thinking they have evolved to godhood and have vowed allegiance to Lucifer. Also notice Bailey's use of the term, *"Global cleansing action."* It has a much nicer ring to it than genocide—don't you think? These *same* mistruths, thinly veiled in safe-sounding Christian terms, have not only penetrated the Charismatic and Pentecostal movement but have seeped into the soil of *most* mainline denominations through the influence of the Latter Rain Movement.

The Latter Rain Movement was said to be a second outpouring of the Holy Spirit similar to Pentecost. According to its proponents, this outpouring would reveal the *Manifest Sons of God*—the New Breed, who would be emboldened by the Christ Spirit to unite the church and establish God's Kingdom on earth.[3]

Joyner believed he was one of the prophets tasked with the equipping of this New Breed—a race within a race. What he was *actually* doing was preparing the church to accept the mass deception of a false Christ to usher in a new, theocratic world government and a one-world church.

The Latter Rain Movement was birthed in 1948 at a Pentecostal Assemblies of God revival meeting held at a ministry school in Saskatchewan Canada. Although the seeds of this movement existed several decades earlier, the movement was given its clarity, cohesiveness, and direction at the Saskatchewan revival.[4]

2. Bailey, A. 1972
3. "Latter Rain and Manifest Sons of God." Way of Life Literature, 2012
4. Wanagas, E.A., 2000

Central to this aberrant doctrine was a man named William Branham whose teachings had indirectly spawned the Saskatchewan revival. Joyner, like many of the Neo-Pentecostals, elevated Branham to cult-like status. It was curious to me how many of the Neo-Pentecostal leaders acknowledged Branham taught heresy, yet still insisted he was a true prophet. How could that be? He was one or the other, but he was certainly not both! If he were a real prophet, he could *not* have been a heretic. If he *were* a heretic, he could *not* have been a true prophet!

In truth, Branham was steeped in the occult, fascinated with both the Zodiac and Egyptology, and openly attributed the supernatural works characteristic of so many of his meetings, to an angel and not to the Holy Spirit.[5] Branham didn't believe in the Trinity, gave jumbled, disjointed sermons, and relied on extra-biblical revelations and false signs and wonders. He also insisted he was Elijah, one of the two witnesses in the book of Revelation.[6] After his death, many of his adherents prayed fervently for him to be raised from the dead. His grave is marked, oddly enough, by a pyramid.[7] He is still in it.

Unquestionably, Branham was accepted as a true prophet based almost *entirely* on the signs and wonders that followed him. Many reasoned that he *had* to be from God, after all, he prophesied and healed the sick! It is always dangerous to accept signs and wonders as the hallmark of a true prophet! Satan can, and frequently does, counterfeit by performing lying signs and wonders to deceive. We simply must not judge by any means other than the infallible word of God or we are ripe for deception, period. After all, isn't it by lying signs and wonders that the Lawless One will deceive the nations?

> The coming of the lawless one is according to the working of Satan, with all power, signs, and lying wonders, and with all unrighteous deception among those who perish, because they did not receive the love of the truth, that they might be saved.
> —1 Thes 2:9–10

The Anti-Christ will be able to deceive many because they will not

---

5. Martin, Rische & Van Gorden, 2008
6. "William Branham: Healing and Heresy." 2008
7. Reckart, G. "The Tragic Car Wreck and Branham's Tomb Stone."

love the Truth; they will love the *experience*. Signs and wonders do not *always* mean that God is present. In fact, it can mean just the opposite.

Much of the Latter Rain Movement's heretical teachings, including Dominionism, were later infused into the Charismatic Movement of the 60's and 70's. Then, these same false teachings resurfaced again in the 80's under the Prophetic Movement. With every cycle through the various decades and movements, the Gnostic and Dominionist ideas of the Latter Rain Movement gained wider and wider acceptance. Suddenly, they were no longer assigned to the lunatic fringe. The same doctrine denounced as heresy by the Pentecostal Assemblies of God in 1948 [8] was now accepted by the majority of full gospel churches and mouthed by many of the big-name ministries. They say that if you repeat a lie enough times, it will eventually be accepted as truth. Not only was *this* lie accepted, but it was also embraced and celebrated!

The revivals of the 90's; Toronto, Brownsville, and others, were a melting pot of Dominionism, Gnosticism, and Latter Rain philosophies. The throngs of foreigners who flocked to these gatherings, whether knowingly or not, enthusiastically enabled these doctrines to circle the globe and gain a foothold worldwide.

Certainly, no one did more to further the Latter Rain lie than the so-called Kansas City Prophets. Members included such notables as Paul Cain, Bob Jones, Rick Joyner, Mike Bickle, Bill Britton, James Goll, John Paul Jackson, and Lou Engle. Paul Cain had been one of the participating ministers in the Voice of Healing Revival initiated by William Branham during the 1950s. These so-called prophets claimed that the Lord was restoring the five-fold ministry back to the church—not that it ever left. They insisted the 1980's would be a time of the restoration of the prophets to the body of Christ and accordingly, would lay the foundation for the restoration of the apostles in the 1990's.

The Kansas City Prophets were certainly a magnet for controversy. Paul Cain embraced the Manifest Sons of God, or New Breed doctrine, a teaching central to the Latter Rain Movement of the 1940's. He was a self-professed alcoholic and a practicing homosexual who firmly adhered to the teachings of heretic William Branham.[9] In fact, Cain openly declared Branham to be the greatest prophet of the 20th century.

---

8. Van Der Merwe, 1995.
9. Grady, Lee J. Charisma Magazine. 2005.

Paul Cain claimed to have been commissioned by Jesus Christ himself and insisted that he saw blue lights, which indicated who to single out for prophetic ministry.[10]

However, none of the Kansas City Prophets were as controversial as Bob Jones. For the sake of clarity, let me emphatically state that he is in no way associated with Bob Jones University. That is a different Bob Jones and mistaking the two is a very common error. According to Jones, an angel announced his call to him, and the Lord himself visited him at thirteen years of age. This experience, he claims, when he was fifteen. After a life of alcoholism, he was finally admitted to a mental health facility where he was told he would remain indefinitely.[11] While there, he outlandishly claimed the Lord appeared to him and instructed him to either kill or forgive twelve people to regain his sanity.

Jones claimed to get between five and ten visions per night and also claimed to see angels ten to fifteen times per week. His ministry was marked by bizarre manifestations, claims of trips to Heaven, angelic visitations, dreams, visions, communication with the dead and even astral projection.[12] Even in the depth of my deception, I was never taken in by Jones. It was inconceivable to me how anyone could consider him a prophet. His bizarre claims were preposterous.

Jones had a far less sophisticated demeanor than Rick Joyner, who carried himself well and had a much more polished and convincing way of speaking. The first time I encountered Jones was at a MorningStar conference at the Adam's Mark Hotel in Charlotte, North Carolina. Believe it or not, I thought he was a homeless man who had wandered onto the conference stage in a stupor. He was an elderly white-haired man whose dress and manner of speaking was more akin to a transient than a conference speaker. His belly hung below his t-shirt, and it appeared to be carrying the ghost of lunches past. I had looked around wildly for someone in authority thinking surely someone would remove him. Those near me had scolded me and told me who he was. I was stunned. Surely this man could *not* be Bob Jones—not *the* Bob Jones! I was unconvinced that this man truly *was* Jones until I spied Julie Joyner several feet ahead of me, arms folded, listening. It *was* him—the legendary Bob

---

10. Dean Robert, Jr. "The Vineyard and the Kansas City Prophets." 2011.
11. Op. Cit.
12. Op. Cit.

Jones, the man revered as a prophet! I listened out of respect, but I didn't believe him. His ridiculous stories and bizarre ramblings seemed to be coming more from a mind in the grip of mental illness, and no one could convince me otherwise.

In one of his more controversial statements, Jones claimed that God had shown him that prophets were not required to have more than a sixty-six percent accuracy rate. According to Jones, the church had not yet *evolved* to a place where it could handle one hundred percent truth. This, of course, provided a cover for his string of failed prophecies, and many used this as an excuse for their own failed predictions. The sheer lunacy of this was staggering to the imagination.

His laundry list of peculiar statements and outlandish claims seemed endless. In one meeting, Jones insisted that the anointing of God resided in our kidneys and that he could take people on trips to the third Heaven simply by holding their hand. At one time, he even went as far as to claim that Kansas City Fellowship was the one true church that all others would assimilate into.[13] Of course, it never happened, but none questioned. After all, God didn't want His prophets being *too* accurate.

Since God *is* Truth, does it make sense that He would deliberately cause His prophets to be inaccurate? God is not a man that He should lie! He cannot and will not lie. He will, however, allow us to believe a lie.

Oddly enough, it didn't seem to matter to his admirers that Jones was publically disgraced in the 1980's for having women disrobe in his office to receive their prophecies, "naked before the Lord."[14] Nor did it matter that he had grabbed a woman's breast when she was at the altar for ministry. I was present at a meeting where he was describing this incident. He did *not* take responsibility for the sexual assault, but rather blamed it on the woman whose demon compelled him to touch her.

Unfortunately, these admitted peccadilloes did nothing to quell his popularity among those who clamored after him for words. He was considered a father to many in the prophetic movement and a high-level prophet. He was also one of the chief disseminators of the Latter Rain, Dominionist, and New Breed, heresies. In fact, Bob Jones claimed it was *he* who introduced Todd Bentley, leader of the now infamous Florida Outpouring, to the angel Emma.

---

13. Gruen, Ernie, date unknown.
14. Op. Cit.

Bentley insisted this angel had been the same one assigned to William Branham. Branham, of course, had credited the angel for the miracles that happened in his meetings. Jones explained that Emma had first appeared to the Kansas City Fellowship in 1980 and that it had been she who helped birth the prophetic movement.[15] I think it should concern us that Jones, by his own profession, *admits* that an angel birthed the prophetic movement—a female angel by the name of Emma.

In later years, Bentley, who was much less savvy in the art of deception, would refer to his angel as Emma O. What a coincidence. Emma O. is actually the name of the Japanese Lord of Hell.[16] It was reasonably self-evident that Emma was a demon; a demon that by Jones' own admission, had birthed the entire prophetic movement.

Evidently, there is nothing new under the sun.[17] The Apostle Paul dealt with similar men in the Colossian church. It too was plagued by Gnostics who valued what they experienced and learned from angels, over established doctrine. Like today's Gnostics, these Colossians *claimed* to believe in scripture but relied more on what they received from angels and spirit guides in the form of visions, and mystical experiences.

> Let no one cheat you of your reward, taking delight in [false] humility and worship of angels, intruding into those things which he has not seen, vainly puffed up by his fleshly mind.
> —Col 2:18

In the 1990's, the Prophetic Movement morphed into what is now referred to as the New Apostolic Reformation, a term coined by its spiritual father, C. Peter Wagner.[18] Wagner, an author, and professor at Fuller Theological Seminary was instrumental in the formation of this worldwide network of self-appointed apostles. The seeds of this were sown when He formed an association with John Wimber, the Vineyard's chief founder. They teamed up at Fuller Theological Seminary, to offer the course, *Signs, Wonders, and Church Growth*. Apparently, they failed to realize that sign-seeking is a clear indication of a spiritually adulterous heart.

---

15. Ray, S.E. "Todd Bentley, Fresh Fire Ministries and Lakeland Revival."
16. Slayford, 2009
17. Ecclesiastes 1:9
18. Wilder, 2011

> A wicked and adulterous generation seeks after a sign, and no
> sign shall be given to it except the sign of the prophet Jonah."
> And He left them and departed. —Mat 16:4

Real signs and wonders will naturally follow blood bought believers
—but they will *follow* them, they will not *lead* them. I can also assure you
that if a miracle does occur, it will not be accompanied by any hype.
Those who are influenced or swayed by such are ripe for deception.
After all, it is by lying signs and wonders that the Antichrist will deceive
the nations.

> He performs great signs, so that he even makes fire come
> down from heaven on the earth in the sight of men. 14 And
> he deceives those who dwell on the earth by those signs
> which he was granted to do in the sight of the beast, telling
> those who dwell on the earth to make an image to the beast
> who was wounded by the sword and lived. —Rev 13:13–14

Those running from this meeting to that one looking for an *experience* will *always* end up in spiritual apostasy and ruin. I know this to be
true. I was one of them.

Through the course, *Signs, Wonders and Church Growth*, Wagner and
Wimber managed to skillfully indoctrinate a whole new generation of
future pastors into valuing signs and experiences over established doctrine. Wagner's goal was a new reformation; the most significant restruc-
turing since Martin Luther nailed his 95 theses to the Wittenberg door.[19]
Luther touched off the Reformation and laid the foundation for the
Protestant church. These imposters are laying the foundation for the
new *global* church.

The apostles of the New Apostolic Reformation believed they are
called and ordained by God to be the government for the emerging New
Order Church. To maintain this governance, they stress strict obedience
and submission to them in all matters. They claim they hear directly from
God, and many claim that Jesus and various angels visit them in person.
The kind of churches that embrace these apostles (and there are many)
are highly authoritative and abusive both spiritually and emotionally.

---

19. NPR, "A Leading Figure in the New Apostolic Reformation." 2011.

Members serve the leaders the opposite of what Christ taught. Their goal, of course, is complete and utter control. They actually *believe* that the world is awaiting the fulfillment of a takeover by a militant church; a church that will arise, conquer and govern the world, both spiritually and politically.

These new apostles are a highly organized group with a global agenda; an agenda well thought out, well strategized and implemented with military precision.[20] They relentlessly press for the dissolution of all denominational walls knowing full well that unity of purpose will be needed to take control. It might astound you how currently entrenched they are in right-wing politics, the GOP, and the military industrial complex. They are making inroads toward their agenda at an alarming speed.

One of their strategic plans for take-over is through the conquest of the so-called seven societal mountains of government; business; education; arts media; family; and religion.[21] This is being accomplished by what they call *Marketplace Evangelism* by *Workplace Apostles*. This effort is assisted through the exorcism of territorial spirits. They appropriately call this *Strategic Level Spiritual Warfare,* a term coined by C. Peter Wagner who formulated the concept. The *Strategic Level Warfare* is accomplished by first determining *which* territorial spirit is in charge of what geographic region by a process called *Spiritual Mapping.*[22]

If you are looking for a biblical precedent for any of this, there isn't any. Nowhere in Scripture are we instructed to do this and most certainly the early apostles did not engage in such a practice. Nowhere in Scripture does Jesus bind and rebuke a territorial spirit before preaching or performing a miracle. While the exhortation to pray is certainly present throughout the entire New Testament, at no time do the apostles or anyone else for that matter, tell us we must bind territorial spirits for the Gospel to prosper. Why would we seek to engage in an activity that clearly has no biblical precedent?

While most assuredly both the Prophetic and Apostolic movement is comprised of Gnostic, and Latter Rain heresies, undergirding it all is the concept of Dominionism.

---

20. Rosenberg, 2011
21. "Seven Mountains." Discernment Research Group, 2010
22. Wagner, C.P. 1997

> Our theological bedrock is what has been known as
> Dominion Theology. This means that our divine mandate
> is to do whatever is necessary, by the power of the Holy
> Spirit, to retake the dominion of God's creation which Adam
> forfeited to Satan in the Garden of Eden. It is nothing less
> than seeing God's kingdom coming and His will being done
> here on earth as it is in Heaven. —Peter Wagner[23]

You see, the purpose of the false teachings of the Latter Rain
Movement with its Gnostic undertones and rabid Dominionism was to
introduce Christians to esoteric teachings and draw them away from the
real Christ and the *real* Gospel. According to Alice Baily, mother of the
modern New Age Movement, Charismatic congregations in mainline
churches were to be used as entry points into the Aquarian Frontier.[24]
She claimed that change-agents would infiltrate the Christian Church to
modify its message while adapting it as a vehicle for the universal Luciferic religion. Using the church as the entry point for a unified Luciferic
religion has *always* been the plan.

Although I have stated it before, it bears repeating: it will not be
possible to bring the kind of radical reforms the Dominionists advocate
without war. If you are converting whole nations and instituting Mosaic
Law, you are going to have to use force—period. This force, according
to the Dominionists, is Joel's Army—an Army they believe will purge
the earth of wickedness and police the nations.[25]

Unfortunately, the term *Joel's Army* has been romanticized and san-
itized to such an extent that most sitting under Dominionist teaching
don't stop to question its meaning. I certainly didn't. Even if I *had* been
told, I doubt I would have believed that the theology I was embracing
included a mandate for genocide.

---

23. Wagner, C.P. May 2007. Letter.
24. Cumbey, C. 1983 and 1986. Print.
25. Dog Emperor, 2008. Web.

TEN
MORAVIAN FALLS

When I first arrived at MorningStar Fellowship in 1997, the community was abuzz with talk of a prophetic retreat being built in the mountains of rural North Carolina. Joyner spoke of it often, and his passion and enthusiasm for this retreat were positively infectious. He referred to it affectionately as the "Moravian Falls Project" due to its proximity to the tiny hamlet of Moravian Falls, nestled in the Brushy Mountain range, part of the foothills of the Blue Ridge Mountains.

Joyner had initially purchased four hundred acres of rural mountain property on Price Road in the Knob Hill community. He claimed this property possessed a unique spiritual destiny, an open Heaven and mystical portals to the spiritual realm.

The community of Moravian Falls fell within a 100,000-acre tract of land purchased by Count Zinzendorf after authorities ousted him from Saxony, Germany in 1786.[1] Joyner was quite enamored with Zinzendorf and held very romantic ideals of his faith and exploits. According to Joyner, the Moravians who first settled in the rural community of Moravian Falls had published a newspaper there called, *The Morning Star.* Naturally, this was sign—everything always was.

The interest in Zinzendorf during my time at MorningStar was extreme. While Rick took great pains to explain his obsession, it never did make sense—at least not to me. Why was a movement that claimed

---

1. "Wachovia." William S. Powell. 2006

God was doing a *new* thing, so obsessed with the *old* thing? If we were going to rally around the faith of a historical leader then why Zinzendorf? Why not John Wesley, or Charles Finney or Hudson Taylor? I knew there was had to be something *underneath* this obsession.

Religiously speaking, Zinzendorf was a Pietist. Pietism was a movement within Lutheranism in the late 17th century that began primarily as a reaction to staunch Lutheran orthodoxy and legalism. It regarded religion as mainly a thing of the heart and relied less on Scripture and more on subjective and experiential stimuli.[2] Feeling and sensing God became more important than the actual written Word. However, a faith built on feelings is a faith built on steadily shifting sands. Emotions can be manipulated by the misguided, the unscrupulous, and the downright demonic. If our faith in God is based on what we *feel* and *experience*, then deception becomes an easy job for the enemy of our souls—an easy job indeed!

When we rely on our feelings, our faith shifts from what we *know* to be true by His Word, to what we *feel* to be true based on our own personal experience. At this point, the enemy need only produce the right circumstances at the right time to manipulate our emotions and change our experience. We then insist something is true because we *experienced* it, even though that experience is contrary or even diametrically opposed to Scripture! This was precisely what happened to those at MorningStar. It was precisely what happened to me.

The Moravians themselves were a Gnostic sect that traced their roots back to the Unitas Fratrum founded in Bohemia in 1457. The Catholic's merciless persecution of Protestant denominations during the anti-reformation drove this sect to near extinction. By the year 1620, the sect's remnants survived by worshipping underground in parts of Moravia, located in today's Czech Republic. Faced with either denouncing their faith or leaving their homeland, they settled, in 1722, on the estate of Count Nikolaus Von Zinzendorf in Berthelsdorf Germany. With Zinzendorf as their leader, they formed a religious community called Herrnhut.[3]

One has little trouble, if motivated to do so, in finding a *very* different Zinzendorf than has been presented in modern texts and inferred by

2. Shantz, D. H. 2013
3. Hamilton, J. T., 1900

Rick Joyner and the neo-Gnostic, new reformation apostles.[4] In 2006, a London Newspaper published an article entitled, *The Lineaments of Gratified Desire*, by researcher Gary Lachman. Lachman wrote that Zinzendorf was involved in the esoteric tradition of Christian Kabbalism, Hermetic Alchemy, and Oriental Mysticism. He described Zinzendorf as a creative theologian and a sexual pervert.[5]

> Zinzendorf preached an intense identification with a fully sexualized Christ, whose circumcised penis was a frequent object of meditation. Zinzendorf's Kabbalism was highly sexualized as well: erotic arousal was necessary for "visionary copulation" with the Shekinah, the divine feminine, so aspirants were advised to maintain erections during prayer.[6]

Mackey's Dictionary of Free Masonry lists Zinzendorf as the head of the Rose Croix (Rosicrucians) from 1744–1749.[7] The Rosicrucians were a secret society of mystics formed in medieval Germany who believed they held ancient esoteric "truths" that needed to be concealed from the masses and revealed *only* to the initiated few. Much like today's new apostolic reformers, these mystics sought a *Universal Reformation of Mankind*.[8] Many current esoteric orders and secret societies are said to draw in part, or in whole, on the Rosicrucian belief system.

Masonic dictionaries also contain a category called Moravian Masonry founded in 1739 and called the *Confraternity of Moravian Brothers of the Order of the Religious Freemasons* An alternative order was the called the *Order of the Grain of Mustard Seed*. Members of the Order wore a ring on which was inscribed in Latin, "Not one of us lives for himself." Its purpose, according to Zinzendorf, was for the extension of the Kingdom of Heaven through Masonic Channels.[9]

I believe that Zinzendorf's Gnostic mysticism and his desire to unite denominations, through the extension of a false gospel to further the Masonic agenda, is what Joyner found so attractive in Zinzendorf.

---

4. Rimius, Henry. 1753(a), 1753(b), 1754(a), 1754(b), and 1757. Print.

5. Lachman, G. 2006

6. Op. Cit.

7. Mackey & Haywood. 2003

8. Jennings, H. 1976 and Heindel, M. 1916. Print.

9. Mackey, & Haywood, 2003 and Row, A. 2008

After all, uniting the faiths is one of the primary goals of the New Apostolic Reformation.

We have *all* been conditioned to think that ecumenism is a good thing—but is it? Think about it. Wouldn't we have to distil Christianity down to its lowest common denominator if we were going to unite *all* faiths? Wouldn't we have to distil it down to things we could *all* agree on and discard divisive doctrines such as the virgin birth, the resurrection, and salvation by faith in Christ alone? Wouldn't we have to abandon *biblical* doctrine altogether as divisive and broaden the narrow way to be inclusive of those who despise the teachings of Christ and disobey His Word? Yes, we *would*, and that is precisely what is happening! The *true* Remnant, the Bride of Christ, is comprised of believers who *love* His Word and *do* His will. Period.

If the unity we are seeking comes at the cost of forsaking God's Word, then it is a false unity and must be rejected! Christ brings division, not unity. To have unity, we would have to discard the *Biblical* Christ, who by the very nature of His message brings division!

> Do [you] suppose that I came to give peace on earth? I tell you, not at all, but rather division. "For from now on five in one house will be divided: three against two, and two against three. "Father will be divided against son and son against father, mother against daughter and daughter against mother, mother-in-law against her daughter-in-law and daughter-in-law against her mother-in-law. —Luk 12:51–53

The Bible does not teach that the *true* Church will unite; it shows that this age will end in apostasy! Ecumenism teaches us to be tolerant of unbiblical beliefs and actions within the church. *Real* love tells people the *truth* about their condition! Truth divides—it costs something! It always *has*. If we do not believe and obey the Word of God, we have no right to call ourselves Christians.

Make no mistake, it is Lucifer that desires to unite all men and religions. In fact, this very thing was tried once at the Tower of Babel by Nimrod.[10] The Tower of Babel was, in essence, the first attempt to establish a New World Order and a united world religion. As such, Nimrod

---

10. Genesis 11

was a type and shadow of a man to come who will try to unite the world under one government and one religion. This has always been the plan.

I have had some Christians accuse me of being a conspiracy theorist thinking they are insulting me—they aren't. The Bible lays out the biggest conspiracy the universe has ever known, and yes, I believe it.

According to Joyner, Moravian Falls was to be the hub of MorningStar's ministry with all the spokes of the wheel spreading outward from that point. Fellow false prophet, Bob Jones, had called Moravian Falls the heart of the God-man—whatever *that* means. As Joyner explained to us, the Moravian Falls Project was to be a place where the misunderstood prophetic community could be gathered, fed and restored. In a description taken from MorningStar's website, Rick Joyner stated that the Project was to include a:

> ... center for 24-hour worship, a Teaching Center, and
> a Prophetic Community, The Sabbath Rest Center, the
> International Fellowship Center, Youth Camp, as well as the
> home of MorningStar Ministries, the MorningStar Fellowship
> of Ministries, and the MorningStar Fellowship of Churches.[11]

Joyner was very adamant that *God* had instructed him to build the project. He also insisted that he had been told to use quality material and craftsmanship to enable it to last a thousand years. Although I didn't understand it then, his statement now makes perfect sense in light of his Dominionist worldview. He believed that it would be he and his fellow Dominionists that would usher in the millennium and incidentally, the ones ruling and reigning throughout it.

Joyner was never shy about asking for contributions. He stated that one hundred percent of the designated contributions would go to these projects. We believed him. The aspect that seemed to garner the most

---

11. Quote taken from Earl, Terri Lee. "Footnotes for: Prophetic Mandate."

attention was the plan for a 24-hour worship center where non-stop worship would be offered before the Lord. There would be parcels of land where people could live full time and also cottages where people could come for rest and restoration. It sounded idyllic; it sounded feasible—it even sounded *believable*.

Rick petitioned donations from the Charlotte fellowship, from the MorningStar conference attendees, and from his international base of fans and supporters. He told us he was going to prepare a place for us, and we would wildly shriek and clap. His vision for this prophetic utopia was certainly no secret. He talked about it frequently, openly and passionately. People were *eager* to invest in the vision for this community. They trusted that Joyner would do as he said.

I remember, even back then, questioning the fact that Joyner said he would be selling lots, cabins, and homes in Moravian Falls *to those whose purpose for having land there fit within the vision of the community*. I wondered why he was asking for donations if his intention was to divide and sell the land he already owned. Wouldn't the sale of these lots pay for the planned development? It seemed unscrupulous to me that he was taking in donations and then selling the land.

Several people from MorningStar bought land for personal use and the land prices in this small farming community sky-rocketed. The locals were unhappy. The land was being priced out of reach for many locals and whispers of MorningStar's mysticism made this highly conservative Baptist-church-going community very nervous.

Male students from both the ministry school and the Charlotte fellowship were petitioned for assistance and Rick was sure to praise them publically for helping to "build the Kingdom." There seemed to be a steady stream of young men going to Moravian Falls to assist in the "Project." Of course, there was no remuneration. They served at their own expense, and many starry-eyed students were happy to do just that, gushing over the fact that they were helping Rick. If Joyner had need of them, they were pleased to serve, whatever the cost, believing that by doing so, they were serving God.

However, there was murmuring among some of those same young men upon returning, but it was hard to get anyone to speak openly about it. No one wanted to speak against, the "Lord's anointed." I remember cautiously quizzing one of the young men who had been volunteering his time. He told me there really was no project. I had stared at him incredulously and asked what he had been doing up there in Moravian Falls if that was the case. He changed the subject. It was quite evident by his folded arms and scowl that the conversation would not continue in the direction it was headed.

I asked several people around that time *where* the Moravian Falls Project was *actually* located. However, few of the Charlotte fellowship knew how to get there. Others would insist that it was tough to find unless you knew the area and knew exactly where to go. This was curious to me. After all, it was supposedly being built as the ministry's base of operations and funds for the project were being raised on an ongoing basis. I would have thought that they would *want* the Charlotte fellowship to see it. In fact, I would have thought that they would have shown us pictures, slides, anything to keep us all interested and contributing our money, skills and time.

One thing was sure—I was *going* to find it! Perhaps seeing it for myself might settle some things for me. If it actually *was* being built, well, maybe I could relax. If it *wasn't*, well, I didn't have to think about that. It *was* being built. It was *there*—of course, it was *there!*

I am in my little red car, singing loudly, windows down, hair whipping my face in the warm mountain breeze. I clutch the directions in one hand trying to read the fluttering paper while watching the road. *Price Road, Price Road, where are you?* I squeal excitedly as I see the sign come into view. I'm almost there! I turn onto the road and drive past the houses clumped together at the base of the mountain, gearing down as my car chugs and sputters up the winding road. When I finally see the small stone pillars that mark the entrance to the property, I sigh with relief. *I found it. I'm here!* I grin and take a quick look at myself in the rearview mirror. My tousled appearance startles me. *I'm never going to get those knots out of my hair.*

As I reach the stone pillars and enter the property, I pass a smattering of apple trees and a large meticulously-kept log home with a red tin roof. The scrubby road continues to wind around, eventually coming to a fork; the left leading to a lodge and the right, to Joyner's massive home. I know the lodge is not owned by MorningStar Ministries, so I begin to look around. Where is the rest of it? There is nothing here! All the talk, all the hype, and *this* is it? Even though I am now seeing it with my own eyes, I am slow to believe. I had been told it existed so many times that now, not even the facts could convince me it wasn't true. No *wonder* the men had been unwilling to talk! They had in all likelihood been working on Joyner's personal home.

At that time, all that existed was Joyner's own personal home, another privately owned home, and Apple Lodge. Apple Lodge was always spoken of as part of the Moravian Falls Project, but in actuality, it was not. It was independently owned by Harry and Louise Bizzell.

Harry and Louise Bizzell were a pleasant couple, who were well spoken of by all who knew them. They had an unusual mixture of sophistication and down-home Southern charm that made them particularly engaging. Harry was a kindly man with warm eyes and a voice that inspired trust while Louise was the perfect hostess whose cooking was divine. They had built a beautiful bed and breakfast lodge on Apple Hill, which could be reserved for groups or retreats. This did *not* belong to Joyner nor did it belong to MorningStar Ministries. It was built and paid for by the Bizzells, and they were its sole owners. The log home I had passed coming up the private drive past the stone pillars had also belonged to the Bizzells. It seemed very odd to me that the only structure at the Moravian Falls Project, owned and paid for by Rick Joyner and MorningStar Ministries was, in fact, Joyner's personal home!

So, how did the Bizzells come to be so intricately linked, (and subsequently unlinked) to Rick Joyner? Joyner gives a very telling explanation in the *MorningStar Journal* of how he and the Bizzells came to live in Moravian Falls.

> A couple of weeks after I met Bob Jones, I received a call from him. He told me that the Lord had called me to the mountains of North Carolina and that he had seen the place that I was to go in a dream. Having been told myself to go to the mountains of North Carolina, but seemingly not being able to get past Charlotte, I was more than a little interested in this dream.

Bob went on to say that I was called to a place that was 100 miles from where I was (The Lamb's Chapel) and 40 miles from the Tennessee border. To get to this land, we would have to go almost due North on a major highway ... and then west on another highway. He then described the property itself, saying there was a mountain overseeing the property that had a rock face, and there was a beacon on another mountain close by that could be seen from the property. He said that the gospel would go out to the world from that mountain. –Rick Joyner[12]

So, to boil it down, Joyner is told by God to go to the mountains of North Carolina, but unable to get past Charlotte, starts his fellowship there in Charlotte. Bob Jones subsequently calls Joyner and tells him about a dream he had. He gives Joyner the exact location of the mountain where God wants him to settle. Joyner tells Harry Bizzell about Bob's dream. Now, let's continue with Joyner's narrative.

Harry was excited about this dream, but for me, not him. He and Louise were *sure* that their destiny was in Charlotte and that they would not leave their present location at The Lamb's Chapel. As Harry was telling me this, I looked at the picture hanging above him, and I suddenly felt a prophetic anointing. The picture was of a chair that I recognized in the Bizzell's back yard, but it had mountains in the background. I asked Harry who had painted the picture. He said that his sister had painted it in their backyard and gave it to them as a gift. I then asked why she put mountains in it, and there was a heavy presence that seemed to engulf us both. I could tell Harry felt it too, *but he was adamant that they were not supposed to leave Charlotte.* I disagreed but knew the Lord would have to persuade the Bizzells. –Rick Joyner [emphasis mine][13]

So, despite Joyner's persistence, Harry and Louise Bizzell *insist* that the Lord wants them to stay in Charlotte. Why do you suppose Joyner

---

12. A Prophetic History Part III by Rick Joyner. Triune Last Days.
13. Op. Cit.

continued to push? Is it possible Joyner wanted them in the mountains because he needed their financial backing? It is certainly no secret the Bizzells poured a significant amount of money into MorningStar.

Whatever the reason, Joyner continues to put pressure on the Bizzells by insisting that their decision holds life or death consequences for their family.

> Soon after this the Lord spoke to me and said that Harry and Louise's destiny in the mountains was so crucial that it actually held "life and death consequences" for their family. I felt a terrible burden from the Lord about this, but I didn't feel that I could share this with the Bizzells without it seeming manipulative. Even so, I knew I had to share it with them for their sakes. I was very clumsy when I shared this burden with them, but they took it very graciously but still remained adamant that they were called to Charlotte. I felt that I had done all that I could and would not say anything else, even though the burden did not go away.
> —Rick Joyner[14]

So, Bizzells continue to insist that the Lord wants them to stay in Charlotte even after Joyner tells them their decision to move holds "life or death consequences" for their family. Then, coincidently enough, Joyner's good friend Bob Jones confirms Joyner's prophecy with one of his own. How convenient.

> A few months later, Harry accompanied me to Kansas City where we spent some time with Bob Jones. When praying for Harry and Louise, Bob saw a death in the family coming before the Bizzells moved into their purpose. Not long after this, Harry and Louise's young granddaughter died in a tragic car accident ... I was shown that Spicer had prayed and offered herself for the purposes of God, even to the taking of her life. She had done this with great sincerity, and in Heaven, she is a martyr who lay down her life for the purposes of the Lord. Spicer Wallace did not die in vain, and she has a great

---

14. Joyner, R. (2008). A Prophetic History Part III.

investment in her family's destiny and in the Moravian Falls project. Soon after her death, the Bizzells, who had land in Moravian Falls, were living there preceding me by several years. —Rick Joyner[15]

So, to sum it up, according to Joyner's *own* testimony, the Bizzells did not believe that they were to be involved in the Moravian Falls Project. However, Joyner cautioned them that their move to Moravian Falls was, in fact, the will of God. Joyner additionally cautioned them that should they disobey, there would be life or death consequences for both them, and their family. When the Bizzell's grand-daughter subsequently dies in a car accident, Joyner insists that God revealed to him that she had offered herself to God and was thus a martyr. Her death, he believed, was an *investment* into the destiny of the Moravian Falls Project.

In what sick twisted world is the death of an innocent young girl considered an investment into a building project? God has *never* required human blood sacrifices. Human sacrifices have *always* been a strictly pagan practice. Does it make sense that God would demand Spicer's life because of her grandparent's disobedience, *if* indeed they were disobedient?

Joyner's claim that Spicer is a martyr is downright ludicrous. Dying in a car accident does not a martyr make! Joyner seems to want people to believe that Spicer somehow *allowed* God to kill her to punish her grandparent's disobedience. Joyner also wants people to accept that Spicer's spilled blood was an investment in the Project because in resulted in the Bizzell's *obeying* and moving to Moravian Falls. This is entirely unscriptural. God did not kill Spicer because of her grandparent's disobedience (*if* they did disobey). Spicer's spilled blood was not a sacrifice for Joyner's building project. Jesus spilled his blood once and for all as a sacrifice for our sins. Human sacrifice has always been the doctrine of Lucifer, not Christianity.

Joyner spoke of another man in connection with the Moravian Falls Project, who was allegedly punished for his disobedience—Tom Hess. Hess headed *The House of Prayer for All Nations* near the Mount of Olives in Jerusalem. He had been given a few tracts of land in the United States, and the donor had apparently instructed him to use these tracts of land

---

15. Joyner, R. (2008). A Prophetic History Part III.

for a "prophetic" purpose. One of these tracts just happened to be in Moravian Falls.

Hess met with his board, and they decided to give Joyner a 99-year lease on the property for a dollar per year. However, Joyner claimed he had been warned by the Lord not to accept anything with strings attached and subsequently declined the offer. Joyner claimed that donations to Hess's ministry immediately dried up.

Paul Cain, Joyner's cohort, and fellow false prophet prophesied to Hess. Cain told him that he (Hess) had some land that had a *prophetic destiny* and that this land was being wrongly tied up. Cain further said that he (Hess) needed to release the land back to those who had given it to him to avoid God's judgment on his ministry. As Joyner tells it, Hess *immediately* started receiving donations again once he released the land.[16] Joyner claims that Cain had known *nothing* about the situation. However, knowing how this movement uses lies and half-truths to manipulate, control and deceive, I personally find that hard to believe.

Paul Cain was an alcoholic actively engaged in a homosexual relationship. It is odd that he believed that God would judge Tom Hess for not freely giving the land to Joyner but not judge him for his alcoholism and illicit affair. In this strange world, you can see what sorts of things brought the greatest judgment and punishment. How was it that these "prophets of the Lord" saw clearly concerning things that benefited them financially, but could not see when one of their own was in sin? Curious, isn't it?

While Harry and Louise Bizzell were never *officially* part of MorningStar, Joyner nevertheless claims they helped lay the foundation for the Moravian Falls Project. The Bizzells had built their lodge in the middle of an apple orchard in the mountains of Moravian Falls; an orchard that, according to Joyner, had been planted by Johnny Appleseed. A ridge of land ran above the property and Joyner purchased that 46-acre tract as well as a small cabin below the ridge. It was in this cabin that Joyner penned his mystical New Age epic, *The Final Quest*.

I remember being in a service where Joyner spoke fondly of the cabin and the "spiritually active" environment there. He added that he no longer let anyone else use it because they were "polluting the atmosphere" and "interfering with the spiritual activity." It had struck me as

---

16. Joyner, R. "A Prophetic History Part III." 2008

an odd thing to say. In retrospect, this should not have been so strange. After all, it was common for those associated with MorningStar to claim angelic visitations. In fact, Joyner claimed to see apparitions of people dressed like pilgrims roaming around the Moravian Falls property. MorningStar *now* contends that Moravian Falls is the second most active angelic portal in the world, second only to the Mount of Olives.[17]

Later, Todd Bentley of Lakeland Florida fame would claim he saw angels playing there. He talked about a particular rock on Joyner's Moravian Falls property, which supposedly had some mystical power. He claimed to have seen three young angels "horsing around, wrestling, getting each other in headlocks and giving each other noogies." According to Bentley, these were the "worship angels" who oversaw the worship center.[18]

Now, let me state emphatically, that there really *is* no 24-hour worship-center. What they referred to, (and still refer to), as the worship center is just a tiny ramshackle building secured with a rusty padlock. Like everything else on this property, it was never open to the public, nor could just *anyone* from the Fellowship access it.

Claims of angelic visitations were commonplace among the leaders of MorningStar. Generally, these visitations would give them some special revelation or impartation not common or accessible to all. It is interesting to note that claims of special knowledge revealed by angelic visitation have been a thread common to almost all cults. These cults do not depend on Scripture, which is the only *sure* Word of prophecy, but allow themselves to be seduced by deceiving spirits. These spirits convince them that God is doing a *new* thing and that they have been chosen to receive ongoing or progressive revelation, not available through Scripture alone.

Some, like Todd Bentley, are brazen enough to command the angels and call them forth. Of course, is no Scriptural record of anyone *ever* giving instruction to an angel, either directly or indirectly, in the name of Christ. Angels do *not* respond to the commands of men! They are *God's* Holy angels and are sent to do *His* bidding, not ours. We are lower than the angels while here on earth and have *no* authority over them.[19]

17. "Prophetic History of the Moravian Falls Land and Mountain View Retreat Center."

18. Bentley, Todd. "Stirring Up the Spirit of Wisdom and Revelation." 2003.

19. Hebrews 2:7–9; Psalm 8:5,

As an aside, I want to strongly caution you to avoid anyone who claims to be a brother or sister in Christ who practices the opening of portals, the calling forth of angels or orbs, spirit travel, fire tunnels, grave sucking, or any of the other occult nonsense prevalent in this movement. God does *not* need an open portal to minister to us—He is God! If the God you serve is so feeble that he needs *you* to open a portal for him, then I think you are serving the wrong God. It is the mystery religions, Luciferians and the New Age that actively seek to open portals. They do this to allow the Ascended Masters (demons) through so they can gain wisdom (gnosis) and enlightenment from them.

Since God's Holy angels do *not* respond to *our* bidding but to the Lord's alone, does it make any sense whatsoever that they need us to summon them forth and open a portal? Is there *any* scriptural example of an angel of God being trapped in the Heavenly realm and requiring human intervention to open a portal? There isn't!

Now I do feel that I need to add something here because inevitably, people in this movement use Daniel chapter 10 to defend this practice not realizing that it proves just the opposite. In the third year of the reign of Cyrus, Daniel had been mourning by the Tigris River for three weeks when an angel appeared. The angel was sent by God to give him understanding regarding the future of Israel. During their conversation, the unnamed angel said to Daniel:

> ... Then he said to me, "Do not fear, Daniel, for from the
> first day that you set your heart to understand, and to humble
> yourself before your God, your words were heard; and I have
> come because of your words. "But the prince of the kingdom
> of Persia withstood me twenty-one days; and behold, Michael,
> one of the chief princes, came to help me, for I had been left
> alone there with the kings of Persia. "Now I have come to
> make you understand what will happen to your people in the
> latter days, for the vision [refers] to [many] days yet [to come].
> —Dan 10: 12–14

Scripture tells us that when Daniel set himself to humble his heart before the Lord, the Lord heard his words. Daniel was not opening portals and summoning angels forth from the Heavenlies—he was humbly seeking God! In response to this prayer, God sent His messenger,

Gabriel. When Gabriel was subsequently detained, Daniel was not needed to "pray him through." No, Gabriel was *God's* messenger on *God's* mission. God sent Michael the Archangel to assist Gabriel so he *could* complete that mission. Human intervention was not needed.

Seeking guidance or illumination from *any* supernatural source aside from God is witchcraft. Satan's goal has *always* been to divert our hearts away from the worship of the One True God

MorningStar eventually backed out of their plan to move all their operations to Moravian Falls. The Project was located in Wilkes County, North Carolina and a dispute developed between county officials and Rick Joyner over unpaid taxes. The entire dispute centered on the denial of his property tax-exempt status. County officials naturally questioned whether the land was being used for ministry or for business purposes. They claimed that more than half of MorningStar's revenue was derived from book and CD sales and thus it was more of a business than a church. Joyner considered taking civil rights action or at least threatened it. He told the *Wilkes Journal-Patriot* that "The County is trying to set legal precedent. They are getting into defining what a ministry is." However, Joyner apparently didn't want to wait around for the outcome of his threatened legal action, which he subsequently lost. He told the *Wilkes Journal-Patriot*, "We just can't wait that long. We think this could be a constitutional thing and drag out for a long time. It could be ugly."

Joyner had already moved the publishing and distribution part of the ministry to the Wilkesboro area, a few miles from Moravian Falls. However, the *Wilkes Journal-Patriot* claimed that Joyner told them the ministry's publishing efforts were returning to Charlotte and that its conference program would revert there in a year or so. The interview that appeared in the *Wilkes Journal Patriot* ended up being quoted by the magazine, *Charisma News*.[20] Joyner refuted these statements, in effect calling the *Wilkes Journal-Patriot* liars. His comments follow.

---

20. Grady, L. J. Charisma Magazine, 10 Dec. 2000.

> On another note, if you saw the news report in Charisma
> Magazine stating that we were abandoning our base in
> Moravian Falls, please know that we have never even
> considered such a thing. We are, in fact, buying more land
> and expect to start more construction this spring. Charisma
> also reported that we have an annual income of 88 million
> which was only off by about 81 million, but we hope they
> were prophesying on that part! ... We do not believe that
> there was any malice behind the Charisma report, but it did
> nevertheless hurt us financially. You can believe that if you
> ever hear of a report that we are abandoning anything, it is
> probably a false report. —Rick Joyner

He had to save face, after all, he was angry with Wilkes County and probably didn't think what he said to a small town newspaper would ever make national coverage. However, it seems the *Wilkes Journal- Patriot* was correct after all. MorningStar *did* abandon their publishing and distribution center in Wilkes County.

MorningStar's conferences at that time were being held in a place called Jubilee Junction, an old Honkey-Tonk bar they had rented for both their conferences and for the Wilkesboro MorningStar Fellowship. The conferences held there ceased and reverted back to Charlotte just as the *Wilkes Journal-Patriot* claimed Joyner had told them. Evidently, Joyner had lied to *Charisma.*

I find it interesting that Joyner claimed that Charisma's reporting of MorningStar moving back to Charlotte had hurt his ministry financially. Why would that report have *hurt* the ministry unless perhaps people stopped giving to the Moravian Falls Project when they heard it was being abandoned? He certainly would not have wanted *those* donations to dry up.

When the publishing and distribution center reverted back to Charlotte, the staff had to endure the fall-out. I knew one employee who had sold her home in Charlotte and bought one in the Moravian Falls area when the publishing part of the ministry moved to Wilkesboro. After settling in Moravian Falls at her own expense, her job reverted back to Charlotte again, seemingly overnight. She was left with a home to sell in Moravian Falls, and nowhere to live in Charlotte.

Contrary to the statement that MorningStar was *buying* more land in the Moravian Falls area, they started to sell. They divided the land into lots and began selling the vast parcels of land off piece by piece. MorningStar's for-sale signs dotted the road up and down that mountain. Then mysteriously, those blue lettered for-sale signs with the MorningStar symbol came down and were replaced with signs with a different company name. They had taken in an inestimable amount of money to build the Moravian Falls Project, but much of the land they had purchased was then developed, divided into lots, and sold. So, where did the money go? There had been years and years of collecting money from an international audience for this project. What did they have to show for it? Where did it all go? The only thing that the Moravian Falls Project contained was a thirteen thousand square foot residence owned by Joyner and some other homes for MorningStar's higher initiates. There was certainly no retreat center. I've heard they have now built a small guest house with eight rooms. However, it is precisely that—a guest-house for *invited* guests.

Aside from the money, what happened to the revelation from the Lord telling Joyner that it was to be the head of their ministry and publishing efforts? What about the 24-Hour Worship Center or the Teaching Center? What about the Sabbath Rest Center, the International Fellowship Center or the Youth Camp? What happened to it being the home of MorningStar Ministries, MorningStar Fellowship of Ministries, and the MorningStar Fellowship of Churches? Did God change His mind about their operations there? Did God make a mistake? Did God not realize before He allegedly spoke to Joyner that Wilkes County would demand land tax? What about all the other prophesies? It's amazing how quickly Joyner could abandon what he had previously claimed to be from the Lord when his pocket book was involved.

While I was writing this chapter, I happened upon something that made my stomach turn. MorningStar is at it again! This time, they are raising money for a missionary base in Moravian Falls. After all, it has been the better part of twenty years since they raised funds for the Moravian Falls Project. Surely their fan base has changed now, and people have forgotten. Their website asks visitors to "pray for the completion of this project's first phase and pray about sending in your investment to help us in reaching the nations through the writing and teachings of

Rick Joyner and MorningStar."[21] We do not need to reach the nations through the Gnostic, New Age writings of Rick Joyner and MorningStar Ministries. We need to reach them with the Gospel of Jesus Christ – the *real* Gospel.

---

21. Parrott, J. "Mission Base Update." 2013

ELEVEN
EVERYWHERE A SIGN

I f you were looking for a sign, you were sure to find it at MorningStar. I remember Robin McMillan, a member of the leadership team, picking up trash from the street on his way to service. He held up each item before us as a prophetic symbol and told us what God was speaking to us through each piece. This was meant to show us, according to McMillan, that the Lord could even prophesy through garbage.

Everything seemed to be a sign at MorningStar! Leaves blowing in the wind might be a sign that God wanted us to turn over a new leaf. Finding a penny in the street might make us believe it was time for *change*. Glancing at a clock at 5:55 might mean God was pouring out a triple portion of His Grace. Literally, everything was interpreted as either a sign or a prophetic symbol.

We *lived* like this! We lived by these signs, omens and portends and that is precisely what they were—although we would have been loath to call them such. We ignored the fact that Scripture *forbids* the seeking of such and we likewise ignored the fact that the rest of the Christendom did not live this way![1] In our twisted minds, it was *them* who had the problem, not us. It was *normal* to us. After all, when you live in the Land of Oz, seeing colored horses and tiny men singing *Oompah*, isn't strange at all.

I had learned to shut my mind down and allow myself to experience

---

1. Deut. 18:10, 18:14, II Kings 17:17, II Kings 21:6, Isa. 2:6, Eze. 13:7, Mic. 5:12

the manifestations without questioning them. It was the only way to survive without going mad in this environment. Some *did* go mad—literally. MorningStar was a giant eclectic collection of mentally ill people congealed in one location! I often wondered if they were crazy before they came or if it developed while they were there. In other words, did MorningStar draw the unstable or did it cause the instability? I suspect it was a bit of both. However, mentally ill or not, the ministry *never* lacked followers. It was a giant turnstile—the wide-eyed initiates streaming in, and the broken and disillusioned streaming out.

Oh, and lest you think I am leaving myself out of the aforementioned mix, I assure you, I am not. If there wasn't something wrong with me before I got to MorningStar, there most certainly was by the time I left. It took me a very long time to be free of the influence of this movement, and it has not been an easy journey.

You see, when I first arrived at MorningStar, my questioning mind had produced a great deal of inner turbulence. However, the longer I was there, the better I became a rationalizing away the significance of almost *any* opposing evidence. If I had stopped to think about it, I would have realized that I was literally being brainwashed into shutting down my rational thoughts and natural discernment. We were inundated with thought-stopping Biblical phrases invariably quoted out of context. Phrases such as; *judge not, touch not the Lord's anointed* and, *do His prophets no harm*. We were admonished to set our questions aside and just accept and receive the experiences and manifestations as an act of faith. Real biblical discernment and any form of logical thought were discouraged and derided as being a kind of religious bigotry. Those who questioned were told they had a religious spirit. Mindless submission was encouraged and lauded, and these were the people who were given places of honor and leadership. The widening gap between what we knew to be true and this newly created reality caused a disconnect—or what is commonly referred to as, cognitive dissonance.[2]

Cognitive dissonance occurs when you continue to hold to a belief *even though* evidence contradicts that belief. Naturally, our minds cannot hold two opposing views at the same time so we strive to bring them closer together through rationalization.

Let me give you an example. Let's say you have been in a loving

---

2. Spencer, Myers, & Steven. Social Psychology. 2006.

marriage for thirty years to a Christian man you adore. One day you hear a knock at the door, and you open it to find a police officer who informs you that your husband has been arrested on several counts of pedophilia dating back two decades. Your mind is reeling. How can your well-respected husband have been a good and faithful partner for thirty years and *also* a pedophile? Your mind says it can't be true because the belief that your husband is a moral man is so ingrained in you that you immediately disregard evidence to the contrary!

You begin to rationalize. Maybe they have the wrong *house*, maybe they have the wrong *man!* It *has* to be a misunderstanding! Surely, your husband will be able to explain all this and clear it all up. However, as evidence mounts, and the witness list grows, sooner or later the acid of truth eats through your wall of denial and your view of your husband swings to the other side. You realize now your husband is *not* a good, moral, decent man. He is a predator and a pedophile who destroys the souls of children for his own sexual gratification. With this realization, your world comes crashing down.

You have just experienced cognitive dissonance. You cannot hold the belief that your husband is a good, faithful Christian man and *also* hold the belief that he is a pedophile. One of those has to go and at this point you only have one of two choices. You either retreat into fantasy, believing it can't be true, or you accept the reality and all that comes with it—even if it wrecks your world. The cognitive dissonance will continue until a decision is made so there is never an option of straddling the fence.

With the mounting evidence against MorningStar, I experienced this very thing. I kept shoving the contradictions in a closet and shutting the door because I wanted to hold on to that beautiful lie. After a while, the closet got so full that it became harder and harder to keep the door shut. As the contents of that overstuffed closet began spilling into my conscious mind, I started believing less of what I hearing and questioning far more

I remember in one meeting, Bobby Connor, a frequent speaker at MorningStar's School of the Spirit, telling us about a recent visitation from the *Lord*. According to his testimony, an electric blue light streamed through his window, into his room, and above his bed. He claimed that it felt like a wind current so he played in it by dipping his hand into and out of the air flow.

Suddenly, the *Lord* materialized and asked Bobby if he recognized him. Bobby told him that he did indeed recognize him. The *Lord* then morphed into an old lady and asked Bobby again, if he recognized him. He replied that he did. Next, the *Lord* morphed into a small child and asked him again. On and on it went, each time the *Lord* changing appearance and each time Bobby affirming that he still recognized him. Finally, the *Lord* morphed into a dreadful and repugnant creature. Bobby said he was frightened, but the creature spoke to him with the voice of the *Lord* asking him if he recognized him *now!*

I was horrified when I heard this story. This man, so revered by MorningStar leadership, actually *believed* this experience was from the Lord. He claimed it was meant to show him that good is often masked in evil. Even then, I knew that was a lie.

The idea of good being hidden in evil or light being surrounded by darkness is Luciferian in nature. It is *Lucifer* who appears as an angel of light! The real Lord *would* not and indeed *could* not, appear as an agent of darkness. The one true God, the God of Abraham Isaac and Jacob, cannot self-contradict! God would not tell us in His Holy Word to *avoid* the very appearance of evil if He was going to cloak himself in it![3] So, while Bobby's experience might have been from the Lord, it was obviously the wrong Lord.

Luciferianism is the religion of Freemasonry, the New World Order, the New Age, and the mystery religions. It is the polar opposite and the complete twisting of true Christianity. Luciferians believe that Lucifer is the *real* God, the *kind* and benevolent God, the creator God. Consequently, they believe the God of Israel, the one *true* God, the God of Abraham, Isaac, and Jacob is a lesser God—an evil and vindictive God who has imprisoned mankind on earth and kept him ignorant of his own divinity. This is diametrically opposed to what we Christians believe. Interestingly enough, Luciferians believe they are worshipping the Day Star or Morning Star mentioned in Isaiah.

> How you are fallen from heaven, O Lucifer, son of the morning! [How] you are cut down to the ground, You who weakened the nations! —Isa 14:12

---

3. I Thessalonians 5:22

It is evident here that this verse is referring to Lucifer. Luciferians do not believe they are worshipping the being named Satan. They believe that Christians have it wrong. They insist that Lucifer is really the *right* God the one that is trying to *help* us, illuminate us, liberate us. In their eyes, the real God, our God, was evil—a malevolent taskmaster trying to enslave us.

Now, I realize that Jesus is referred to as the Morning Star in the book of Revelation, and this is where some of the confusion comes in. The word Morning Star in Isaiah should actually be translated Lucifer. Some of the newer Bible translations have replaced Lucifer with Morning Star in the verse in Isaiah, but it should not be so. The original Hebrew word for Lucifer is Helel (hay-LALE) which means son of the morning. This Hebrew word *Helel* only appears *once* in the Word of God, and that is in this verse in Isaiah. His crime is described in Isaiah Chapter 14. He exalted himself above the other stars of God, he wanted to *be* God. After God had cast Lucifer (Helel) out of Heaven, he became Satan. So to make it simple, Lucifer (Helel) and Satan are the same being—called Lucifer (Helel) before the fall and Satan after.

So having cleared that up, let me state emphatically that Jesus is the *real* and *only* Morning Star and the Hebrew root *Helel* has been translated Morning Star in both Isaiah and in Revelation but are from two *different* Hebrew words. They are *not* the same person.

> "I, Jesus, have sent My angel to testify to you these things in the churches. I am the Root and the Offspring of David, the Bright and Morning Star." —Rev 22:16

Jesus is *the* Light of the World, and Lucifer is only a *created* being—a created light.[4] He has been cast down from Heaven and is now a dark and deceiving light—a light that masqurades as the real thing. This is precisely what Jesus meant when he said the following:

> Therefore take heed that the light which is in you is not darkness. —Luk 11:35

Although I am not a fan of the New Living Translation, I do like

---

4. John 9:5

the way it interprets this verse. "Make sure that the light you *think* you have is not actually darkness." That is powerful.

Now, I think before continuing I should clarify something that frequently comes up. There *is* a big difference between Satanists and Luciferians. While both Satanists and Luciferians are, in essence, both worshipping the devil, there is a fundamental difference between the two. Satanists *know* that Lucifer is who the Bible portrays him to be yet they choose to worship him anyway. Luciferians, on the other hand, believe they are worshiping Lucifer but believe him to the real God— God Most High.

The quote below encapsulates precisely what it is that Luciferians believe. Notice they capitalize God when speaking of Lucifer but do not capitalize it when speaking of our God.

> Yes, Lucifer is God, and unfortunately, Adonay is also god. For the eternal law is that there is no light without shade, no beauty without ugliness, no white without black, for the absolute can only exist as two gods; darkness being necessary for light to serve as its foil as the pedestal is necessary to the statue, and the brake to the locomotive.[5]
> —General Albert Pike, Grand Commander, Sovereign Pontiff of Universal Freemasonry.

The Luciferian idea of God being found in darkness was a prevalent theme at MorningStar. On more than one occasion, I recall Joyner telling us that the Holy of Holies, the inner sanctuary of the Tabernacle, and later the Temple in Jerusalem, was pitch black. God, he explained, surrounded Himself with darkness, and to experience real intimacy with God we had to go *into* that darkness. What a lie!

In the Old Testament, the Light in the Holy of Holies was God's Glory. There was no lampstand in there because God *was* (and is) the light! In the New Testament, *Jesus* is the Holy of Holies, and we enter in through our relationship with *Him* and the acceptance of His sacrifice. There is no darkness or shadow in Him!

This is the message which we have heard from Him and

---

5. Brent, 2006

declare to you, that God is light and in Him is no darkness at all. If we say that we have fellowship with Him, and walk in darkness, we lie and do not practice the truth. —1 Jo 1:5–6

So, if this doctrine is Luciferian then why was it being preached at MorningStar. Why, indeed! It is quite evident when one becomes familiar with what is taught there, *who* they are serving. However, to make it even more clear, let's compare Isaiah 14:12–14 to words taken directly from Rick Joyner's, *The Final Quest*.

How you are fallen from heaven, O Lucifer, son of the morning! [How] you are cut down to the ground, You who weakened the nations! For you have said in your heart: 'I will ascend into heaven, I will exalt my throne above the stars of God; I will also sit on the mount of the congregation On the farthest sides of the north; I will ascend above the heights of the clouds, I will be like the Most High.'

Notice Lucifer's five "I will's" in the verses of Scripture above.

- I will ascend into Heaven
- I will exalt my throne above the stars of God
- I will sit on the mount of the congregation (mount of assembly)
- I will ascend above the heights of the clouds
- I will be like the Most High.

Now, let's look at a quote from Rick Joyner's book, *The Final Quest*.

Let us understand, the Lord wants us to ascend to Heaven; He wants us to sit on the mount of the assembly; He wants us to be raised above the heights of the clouds, and He wants us to be like Him. —Rick Joyner, *The Final Quest*

Now, since the *real* God, the one *true* God, is *condemning* Lucifer for these things, do you really think the real God would be encouraging us to do the same? Yet Joyner tells us in the quote above that the Lord *wants us* to:

- ✠ To ascend to Heaven
- ✠ To sit on the mount of assembly
- ✠ To be raised above the heights of the clouds
- ✠ To be like Him (meaning to be Him- become Him)

Again, I have to ask you, which *Lord* is he referring to? Certainly not mine.

In another recalled incident from MorningStar, Bobby Connor told us about losing his pocket knife. The knife held significant sentimental value, and he was understandably upset about its loss. In exasperation, he told God that he wanted his knife back. Immediately, according to Bobby, the knife materialized and dropped onto the bed in front of him.

If this actually happened, and that is a big *if*—it was a manifestation through witchcraft and *not* the Holy Spirit! Demons can, and frequently do produce manifestations. There are *no* instances of anything of this nature occurring in Scripture. There are, however, plenty of cases of this happening in witchcraft and the occult. Manifestations in and of themselves, mean *nothing*. The materialization of objects is a hallmark of Eastern mysticism and the occult.

At Mahesh Chavda's All Nations Church in Charlotte North Carolina, I remember seeing Ruth Heflin speak while covered in a substance she claimed was gold-dust. She insisted it just materialized out of thin air everywhere she spoke. Later examination, however, proved it to be nothing more than cheap poster glitter.

Ruth Heflin died of cancer at the age of 62. Bob Shattles, another great purveyor of the glory dust phenomena, died of liver cancer at age 65. I would never have wanted harm to come to them but by their fraudulent claims, they were mocking the Glory of God and that is very dangerous territory.

The manifestation of gold dust is not of God. The only time gold dust is mentioned in the Bible is when Moses came down from the mount of transfiguration and found the Israelites worshipping the Golden Calf. Angered, he pounded their idol into dust and made them drink it.[6] Something to ponder.

Another manifestation, which far exceeded gold dust in its foolishness, was that of angel's feathers. Not once in Scripture are angels presented as having wings. Seraphim and Cherubim have wings but not angels in general. The purpose of the Seraphim and Cherubim is to surround God's throne and worship him. While technically they are classified by most Biblical scholars as angels they are considered to be of a higher class. However, no *other* angels are presented in Scripture as having wings.

So, if this manifestation is really from God, then we would first have to accept the fact that the feathers are coming from either the Seraphim or the Cherubim that surround God's throne. We would also have to accept the fact that they molt! If there is no death or decay in Heaven how could they possibly molt? Are they defective? Does God have defective angels worshipping him and dropping feathers on the throne room floor? Do you see how ridiculous this gets?

In all fairness, I never saw the "feather manifestation" at Morning-Star, but I *did* witness it in other churches in this movement. It looked, to me, like someone had opened the inside of a feather pillow. Seriously, the feathers were tiny and looked suspiciously like chicken feathers—just saying.

Equal to angel feathers in its sheer goofiness was the phenomenon of gemstones being dropped from Heaven in revival services. I have been in services where they claimed that gems fell from Heaven or that God filled their teeth with gold. Please do not misunderstand me, I believe in miracles. However, miracles and manifestations in and of themselves, mean nothing. The occult claims these same manifestations! We *have* to use discernment and *love* the Truth, or we will easily be led astray by such things.

We also need some common sense! Do you really think the God of

6. Exodus 32

the universe that knit you together in your mother's womb would give you a gold tooth instead of say, I dunno, filling it with actual tooth material? Wouldn't that be like Jesus giving the deaf man a hearing aid instead of actually healing his ears or like giving the blind man glass eyes?

Remember, Pharoah's magicians could duplicate most of the miracles that Moses performed. Yes, God *does* confirm his word with signs following according to Mark 16:20, however, God will not ever confirm a false message! If false doctrine is being preached why would God approve and affirm that with a sign? The author of the message is the one affirming it, and if the message does not conform to Scripture, you can be sure that God is not the one confirming it no matter how convincing the sign.

After getting out of this movement, I had to take a very long and painful look at what was lacking in me that made me so vulnerable to this kind of spiritual deception and manipulation. My conclusion: I was deceived because I did not love the Truth—not enough, anyway. I have always been an adventure seeker, and this was an adventure. I wanted the experiences, the thrill.

I don't place the blame on those from whom the deception came. No. I place the blame squarely on my own shoulders where it belongs. Just like Adam who complained that the woman had deceived him, we are all responsible for our *own* decisions. We are all without excuse before God. We have to love Truth and value it above all else.

TWELVE
LOST TIME

I am at MorningStar. I feel peculiar, spacey, a strange floating sensation pulling at my belly. I am under, drifting, floating, blissfully numbed. Suddenly, I awake. Something is wrong. I'm standing with my arms raised, swaying. I drop my arms down and look around anxiously. I am disoriented. What is happening? I quickly scan the room noticing the homogenized mass of swaying bodies with oddly vacant looks pasted to their faces. Dan is standing in the row behind me, hands raised, eyes closed, head cocked to the side. He looks as if he has left his body. I turn back toward the front and listen to the worship team. Leonard Jones is leading. My eyes widen in horror as the realization of what is being sung washes over me.

Oh, stinking death we drink your cup....
Here comes the Sun all dressed in black

I turn around. "Dan!" I hiss loudly, "Dan!" There is no response. "Dan!" I whisper louder, "Dan!" Again, no response. "Dan, please!" I cry louder, poking him hard in the chest. "Please listen, please—*listen!*"

His eyes flutter open. "What?" he moans, brows knitting together tightly. "What do you want?" He is angry.

I'm pleading now. "Listen—please listen to what they are saying!" His eyes close again then suddenly snap open. He is fully alert now. A look of shock crosses his face as he listens for a moment. "*What* are they singing?" The band has now gone into a Beatles song ...

Here comes the sun, doo doo doo doo
Here comes the sun, and I say
It's alright
Little darling
It's been a long, cold, lonely winter
Little darling
It feels like years since it's been here
Here comes the sun
Here comes the sun and I say
It's alright ...[1]

Dan grabs my arm and jerks it toward the door, "We need to get *out* of here!" We surge through the door and out into the night, standing together for a while at the edge of the parking lot before either of us speak. "What are we involved in?" Dan asks, looking back toward the light spilling from the glass doors.

"I don't know. I really don't know." I look toward the Charlotte skyline sparkling like a jewel against a starless sky. I wonder how many people are represented by that skyline. Countless people leading normal lives, doing normal things, oblivious to *this* world—this *madness*. I'm struggling to make sense of where I am, of what just happened. "Dan, do you remember *anything* before I poked you?"

"No, no I don't. What about you?"

"Well, I remember the worship starting ... I think. I don't know—it was like I just woke up all of a sudden. I woke up and started listening and ... they were talking about death—about drinking a cup of death! Am I crazy? *You* heard them say it, didn't you?"

"*Yes!* I heard it!" Dan is staring blankly past me as if in shock.

"Where *were* we? I ask pleadingly, "where did we *go?* Why can't we remember? Were we hypnotized? Are we mind- controlled? Are we nuts?"

"I don't know, but what we just experienced was *not* God!" He pauses for a moment as if afraid to continue. He looks around quickly to ensure there is no one within earshot. "There is something *really* wrong here," he whispers.

---

1. The Beatles. Here Comes the Sun. Abbey Road EMI-Electrola. 1979

"Heck yeah, there is something wrong here!" I pause for a moment looking down, kicking at a small stone, thinking.

"My family thinks I'm in a cult," Dan offers, after several minutes.

"We *are* in a cult!" I quickly retort. Dan snorts and looks away, but when our eyes lock several minutes later, there is an understanding there. We both know it is true.

"What does your family think of all this, Mishel?

"Mine? Are you kidding me? My family would have me committed if they knew what I was involved with. I don't discuss it with them, or *anyone* for that matter. I mean, really, what would I say? Can you imagine? I would be like, 'Hey mom, the other day I was worshiping in church, and I must have been hypnotized or something because I woke up and they were singing a Beetles' song and talking about drinking a cup of death.' How do you think that would go over?"

Dan laughs. "I can picture your mom right now—your poor sweet conservative mom. I can imagine the look of *horror* on her face. I would love to be a fly on the wall for *that* conversation."

I sigh heavily and roll my eyes. "We are the only ones who think this is normal, and *we* don't even think it's normal—anymore!"

A serious almost pensive look registers on Dan's face. "No, it's definitely *not* normal."

"Dan, sometimes what MorningStar calls the anointing, feels— umm, it feels, well almost, you know, like—well like, umm ..."

"Say it, Mishel! Go ahead and say it. Evil—it feels evil!"

"Yes! It feels *evil*. I said it! I felt it the first day I came, but then I shoved it down because I thought it must be me. I didn't even want to *think* about the fact that I could be right about what I was feeling. It was easier to think it was *me*, that there was something wrong with *me!* But it's *not* me! There is something *evil* here. There is—and I don't care what *anybody* says or *how* they explain it away!"

"So what do we do now?" Dan asks soberly.

"I don't know. I don't even want to think about it. My *life* is here, my friends—I mean I *moved* here for this! I just don't know."

"Come on, Mishel. Leave your car here. Let's take my truck and go downtown, Charlotte. Let's just forget this place and go walking in the city. It's so beautiful this time of night. Let's forget about all the questions and confusion and just laugh again. How long has it been since you laughed?"

"I don't honestly remember, Dan. My spirit has been so heavy lately."

"Do you remember when we first came, how we all laughed? We had all come to seek God, and it seemed like such an adventure. Not just you and me, but the others, too. We all seem so burdened now. It's *changed* us." Dan pauses, sighs, and then looks at me with a mischievous lopsided grin. "Let's do something *spontaneous!* Let's go downtown, run through the streets and laugh like we *used* to laugh. Let's find our joy again."

"Tonight?"

"Why not tonight?"

"Like, right now?"

"Right now."

"Alright! Let's do it. But can we stop for a Coke first—that cup of death made my mouth dry."

I drifted in and out of MorningStar for many months after that, struggling to get free. However, my friend Dan pushed the fear and confusion aside and immersed himself deeper.

THIRTEEN
KING ARTHUR &
THE LUCIFERIAN LIGHT

I was there the night the following words were spoken. Words that were transcribed and immortalized on the internet by someone who had obtained a tape of that evening's service, albeit, an edited tape. I remember it so plainly. I remember the expressions, the hand movements, and even where I was sitting. Rick was the speaker that evening and the following is the transcript taken from the audiotaped session.

> Bob would fall into a trance as soon as he crossed the South
> Carolina border, and an incredible prophetic anointing would
> come upon him. And we're flying along, Bob's talking, and
> all of the sudden the anointing comes on the airplane. And
> Bob goes, and he's in it, and he starts prophesying and believe
> me when he hits that anointing, it is a high level. Bob told me
> many, many years ago—he said 'You're gonna be in London
> on the first of spring,' and I'm just gonna share briefly what
> he said. He said the Lord told him that I was Arthur, and he
> spelled it out, and also an author, and he spelled it out again.
> This is years ago—I believe Bob got this before we ever met.
> He said, 'You're gonna be in London on the first of spring
> and God's gonna show you where a sword is stuck in the rock
> and you're supposed to pull this sword out of a rock.' And he

said, 'And then you're gonna start the Round Table.' Anyway, I'd forgotten that years ago.

—Rick Joyner[1]

Now, let's take a moment and recap what we have to this point so we don't get tangled in the narrative.

- ✠ Bob Jones falls into a trance on an airplane just over the South Carolina border.

- ✠ While in the trance, the *Lord* shows Bob that Joyner will be in London on the first day of spring.

- ✠ While in London the *Lord* is going to show Joyner a stone with a sword stuck in it.

- ✠ Joyner is going to pull the sword out of the stone and start the (Prophetic) Round Table.

Now, let's continue with the rest of the narrative and continue building the foundation as we move through the rest of the transcript.

Three years ago, January, when Bob was here for our New Year's Eve meeting, we were sitting in our kitchen. He said 'When ya going to London?' and I started thinking and I said 'I'm going this year.' He said 'Yep, probably about the first of spring.' I started thinking, and I said 'Bob, I'm gonna be there on the very first of spring.' He said 'Yep'—you know how he does—says, yep, yep. He says, 'How long has it been since I gave you that prophecy?' I said 'Five years.' And I went back and counted. I said five years since he told me I was gonna be in there. He had told me about the sword and all that. I don't remember exactly, but when he told me I would be there on the first of Spring, I believe it had been about five years. I said 'Bob, I think it's been about five years.' He said 'How many kids ya got now?' I said 'Five,' said 'How many times did the Lord lay hands on you?' And I had a visitation when the Lord literally came and laid hands on me five times. I thought He

1. Joyner, Rick. Words for the Coming Times. Dec 31, 1997 Cassette.

had killed me five times. But that happened. He said 'How many times did the Lord lay hands on you?' I said 'Five.' 'How old is Amber now?' He said 'Five.' You know, five—all these fives are lining up. He said 'Yep. You'll be there on the first of Spring, and that will be the time of your commission.'

And I was there sitting in my hotel room, and I had an extraordinary visitation of the Lord. I was carried places by the Lord—given things—I was given five things by the Lord in that visitation. It was just one of those deals. You know, I think it was in a lot of ways a commission.'—Rick Joyner, Signs of the Coming Times.

So, to encapsulate what was just spoken, Bob was at Morning-Star for the 1995 New Year's Eve Service. While there, Bob reminds Joyner of what he (Bob) had prophesied in the airplane years earlier (by asking Joyner when he will be in London). Joyner tells him he is planning to be in London on the first day of spring. Bob subsequently tells Joyner that this will be his commissioning. In other words, Bob tells Joyner that this will be the fulfillment of the earlier prophecy. On *this* trip, Joyner will draw the sword from the stone and later start the Prophetic Round Table. Now, I also want you to pay attention to the emphasis on the number five as we will be coming back to this a bit later.

In the next part of the narrative, which takes place in December 1997, Bob asks Joyner for a *second* time if he will be in London on the first day of the coming spring (1998). What a coincidence—he *IS* going to be in London on the first day of spring! This isn't *quite* the coincidence that it seems, but let's push on with the narrative.

Then Bob comes up again—you know—the other day and he goes 'You're gonna be in London again on the first of spring.' I'm thinking back—I do go to London this year. It's the first of spring! How old is Amber? All these eights start lining up, you know. It's an important trip to London. I will be in London again on the first of spring. And it's eight. And it's gonna be a major beginning. A major beginning for me personally and for us—you know –as a ministry.[2]

2. Op. Cit.

I may be belaboring this but it is imperative that you understand what is being said here to build a foundation for what is to come. According to Joyner, Jones had prophesied, sometime in the early nineties, that:

- Joyner would be in London on the first day of spring.

- The Lord would show Joyner a sword in stone.

- Joyner would draw the sword out.

- Joyner would start the Prophetic Round Table.

- Joyner found significance in the fact that "all [the] fives [were] lining up."

So, Bob is at MorningStar for the New Year's Eve Service, Dec 31, 1994. He reminds Joyner of that prophecy and coincidentally, Joyner *just happens* to be going to London for the first day of that coming spring, (March 21, 1995). So, according to Bob's prophecy (and what Joyner himself has stated here) Joyner would have "pulled the sword from the stone" on March 21, 1994, and started the Prophetic Round Table sometime after that.

Now, I don't want to get too far off track here but I do want to mention this. The Prophetic Round Table met at MorningStar for the first time on December 4–6, 1995. Its purpose, according to Joyner, was to "discuss important issues now facing the church in America and to make a common statement about our position concerning those issues."[3] Those in attendance at the first Round Table meeting were Larry Alberts, Paul Cain, Mahesh and Bonnie Chavda, Bobby Conner, Don Cousins, Jack Deere, Reuven and Marylou Doron, Don Finto, Francis Frangipane, T. D. Hall, Dudley Hall, Peter Lord, Steve Mansfield, and Bob and Rose Weiner[4] I mention the start of the Prophetic Round Table and those in attendance only as a matter of interest and not as a matter of focus. So, at the risk of getting off track, let's return to the narrative.

Now, the last part of the recorded tape brings us to the present, not *our* present, but present as in the night of the recording. Joyner is speaking here at the New Year's Eve Service Dec 31, 1997. He informs

---

3. Joyner, Rick. "Report from the Round Table." Prophetic Bulletin #15
4. Op. Cit.

us (and I say us because I was present that evening) that Bob told him (the other day) that he (Joyner) was going to be in London *again* on the first day of spring that year (March 21, 1998). Joyner confirms that yes, he WILL be in London on the first day of spring and states that it will be "an important trip to London." Then, by way of explaination, he says "I will be in London again *on the first of spring.*" Evidently, that date is very important to him. As to his second reason, he states that the "eights are lining up." He mentions this about the eights because one, he will be going in 1998, and two, because his daughter Amber will be eight years old. This is significant because Joyner believes that the number eight is the number of new beginnings. He interprets this to mean that it will be a new beginning for him personally and for the ministry.

Now, I realize I have belabored this narrative somewhat, but it is critical to what I am about to show you. When Bob "prophesied" that Joyner would pull a sword from a stone, he was referring of course, to King Arthur. This was in reference to the 1995 trip, the one in which Joyner made a point of telling us that the fives were lining up.

According to legend, King Arthur supernaturally removed a mystical sword from a stone that none could draw out, save he who was the rightful king. King Arthur then gathered a group of knights who were reportedly the best in the kingdom, and they met encircling a round table in the king's castle. These Knights of the Round Table spent years traversing back and forth across Britain in search of the Holy Grail.

Now, obviously Joyner would not have told us this so-called prophecy from Bob Jones if he didn't actually *believe* it. Therefore, it is safe to assume that he believed himself to either be the *real* King Arthur, (whom legend says will return) or a type and shadow thereof.

Now, if we take this at face value we would have to believe that Joyner stumbled on an actual rock on the first day of spring in 1995, and this rock had a sword embedded in it which he managed to draw out. Presumably, this would somehow show Joyner's worthiness for the task he was predestined to fulfill. In this case, according to Bob Jones, starting the Prophetic Round Table.

Now, I think we can agree that a *literal* interpretation of Joyner drawing a sword out of stone is highly unlikely and a bit preposterous. So, I believe that it is safe and *reasonable* to assume that Bob's prophecy to Joyner was meant to be more *symbolic* than literal. But what was it a symbol *of* and why the emphasis on the first day of spring?

Interestingly enough, this date is the Vernal Equinox. It is a day celebrated by many esoteric groups and considered to be the Luciferian New Year. Coincidence? Maybe—but you have to realize that Joyner seemed to place an inordinate amount of importance on days the occult considers Holy. Oddly, many of the conferences seemed to coincide with these dates. I was not the only one who noticed this fact during my time at MorningStar. Many had commented on the oddity of it. To further illustrate this point, I took an excerpt from a 2008 MorningStar Prophetic Bulletin.

> We are close to the birth of something we were created for, that we believe will begin this fall, around September 21 ... Because of this, we moved our Harvest Conference to begin on September 18, and the Worship & Warfare Conference to begin on September 22, so September 21 will be the Sunday in-between ... We will have midnight bonfires, roaming worship and ministry teams, and other events that will create a festival atmosphere that is conducive to members of the body getting to know one another. Many important bonds between them will begin at this event.[5]

Notice this "new beginning" was to fall *exactly* on the summer solstice. Notice as well, that Joyner moved two conferences so that this date fell in the middle. Oddly enough, he chose to celebrate this date with *midnight* bonfires on September 21, *precisely* the time and date that the summer solstice is celebrated by occult communities through the lighting of the Baal fires.[6] This *can't* be a coincidence.

So, returning to our narrative, Joyner was going to be in London on the first day of spring, the Vernal Equinox—the Luciferian New Year. There, he would do something symbolic that represented removing a sword from a stone. So whatever this removal of a sword from a stone signified, it was important that it be done on *that* particular date. It was also significant to Joyner that all the fives were lining up. Remember, as well, that Joyner claimed to have experienced a visitation where the *lord*

5. Joyner, Rick. "The History and Future of the Present Revival Part 8."
6. Franklin, Anna. 2002

came and laid hands on him five times, each time, making him feel as if the *lord* had killed him.

I posit that Joyner was in London on the Luciferian New Year because he was undergoing an initiation. It is fairly well known that pulling a sword from the stone symbolizes the path Luciferian initiates take toward enlightenment.

Modern Luciferianism's roots are in Gnosticism and the ancient mystery schools. Their beliefs mainly parallel that of the Theosophy and the New Age. They believe that we are born with a divine spark (sword) within us that is trapped, or imprisoned in the gray matter (stone) of our lower minds. This divine spark is the seed of our own divinity –our godhood, if you will. Through ascending the levels and initiations, the divine spark (sword) can be released from within and we can achieve at-oneness with the divine (Lucifer) and become gods ourselves. At this stage we return, metaphorically speaking, to the garden.

The key to awareness and to releasing that spark is through secret gnosis or knowledge. This freeing knowledge is delivered to us via the ascended masters and messengers of light (demons). Now, lest there be any confusion, let me emphatically state that this divine spark is *not* the Christian God but rather Lucifer.

One Luciferian puts this concept rather succinctly in the following quote.

> We have said that Lucifer came to the world to wake man up, to help him remember his divine origin, the divine origin of his Spirit, and to help him free himself from the body-soul in which he is trapped.[7]

Gnostic Luciferians seek higher and higher levels of illumination in order to undergo an apotheosis and reach godhood. As an aside, the entire Apostolic and Prophetic movement talks incessantly about "levels." This concept is *not* found in Scripture but comes directly from the idea that one must ascend through increasingly more challenging levels on the path to becoming divine. If you have been anywhere near this movement, you will recognize the saying, "higher levels, bigger devils." How true that is—but not for the reason they suppose!

---

7. Herrou Aragon, Jose Maria. The Forbidden Religion. Pg 37.

David Spangler, one of the founding members of the New Age Movement and a self-avowed Luciferian shows us why we, as Christians, cannot depend on traditional Christian definitions anymore. One can *say* they serve Christ and *still* be a Luciferian.

> Christ is the same force as Lucifer … Lucifer prepares man for the experience of Christhood. (He is) the great initiator. Lucifer works within each of us to bring us to wholeness, and as we move into a New Age … each of us in some way is brought to that point which I term the Luciferic Initiation, the particular doorway through which the individual must pass if he is to come fully into the presence of his light and wholeness. Lucifer prepares man in all ways for the experience of Christhood … The light that reveals to us the presence of the Christ … comes from Lucifer. He is the light-giver, he is aptly named the Morning Star.[8]

Of course, no one has done more for Gnostic Luciferianism than Alice Bailey of the Theosophical Society. She started Lucifer Trust (now known as Lucis Trust) the publisher for all U.N. material. On the Lucis Trust website, Wendy Boyd explains what drawing the sword from the stone is meant to symbolize.[9]

> Arthur may be likened to sharing a similar role as the Christ principle [Lucifer] in that his presence or appearance is key to unlocking the sword from the stone. In this context it is representative of the transition from the "stuckness" of the lower concrete mind to the higher rapier-like speed of the intuition, giving the Great Invocation a transformative effect upon the mental plane.

So, the sword is the Divine Spark that is trapped within the lower mind—the gray matter represented by the stone. Now, this spark as we have stated earlier, is not Divine at all but demonic in nature. It is the sin nature present within us all as a result of the fall. Gnostic Lucifereans

---

8. Spangler, D. "Reflections on the Christ." P. 44–45
9. Bailey & Boyd. "The Great Invocation, the Sword of God (Lucis Trust).

believe that it is *this* spark that communicates with the Aeons and Ascended Masters (demons). Through this communication, they gain what they believe is sacred knowledge—the wisdom to ascend. This is accomplished through direct connection via trances, mystical experiences, and rituals. Generally, this contact will produce feelings of ecstasy and well-being which is one reason we should never rely on our emotions or what we *feel!*

Here is another quote by Wendy Boyd of Lucis Trust that further elucidates the symbolism of the sword in the stone.

> However, the sword, like Excalibur, has still to be pulled from the stone, the concrete boulder of the lower mind. The Great Invocation can be seen as the Excalibur that is released from the stone and comes to life for all who apply the will-to-good to use it—the sword in the stone waiting to be seized and fulfill its destiny, the promise of paradise regained.[10]

And to show you that the sword-in-the-stone symbolism is well known to Gnostics, here is a similar quote from another Gnostic website.

> The Lesson of The Sword is an Esoteric and Sacred Instruction. It teaches us that by putting our Mind to Its highest and best Spiritual use, each one of us can Pull Our Sword from The Stone and Re-enter The Garden Of Eden! (sic)[11]

On Joyner's *first* trip to London (the trip in which he symbolically withdrew the Sword from the Stone), he emphasized the number five. I have hopefully established the fact that in all likelihood this was a ritual initiation that symbolized ascending through the levels and attaining at-one-ment with the divine. It is worth noting that there are five major initiations one must pass through on the path to enlightenment.

Benjamin Crème a student of both Helen Blavatsky (founder of Theosophy) and Alice Bailey (founder of the New Age Movement) states that:

---

10. Op. Cit.
11. Panek, Joseph. "A Seeker's Thoughts." The Sword

The evolutionary journey on which we are engaged is marked off by five major points of crisis, major expansions of consciousness, which are the five steps to Liberation and Mastery. These are the five planetary Initiations which free us from further incarnational experience on this Earth. All of the Masters have taken these five Initiations.[12]

In another article, Benjamin Crème describes the goal of these five initiations.

There are a great many minor, but only five major, planetary initiations. Each one represents a definite stage of integration and at-one-ment reached by the initiate. The goal is achieved when, at the fifth initiation, the liberated Master stands in full at-onement with the Monad, His Father in Heaven [Lucifer].[13]

There was an overarching fascination with King Arthur, knights, conquests, and the elusive Holy Grail at MorningStar. This was the latter half of the 90's and at that time, Joyner was busy trying to defend himself over being knighted by the Knights of Malta. There were whispers of swords being used in men's meetings to knight them and likewise at the children's meetings.

In a 2001 *Charisma Magazine* article, a former ministry staffer told the magazine that he got concerned when Joyner began urging friends in the inner circle to be knighted. "I never felt a peace about it," the former employee said. "It is an elitist club. People started vying for position so they could be knighted. The ones that were knighted had a special bond with Rick."[14] Everyone present at MorningStar during the late 90's *knew* about the knighting ceremonies. It was impossible to miss the constant talk about knights and conquest, and equally impossible to miss Rick's animated tales of his induction into the Knights of Malta.

In fact, Joyner laughed about others being likewise knighted as he had been. He joked that Bobby Connor had been dubbed Sir Bubba while Mahesh Chavda of all Nations Church had been dubbed Sir Loin. Even then, I wondered why these fables and legends of the dark ages

12. Creme, Benjamin. "The Gospel Story and the Path of Initiation."
13. Creme, B. "The Requirements for Initiation."
14. Harnon, C. "God's Lightening Rod." 2001. Print.

were becoming so prevalent in a church which claimed that God was doing a *new* thing.

As if the focus on knighting was not enough, Joyner unashamedly urged us to seek the Holy Grail. In Joyner's, *Report from the Round Table* published on the ministry website, Joyner wrote the following:

> When the legendary King Arthur called for Knights, it was a call for those who would:
>
> 1. Follow the king;
> 2. Do exploits;
> 3. Slay dragons;
> 4. Find the Holy Grail, which was the cup the Lord used for the Last Supper.
>
> We believe the Lord is putting forth the same call today. He is seeking those who will lay aside everything to follow Him, who will do exploits in His name, who will go about seeking the powers of darkness to destroy them, and who will never give up the quest to find the vessel of true communion.
> —Rick Joyner[15]

So according to his own words, Joyner believed that God was issuing the same call to us as the one King Arthur issued to his Knights of the Round Table.

Now, let's think about that for a minute. Why do you suppose Joyner was so quick to explain that the Grail was the *cup* Christ used at the Last Supper? Why would he feel the *need* to explain that? Wouldn't most people just *assume* he was referring to the cup? Well, of *course*, they would! He emphasized the fact that the Grail was a *cup* because it was a coded message not meant for the uninitiated. He was *not* referring to a cup at all! If he *had* been, then what he said would have made no sense. Think about it. Why would *that* cup be any more Holy than say, the cross on which Christ died or the linen they wrapped His body in after death, or the nails that pierced His hands and feet, or His seamless robe? Why would *this* vessel be so worthy of the centuries-old quest to obtain it? Furthermore, why would Joyner equate finding this cup with

---

15. Joyner, R. "Report from the Round Table." 1996.

"*true* communion?" Could it be that the Holy Grail he was referring to was something else—something far more arcane and mystical?

It is well known among occultists that Arthurian Grail romances are Gnostic and Kabalistic teachings disguised as tales of knightly quests. By concealing the secret knowledge in myths and legends, the keepers of the ancient knowledge were able to pass on heretical doctrines without arousing the suspicions of the Catholic Church. By concealing the secret, those adepts initiated into the Luciferian Light, having attained what the New Age refers to as "Christ Consciousness," avoided being hung or burned as heretics. This so-called, *Christ Consciousness* had nothing to do with serving Christ but rather with *becoming* Christ. This was the original lie whispered to Eve in the Garden by the serpent—her eyes would be opened, she would be illuminated and she would become like God. Incidentally, this is the same lie being whispered today. One New Age teacher puts it quite succinctly.

> Ultimately, what we are dealing with here are the many gradients of higher consciousness ... To find the Grail is to reach the higher stages of consciousness. The highest human stage of consciousness in Western terms is Christ Consciousness.[16]

Certainly, Joyner was *not* telling us to search for the actual cup. That would be ridiculous. After all, the real vessel that Christ drank from has *never* been associated with "true communion." It has *always* been related to profound mysticism, alchemy, gnosticism and the occult. The process of Luciferic enlightenment symbolized by the quest for the Holy Grail is at the heart of *all* esoteric doctrine.

It is interesting to note that Hitler, as one deeply steeped in Luciferian doctrine, was obsessed with King Arthur and the Grail lore. He fancied himself to be King Arthur and his aristocracy, the Knights of the Holy Grail. It is well documented that Hitler underwent a Luciferian initiation under the tutelage of his spiritual mentor, Dietrich Eckart. Meister Eckart is quoted as saying:

> "I shall have influenced history more than any other German. Follow Hitler! I have initiated him into the secret doctrine,

---

16. Piccolo, B.J. July, 2008. Vol. 1. The Grail Newsletters.

opened his centers of vision and given him the means to communicate with the Powers."[17]

In the book *Hitler and the New Age*, author Bob Rosio explains that Hitler underwent a Luciferic initiation:

> "He established communication with Lucifer, from whom he openly coveted possession ... entering the service of Satan through a Luciferic Initiation."[18]

I firmly maintain that Joyner has likewise undergone a Luciferic initiation. First of all, if you dig deep enough into his own writings and things he has publically stated, it becomes increasingly evident what he believes. However, there is another reason, I so firmly maintain this.

At one point, near the end of my time at MorningStar, I happened to have a conversation with a friend, Cynthia. She had been very close to the Joyner's and had, at one point, been a nanny to their children. She had an interesting history, and there are still far more questions about who she was, and how she ended up at MorningStar than I will ever have answered. She was found dead at her home in Virginia in 2009 at the age of 52. I have never heard the cause of death.

During my days at MorningStar, Cynthia had mentioned to me that her husband was in prison. She disclosed to me that Joyner believed her husband to be the biggest false prophet in America— and one of the most dangerous. I had questioned her about this. Surely it was a gross exaggeration on Joyner's part, but she assured me it was not. She also added that her husband had connections to some *very* dangerous people. I asked her several more questions, but it was clear she was uncomfortable, so I let it go. I didn't know her well enough at *that* point to determine whether she was a liar or just plain crazy. As it turns out, she was neither.

After I had known her a while, Cynthia revealed to me that her husband had been the subject of numerous Chick Tracts. I used to *love* those little cartoon tracts, so it piqued my interest. In the 70's and 80's, American publisher Jack T. Chick published numerous short evangelical

17. Rosio, B. Hitler & the New Age, 1993. 137- 144. Print.
18. Op. Cit.

cartoon booklets in the form of tracts. These were hugely popular at the time and came to be known as Chick Tracts. Christians would buy these tracts as a witnessing tool and leave them on restaurant tables, bus stations, trains, phone booths and wherever else they found to leave them. Years after my time at MorningStar, someone inadvertently sent me an article about a man named John Todd Collins. The article mentioned that he had been the subject of several Chick Tracts. It finally clicked—all the bits and pieces Cynthia had told me fell into place with a sickening thud. *This* was who she had been married to! *This* was the man Joyner claimed was the most dangerous false prophet in America.

John Todd, also known as John Todd Collins, was a relatively well-known speaker who made the rounds in fundamental circles in the 70's and 80's. He claimed to be a former occultist born into one of the top ten Illuminati bloodlines before converting to Christianity. Once converted, he became very popular among both fundamentalists and conspiracy theorists. He actively spoke out against the Illuminati, Christian Rock, Catholicism, and Neo-Paganism. Eventually, he went to prison on rape charges—charges he vehemently denied. He claimed he was set up, but there seems to be a tremendous amount of evidence against him. I don't know. It is not my intention to defend or accuse John Todd. I just don't know enough about the facts to intelligently comment one way or the other.

The *official* story claims he was released from prison in 2004 into the care of the Behavioral Disorder Treatment Unit run by the South Carolina Department of Mental Health. According to their records, he died in their care in 2007. Todd would have been only 52 years of age.

In many conspiracy circles, it is believed he was killed deliberately while in the care of the prison system in 1979. However, that cannot possibly be true. John Todd was certainly alive during my time at MorningStar in the late 1990's. Some conspiracy theorist have even claimed he was killed and *replaced* in 1979, but that is just too bizarre for me to seriously consider. Whatever the story, Todd was clearly a fascinating and colorful character who even in death continues to stir a great deal of controversy in conspiracy circles.

Once I had made the connection between John Todd and Cynthia, it became unfathomable to me how the wife of a man who claimed to be a former high-level occultist came to be Rick Joyner's nanny. If Joyner had *truthfully* considered John Todd to be the most dangerous false prophet in America, why did he trust his wife to be his children's nanny?

Interestingly enough, I later found that Cynthia had married John Todd while he was in prison. John Todd's former wife had reportedly divorced him prior to his incarceration. The whole thing seemed odd—but then everything at MorningStar was odd. MorningStar could bend and warp your mind if you let it.

It was from Cynthia that I gleaned the information regarding Joyner's initiation into the Luciferian Light. She shared this information with Dan and I while we all enjoyed some down time in the Blue Ridge Mountains. She seemed genuinely troubled and eventually began to talk about what was bothering her. Hesitantly, she disclosed to us that recently, while visiting at the Joyner's home, Julie had shown her a sequined dress she was planning on wearing to a special event. After showing her the dress Julie asked her advice on what earrings she thought would look best with the dress. Cynthia confessed to us that she had been surprised at Julie's dress choice. The dress was out of character for Julie and most definitely out of place for the backwoods mountain community of Moravian Falls. Cynthia told Julie she thought it was beautiful but asked her where she planned on wearing it. Julie smiled sweetly and motioned toward an invitation on the table. Cynthia looked at the card and was shocked to find it contained an invitation for Rick and Julie to be initiated into the Luciferian Light. When Cynthia questioned it, Julie hastily explained that it didn't mean what she *thought* it meant—that Luciferian did not mean it had anything to do with Satan—that it just meant light, knowledge, and illumination. It brings entirely new meaning to the name *MorningStar* Ministries, doesn't it?

The initiation into the Luciferian light was to take place somewhere in Europe. I always thought I remembered her saying that it was to be held in Great Britain (which of course is where London is located), but then I began to question myself as to whether I remembered that detail correctly. So I don't know for certain but one thing is sure, Cynthia had been very troubled by seeing the invitation—very troubled indeed. She was, however, unwilling to accept what it *really* meant. She would not allow herself to even consider the fact that the Joyners might not be who and what they *said* they were. She eventually left MorningStar but to my knowledge, MorningStar never really left her.

FOURTEEN
NAZIS & THE NEW BREED

Truth can be ugly, especially when the lie has been so beautiful. I saw a momentary flash of truth the night Rick Joyner told us about having a prayer meeting in Hitler's bunker. It was a flash of insight and inner knowing that would stay with me for years, haunting me. It forced me into days, weeks and years of research for answers. What had I been a part of? It was not the gospel, not the real Gospel anyway, but what was it?

Rick had talked about a residual power or energy that was still present in that place. Energy, he explained, left over from what happened there, spiritually. By the look in Rick's eyes, he enjoyed remembering a little *too* much. Whatever residual energy was left there could not have been the presence of the Lord (not the real one, anyway). So, why would he be so excited about holding a prayer meeting there? Additionally, the remains of Hitler's bunker are sealed to the public. So, why had *he* been given access?

Recently, I did a search on the internet to see if I could find others who remembered Joyner talking about having a prayer meeting in Hitler's bunker. I found an interesting transcript of an undated tape that documented the information I remembered hearing. In fact, it is very likely that it is the *actual* audio tape transcript from the night I was present. If it is, then it has been edited somewhat.

Many of those meetings in the mid to late 1990's were recorded, and the cassette tapes mailed to MorningStar's Tape-of-the-Month, subscribers. This transcript was, for the most part, what I recalled from memory, yet parts were missing. Perhaps as I stated, the tape had been edited, or maybe my mind was adding pieces gleaned from other meetings where this was discussed. I don't know.

In addition to the tape transcript, I found some newer videos in which Joyner displayed an odd and alarming affinity for Nazi Germany. In one of the videos, Joyner claimed that his twenty-year fascination with Hitler and the Nazis sprang from a desire to remain vigilant lest history repeat itself. He claimed the Lord had shown him that the same spirit that presided over Nazi Germany would try to gain entrance into America. If you understand what the Dominionist agenda *actually* is, and the nature of the theocracy they seek to *forcibly* institute, it is chillingly similar to Nazi Germany in very significant ways. I found it ironic that Joyner was now warning against the very thing that he was working so diligently to institute!

It is my firm belief that Joyner's affinity for Nazi Germany has *nothing* whatsoever to do with concern over history repeating. After all, Joyner has *no* problem with fascism. He openly admits that the kind of dominion he is seeking to institute will *feel* like totalitarianism.[1] Obviously, it is not fascism that he opposes, but rather any fascism that does not place him and his fellow Dominionists firmly in control.

If you are a student of history, you will realize that Hitler played this card well. He ran for power against the "Godless liberals" and painted himself as a God-fearing Christian man who only wanted to bring back morality to the nation of Germany. Like today's Dominionists, he hated liberalism in all forms. He likewise emphasized how the German people had a "Christian heritage" and that Christian principles had to be adhered to so they could rebuild the country and expand its influence. Does any of this sound familiar? It should! It is precisely the platform of the American Dominionists.

Not long ago, I happened upon a few of MorningStar's *Prophetic Perspectives* videos in which Joyner expounded on his travels to Berlin Germany. In one video, Joyner claimed to have met a man by the name of Colonel Eugene K. Bird; a man who would not only introduce him to some former high-ranking Nazis but would also be indirectly responsible for having him initiated into the Knights of Malta.

If you recall, at the conclusion of WWII there were a series of

---

1. Joyner, R. "Rick Joyner with Dutch Sheets: The True Soldiers." 2007.

military tribunals in which select high ranking political leaders of the defeated Nazi party were prosecuted by the allied forces. These tribunals were known as the Nuremberg Trials. Seven of the convicted war criminals were subsequently held in the Spandau Prison in Western Berlin and guarded in rotating shifts by the Russians, the French, the British and the Americans.

Lieutenant Colonel Eugene K. Bird was the U.S. Commandant of this prison from 1964 to 1972. Rudolph Hess, Hitler's deputy and second in command, was incarcerated at Spandau along with von Schirach, head of the Nazi Youth, and Albert Speer, Hitler's architect. Speer and von Schirach were released in 1966 leaving Hess as the prison's only occupant until his suicide in 1987.

Colonel Eugene K. Bird had been Hess's only friend during his long imprisonment, and it was precisely this close alliance with Hess that ended Bird's military career. He had been collaborating surreptitiously with Hess in writing his memoirs. Colonel Bird had also, brazenly enough, had Hitler's famous architect Albert Speer, design his private summer house while Speer was still incarcerated for war crimes.

Reportedly, Bird moved to Germany permanently at the conclusion of the war and maintained close ties with several former high-ranking Nazi officials. The following quote is taken word for word from MorningStar's *Prophetic Perspectives* video. Rick Joyner is the speaker.[2]

> ... so he [Bird] had spent his time interviewing these top Nazis. Albert Speer, Rudolph Hess, von Schirach, head of the Hitler Youth, and all these who were in the Spandau Prison got to spend about seven years interviewing these guys getting to know them. Albert Spears, who's genius probably extended the war maybe, some estimates have made it as much as two years beyond what it would've taken otherwise. Supposedly the greatest architect maybe in history, designed Col. Bird's house for him and after everything had been destroyed in World War II, the only thing still in existence that the great architect had designed was Col. Bird's house.[3]
> —Rick Joyner

2. Joyner, R. "The History of Moravian Falls, North Carolina Part II." 2012.
3. Op. Cit.

It's odd to me that in the video Joyner seems to be admiring and elevating Speer, who's so-called, "genius" extended a war in which sixty million people died. It's also a bit curious to me why Joyner appears to hold Colonel Eugene K. Bird, in such high esteem. Here is a man who collaborated with Hitler's second in command (Hess) to write a book, *and* had Hitler's architect design his personal summer home. It is no wonder his American military career ended!

However, it gets stranger. In another video, Joyner insists his friend Bird led these three high-ranking Nazi war criminals to the Lord—a claim that is downright ludicrous in light of contradictory evidence.

> Bird was also instrumental in helping to lead von Schirach,
> who was the head of the Hitler Youth, Albert Speer, who was
> supposedly the greatest architect and engineer—they said
> his genius prolonged the war up to two years—and Rudolf
> Hess all met the Lord. We're going to know them in Heaven.
> I mean if that isn't redemption if that isn't restoration.... He
> [Bird] was almost universally recognized as possibly the top
> authority on Nazi Germany. —Rick Joyner[4]

While it is true that some claim Albert Speer was repentant of his Nazi-era actions, others claim his remorse and vigorous claims of ignorance were a self-serving ruse that saved him from hanging. His release from Spandau prison after his twenty-year sentence was a worldwide media event complete with a flurry of reporters and photographers.[5] There was no mention of a spiritual conversion at this event, nor in any of the three books, he subsequently authored. Additionally, after his release, Speer stated in an interview with People Magazine that he had atoned for his sin by fully submitting to the law [Nuremberg trial][6] and made no mention of any change of heart, or feelings of remorse.

The claim that Rudolph Hess was converted by Colonel Bird is diametrically opposed to what Bird *himself* stated—that Hess had remained unrepentant about his Nazi era actions to the end.[7] The fact that the

---

4. Joyner, R. "The Spiritual Significance of the Japanese Earthquake." 2011.

5. Nazi War Criminals Released 1966. 1966 Unused News Reel.

6. Spelman, 1976.

7. DPA. "Former Governor of Spandau Prison Dies in Berlin." 2005.

self-admittedly unrepentant Hess had a lifelong interest in the occult is irrefutable. Hess was a sympathizer of Germanic Nationalistic Pantheist ideas and stayed a devout Nazi up to his suicide in 1987.[8] Think about it; if Hess had *actually* converted, wouldn't this have garnered a great deal of press coverage, or at least *some* coverage, *somewhere?*

The so-called third convert, von Schirach, claimed at the Nuremberg trials, that he had *always* maintained his [Catholic] Christian faith; a faith he evidently believed did not conflict with his devotion to Hitler or the Nazi ideals. Baldur von Schirach admitted that the "Destruction of Christianity was explicitly recognized as a purpose of Hitler's National Socialist Movement."[9]

I find it unlikely given the facts, that these men possessed any *real* devotion to the one true God. After all, had they not worked so feverishly to destroy His people? There is not a shred of evidence, other than Joyner's absurd claims that these men converted and became believers in the *real* Gospel. There *is,* however, an abundance of evidence that shows that they did not.

So, was Joyner just flat out lying? Whatever these men were converted to it certainly wasn't the Gospel of Jesus Christ. For now, let's continue with Rick's description of his dealings with Colonel Eugene K. Bird.

> ... He [Bird] introduced me to some of the famous old Nazis. Even the Colonel, if you saw the movie, when Hitler and Eva Braun killed themselves, how the one-armed colonel went in, picked up the pistol they'd shot themselves with, and had their bodies burned. That Colonel was still alive until a few years ago, still had the gun Hitler killed himself with. And, we were out there at Hitler's bunker one time. Here's the guy who had them buried—and, their bodies burned and then buried. And then, unfortunately, typical of Nazis. Then they killed the ones that did that, who buried them so nobody would know, and he said the Russians never found their bodies ... He showed us where they were buried. If you knew, it is one of the most remarkable stories. I'm not going

8. Klee, 1991.
9. Farah, 2013.

to say here because this program goes everywhere, but I know where they're buried. —Rick Joyner[10]

The historically accepted version of Hitler's death comes mainly from a 1945 report from the British army that is primarily based on eyewitness accounts. The Soviets were the first of the Allied Forces to reach the bunker and strictly controlled its access. For this reason, neither the Americans nor the British were able to conduct a proper and extensive forensic investigation.

Rochus Misch, part of Hitler's elite guard, claimed he saw the lifeless body of Hitler and his companion Eva Braun shortly after their death. He additionally claimed to have seen Hitler's lifeless body being wrapped in a blanket and carried down the hall and outside to the Chancellery Garden.[11]

Hitler had reportedly ordered his aids to burn his body post-mortem, out of fear it would be displayed as a war trophy. However, due to heavy shelling by the advancing Russian army, the aids were unable to fully burn the corpses. The Russians arrived not long afterward and found a corpse they believed to be Hitler's. Evidently, it wasn't.

When the History Channel gained access to the skull the Russians had long claimed belonged to Hitler, the DNA analysis proved it belonged to a woman.[12] Evidently, despite their claims, the Russians did *not* know where Hitler's body was! So, if the Russians didn't know where the body was located, and the Americans, the French and the British didn't know—how was it that Rick Joyner knew?

Joyner's dialogue surrounding his meeting with the one-armed colonel is equally bizarre. Joyner was, of course, making reference to the one-armed Artur Axmann who succeeded von Schirach as Reich Youth Leader. In the last days of the Third Reich, with Berlin surrounded by the Russians, Axmann commanded an army of young boys, some as young as twelve. Without proper military training or equipment, he urged these young boys to continue fighting to their death knowing the war was lost.

---

10. Joyner, R. "The Spiritual Significance of the Japanese Earthquake." 2011.
11. Hattemer-Higgins. 2005.
12. "Hitler's Escape." 2009.

The goal of these boys' fighting and dying was not to stop the Russians from conquering Berlin, which was not even remotely possible. They died to buy Axmann and the Führer more time to keep open the possibility of their escape.[13]

In fact, Axmann had even offered to use two hundred of these young boys as human shields to evacuate Hitler out of Berlin.[14] Doesn't he sound like a lovely fellow—willing to trade the lives of two hundred innocent boys for the life of a murderous madman? Isn't he just the kind of man you would love to have tea and scones with?

Joyner is introduced to Axmann through Colonel Bird and Axman, oddly enough, ends up showing Joyner the weapon Hitler shot himself with![15] Now, the value of this gun has to be astronomical due to its historical value. Would it *really* be something you would bring out to show a guest? I can hear the conversation now. "Here, have an hors d'oeuvre. Oh, by the way, would you like to see the gun Hitler shot himself with?"

Axmann died in 1996, and I suppose it *is* plausible that he had possession of Hitler's gun (despite claims that he discarded it). It is also *possible* that he showed it to Joyner, but why? Why would Joyner be privy to these things—the burial spot of Hitler, Hitler's bunker, his gun? I happen to think these stories are true, or at least partially true, for reasons I won't elaborate on here. However, whether the stories are true or not is inconsequential—if they are true, then the implications are disturbing. If they are *not* true, and Joyner wants us to *believe* they are, then that is disturbing as well.

I think Rick's interest in Nazi Germany is a whole lot deeper than it appears. You see, the National Socialist Movement is almost identical to the society that Dominionists such as Joyner are seeking to construct. The Third Reich was nothing more than an occult-based religious movement to usher in the same New World Order (New Age) that both the Dominionists and the globalists are seeking to institute. In fact, the only difference between what the Dominionists believe, and what the globalists believe, is *who* will be in charge. Don't be fooled, world government is not from God no matter how "Christian" they want to make it sound.

---

13. Selby, 2012
14. Op. cit.
15. Joyner, R. "The Spiritual Significance of the Japanese Earthquake." 2011

It is certainly no secret that the entire Third Reich was deeply steeped in occultism, and this occultism is all likelihood is fueled its meteoric rise to power. However, if you or I had been a resident of Germany at the time Hitler came to power in 1933, I doubt we would have known that. Outwardly, Hitler professed a deep faith in Christ and insisted he was Christian! He claimed that his actions were justified by a Biblical mandate, and even received the accolades of a vast percentage of the German Christian community.

> I may not be a light of the church, a pulpiteer, but deep down I am a pious man, and believe that whoever fights bravely in defense of the natural laws framed by God and never capitulates will never be deserted by the Lawgiver, but will, in the end, receive the blessings of Providence. —Hitler[16]

> May God Almighty give our work His blessing, strengthen our purpose, and endow us with wisdom and the trust of our people, for we are fighting not for ourselves but for Germany. —Hitler[17]

> Hence today I believe that I am acting in accordance with the will of the Almighty Creator: by defending myself against the Jew, I am fighting for the work of the Lord. —Hitler[18]

> As a Christian, I have no duty to allow myself to be cheated, but I have the duty to be a fighter for truth and justice. —Hitler[19]

> I say: my Christian feeling tells me that my Lord and Savior is a warrior. It calls my attention to the man who, lonely and surrounded by only a few supporters, recognized what they [the Jews] were, and called for a battle against them, and who, by God, was not the greatest sufferer, but the greatest warrior. —Hitler[20]

---

16. Hitler, Adolph. Speech delivered on July 5, 1944 (see Flood, 1989 p.208).
17. Hitler, Adolph. Speech delivered Feb. 1, 1933 (see Hitler, 1941 p.147).
18. Hitler, Adolf. Mein Kampf, Ralph Mannheim, ed., 1999.
19. Baynes, Norman. The Speeches of Adolf Hitler, April 1922 – August 1939.
20. Hitler, Adolph. Speech delivered April 12, 1922 (see Flood, 1989, pp. 261–262)

> Even today I am not ashamed to say that, overpowered by
> stormy enthusiasm, I fell down on my knees and thanked
> Heaven from an overflowing heart for granting me the good
> fortune of being permitted to live at this time. —Hitler[21]

Most German Christians didn't question Hitler's allegiance to God, or if he was actually Christian at all. Why *would* they? He used the right words and phrases, quoted Scripture, and even shook a floppy Bible for dramatic effect when it suited his purpose.

Rest assured, the evilest of men will *always* cloak their deeds in righteous and palatable terms to make their causes appear nobler. True evil is always duplicitous—an oppressive darkness wrapped in light to deceive. In Hitler's case, being Christian was nothing more than a brilliant political maneuver. He knew the church would be indispensable to his political cause, and indeed, it was.

If one spends much time reading the literature of the leading Dominionists, the potential for a repeat of this kind of brutal fascism becomes all too real a possibility. The Nazi worldview was, in fact, almost identical to what is being preached in most of the evangelical churches today. Tragically, it is being cloaked so cleverly with pious-sounding words that most will never bother to look beneath its thin veneer to see what's underneath. Those who do find the courage to look will soon realize that the doctrine they've been embracing is actually Luciferian.

THE NEW BREED AND THE ÜBERMENSCH

Certainly of the most blatant similarities between Dominionism and Nazism is the idea of a so-called New Man or New Breed. Believe it or not, this idea is common to *all* secret societies and most cults. They *all* speak of a select few that will be endowed with supernatural strength and energy. Where do you suppose this energy or superhuman strength and ability come from? Demons.

The New Age movement calls them the Ascended Masters—higher order beings who endow the initiated with superhuman traits. The neo-Gnostic, hard-core Dominionists like Joyner, believe these

---

21. Hitler, Adolf, Mein Kampf, Ralph Mannheim, ed., 1999. 161. Print.

superhuman characteristics will appear in a select group of believers who will evolve to the point of complete transformation. They believe they will be transformed *into* Christ! In fact, they hold that Christ is coming *in* his church, not *for* it. In other words, they think the Church *is* Christ.

Attempting to institute a thousand-year reign without Christ physically present is occult theology. This is precisely what Hitler attempted! Hitler called his version of the New Breed, the Übermensch, or God-men. One would be making a very grave error to think that Hitler's Übermensch differ in any significant way from the New Breed that Joyner and leaders of the New Apostolic Reformation espouse.

> All of the force of creation will be concentrated in a new species … [which] will surpass infinitely modern man … Do you understand now the profound meaning of our National Socialist movement? —Hitler[22]

It is more than a little chilling to hear Hitler admit that the advancement of the Übermensch, or New Breed, was the entire meaning and purpose of the National Socialist Movement!

> What will the social order of the future be like? Comrade, I will tell you. There will be a class of overLords, after them the rank and file of the party members in hierarchical order, and then the great mass of anonymous followers, servants and workers in perpetuity, and beneath them again all the conquered foreign races, the modern slaves. *And over and above all these will reign new and exalted nobility of whom I cannot speak.* But of all these plans the militant members will know nothing. The new man is living amongst us now! He is here. Isn't that enough for you? *I will tell you a secret. I have seen the new man. He is intrepid and cruel. I was afraid of him.*
> —Hitler[23] [emphasis mine]

Hitler was obsessed with the Übermensch. He believed them to be a pure race and a *New Order.* It should give us more than cause for

---

22. Hitler, Adolph. Quoted by Hermann Rauschning, Hitler ma'a dit [Hitler Speaks].
23. Rauschning, H. Hitler Speaks. 1937. Print.

concern when we compare Hitler's version of the New Man with that of the Apostolic and Prophetic movement and find they are the same thing.

Hitler sought to bring about the manifestation of the New Man through selectively breeding a pure race. It would be the bodies of this pure race through which the Ascended Masters (demons) would rule. His goal was to bring about the thousand year Reich (the millennium). Dominionists seek to bring about the manifestation of the New Man through ascending levels of spiritual enlightenment with the goal being the attainment of godhood. Their Army of god-men will then slaughter all who oppose them—most notably Bible believing Christians. This, they believe, will usher in the millennium with them ruling and reigning as Christ.

Jack Deere, one of the original Kansas City Prophets, said this army of specially imbued believers will be "large and mighty." So mighty in fact, that there will be nothing to compare them to. He additionally claims that no one will be able to kill them. John Wimber insisted that those in this army will possess such power and anointing that anyone who wants to harm them will have to die. Paul Cain claims this New Breed will not only physically walk through walls but will also cause the nations to tremble with terror. Doesn't this sound suspiciously like Hitler's *god-men* whom he described as intrepid and cruel?

Bob Jones called this army the "dread champions." It should be fairly self-evident that these men are not talking about an army of believer's bringing the Good News of Salvation. This is a supernaturally endowed army bent on destruction and slaughter.

> When this army [Joel's Army] comes, it will be large and mighty. It's so mighty that there's never been anything like it before … begin the slaughter and begin it in the temple and begin it with the elders, the leaders of my people. And they walk through the land, and they start and they begin to slaughter … He has already started the slaughter … and it is coming now among the church. —Jack Deere[24]

> So my point is, that there will be a manifestation of the sons and daughters of God. And it won't be this baloney that we've heard of in the past; I mean, there have been a few people

---

24. Deere, J, "Joel's Army." 1990.

tried to walk through a wall like this over here and knocked their brain loose, but that's not what I'm talking about. I'm talking about a true manifested son of God: if anyone walks through this wall over here, they're not going to tell you about it- I mean, they're just going to do it. And sons of God don't tell you they're sons of God, they'll just show You! Amen! — Paul Cain[25]

Here is an equally disturbing description of Joel's Army by Rick Joyner.

This army of which Joel speaks is about to be revealed … They will take cities. They will burst through the enemy's strongholds and take houses (families). The very Heavens and the earth are about to shake because of this great army … the time has come. —Rick Joyner[26]

Below, Joyner goes further, suggesting that these Joel's Army Churches will be thought of more as military bases for training, equipping and deployment.

As the church begins to take on this resolve, they [Joel's Army churches] will start to be thought of more as military bases, and they will begin to take on the characteristics of military bases for training, equipping, and deploying effective spiritual forces; In time, the church will actually be organized more as a military force with an army, navy, air force, etc. — Rick Joyner[27]

According to Joyner, passive Christians will cease to exist as the militant New Order Dominionists take over. Joyner and others in this movement believe that Joel's Army will be actually warring against "passive" Christians and destroying all who will not unite with them.

We are coming to the times when passive Christianity and

25. Cain, Paul. The New Breed. [As quoted by: Let Us Reason Ministries].
26. Joyner, Rick. Advertisement for a Conference. 1994.
27. Joyner, Rick. The Warrior Nation: A New Trumpet Sound. 2006.

passive Christians will cease to exist. There is a maturity, a discipline, and a divine militancy coming upon the people of God. Those who have succumbed to humanistic and idealistic theologies may have a hard time with this, but we must understand that God is a military God. The title that He uses ten times more than any other in Scripture is *The Lord of Hosts* or *Lord of Armies*. There is a martial aspect to His character that we must understand and embrace for the times and the job to which we are now coming.

—Rick Joyner[28]

Might I add, the word *armies* in the title *Lord of Hosts* or *Lord of Armies* is referring to the angelic armies of *Heaven*. It is being used out of context here as somehow implying that God is behind and approving of the coming slaughter. Joyner is telling us we need to embrace the *military* aspect of God for both the times and the job that lies ahead? What job, you ask? Well, naturally it is the job of slaughtering those whom the Dominionists feel are the enemies of God.

I also want to stress for those of you who have been fooled by Dominionist double speak. We are *not* under the Old Covenant. What Joyner has stated above is diametrically opposed to the message of the New Covenant! Jesus told us to seek peace, to avoid retaliation, to love our enemies, and to do good to those who persecute us.

> You have heard that it was said, 'An eye for an eye and a tooth for a tooth.' But I tell you not to resist an evil person. But whoever slaps you on your right cheek, turn the other to him also. If anyone wants to sue you and take away your tunic, let him have [your] cloak also. And whoever compels you to go one mile, go with him two. Give to him who asks you, and from him who wants to borrow from you do not turn away. You have heard that it was said, 'You shall love your neighbor and hate your enemy.' But I say to you, love your enemies, bless those who curse you, do good to those who hate you, and pray for those who spitefully use you and persecute you.
> —Mat 5:38–44

---

28. Joyner, R. "Taking the Land." 2005.

> Blessed are the peacemakers: for *they* shall be called sons of
> God. —Mat 5:9 ESV

The *real* gospel calls for us to imitate Jesus, to love our enemies, to do good to those who persecute us and to love others even unto our own death. His acceptance of us is based *entirely* on our acceptance of His Son as the sacrifice for our sins. It is not based on our works, and it most *certainly* is not based on our bloodline as Bob Jones suggests below.

> I have called the best of every blood line in earth unto this
> generation ... I have elected to bring them forth in this
> generation ... the elect generation ... even the bloodline of
> Paul ... of David ... of Peter, James, and John ... They will
> even be superior to them in heart, stature and love for me' ...
> Your children will possess the spirit without measure ... They
> will move into things of the supernatural that Christ ... a
> Church that has reached the full maturity of the God-man.
> This generation ... is going to see the beginning of this
> *worldwide New Order.* —Bob Jones[29] [emphasis mine]

In the quote above, Bob Jones is again describing these god-men as moving into the ministry of perfection and actually taking on the Divine Nature of Jesus Christ, (His deity). Alarmingly, he is blasphemously claiming that that not only will these god-men evolve to God-hood but they will also put death under *their* feet and obtain immortality.

> ... There is a ministry after the five-fold called the ministry
> of perfection—the Melchizedek Priesthood ... Your children
> will be moving into the ministries of Perfection ... coming
> into that Divine Nature of Jesus Christ ... they themselves
> will be that generation that's raised up to put death itself
> underneath their feet ... because the Lord Jesus is worthy to
> be lifted up by a church that has reached the full maturity of
> the God-man![30] (Bob Jones).

---

29. Jones, Bob. Vineyard Prophecy Conference, 1989.
30. Jones, Bob. Kansas City Fellowship. 1988.

Rest assured friends, it is Christ himself, not these New Breed, god-men, who deliver the Kingdom to God after He, (Christ Himself) has placed all of His enemies under His feet. Additionally, it is Christ alone who has conquered death.

> They will move into things of the supernatural that no one has ever moved in before. Every miracle, sign, and wonder that has ever been in the Bible—they'll move in it consistently. They'll move in the power that Christ did. Every sign and wonder that's ever been will be many times in the last days. They themselves will be that generation that's raised up to put death itself underneath their feet and to glorify Christ in every way ... and the Church that is raising up in the government will be the head and the covering for them. So that that glorious Church might be revealed in the last days because the Lord Jesus is worthy to be lifted up by a Church that has reached the full maturity of the god-man![31]
> —Bob Jones

Notice, according to Jones, these god-men will be known for signs, wonders, and miracles, but wait. Doesn't the word of the Lord say that it is the *lawless* one, the *antichrist* who will come with all manner of signs and wonders?

> The coming of the [lawless one] is according to the working of Satan, with all power, signs, and lying wonders.
> —2 Thes 2:9

> For false christs and false prophets will rise and show great signs and wonders to deceive, if possible, even the elect.
> —Mat 24:24

Remember that in Mathew 7:23, Jesus describes those who have cast out demons and performed many miracles in His name, but are not his!

---

31. Jones, Bob. Visions and Revelations. Kansas City Fellowship. 1988.

And then I will declare to them, 'I never knew you; depart from Me, you who practice lawlessness! —Mat 7:23

Dominionists claim that the concept of the *god-men* or *Joel's Army* comes from the second chapter of Joel. However, if you take the time to read and study this out, the army being referenced in the book of Joel is is an ungodly Babylonian army that destroyed Jerusalem in 586 BC! Granted, it also clearly foretells a second fulfillment in the armies of Anti-Christ. However, according to the book of Joel, the army that these prophets insist we should aspire to will be completely and utterly destroyed by God! I wonder why they leave *that* part out![32]

Joyner insists that what is about to come upon the earth will change the very definition of Christianity. However, the last thing we need is Joyner redefining Christianity! Jesus defined it quite nicely the first time, and if you don't mind, I think I will stick with His version. According to Joyner, this redefinition will be accomplished by a company of prophets raised up in the spirit of Phineas. We'll get back to Phineas in a moment, first, let's look at Joyner's quote.

> What is about to come upon the earth is not just a revival or another awakening; it is a veritable revolution. The vision was given in order to begin to awaken those who are destined to radically change the course and even the very definition of Christianity. The dismantling of organizations and disbanding of some works will be a positive and exhilarating experience for the Lord's faithful servants. A great company of prophets, teachers, pastors and apostles will be raised up with the spirit of Phineas this 'ministry of Phinehas' will save congregations, and at times, even whole nations.... Nations will tremble at the mention of their name. [33] —Rick Joyner

Joyner claims that the nations will tremble at the mention of *their* name, not the name of the Lord, no, *their* name! This is a clear indication that what they intend to bring to the earth is not exactly the Good News of the Gospel!

---

32. Joel Chapter 2:20.
33. Joyner, Rick. The Harvest. 1993. Print.

The term Phineas Priesthood was first coined by Kelly Hoskins, who justified acts of domestic terrorism up to and including murder, to avenge transgressors of God's law. This so-called "Phineas Priesthood" believed they were justified in murdering those who disobeyed God's law and believed that God actually blessed them for doing so!

> They will put you out of the synagogues; yes, the time is coming that whoever kills you will think that he offers God service. —John 16:2

The reference to Phineas is taken from a Biblical story in the book of Numbers. Phineas was a Levitical Priest who thrust his sword through an Israelite and his Midianite lover at the same time, killing them both. Is this the type of militant Christianity Joyner proposes? Well, interestingly enough, yes it is. Joyner has already stated that passive Christianity will cease to exist and will be replaced with a divine militancy. In other words, if you are passive and not bent on establishing the Kingdom of God in the here and now, then you are to be purged from the earth according to Joyner—period.

So, in light of this, do you really think Joyner was merely warning us of the dangers of Nazi Germany, or do you think there might have been another reason for his fascination with this brutal regime? Hitler's quest to slaughter all who opposed him and to usher in a thousand year Reich is essentially no different that the Dominionist's version of the same.

History *is* repeating itself!

Any doctrine that has a particular class of Christians taking over the earth, subduing nations, and killing those they deem to be enemies of God, comes straight from Hell itself. There *is* no special class of Christian imbued with extraordinary power for the last days. According to Scripture, which is the only *sure* word of prophecy, all *true* believers are part of the elect. They are a chosen generation and a Holy Priesthood.

Joyner, Jones, and the others who repeatedly claim that God has called the very best of all bloodlines to the earth for this elect generation are wrong—dead wrong! Scripture plainly states that all *true* believers are the seed of Abraham. It is not our bloodline that saves us, nor is it our bloodline that sets us apart. We are saved because of *His* blood. Bloodlines are crucial in occult doctrine but not in the doctrine of Christ. We cannot earn our righteousness nor can we obtain our calling by virtue of our bloodline. Our natural bloodline is of no concern to God! He does not choose the best bred, He chooses the foolish, the downtrodden, the poor, the weak, and the rejected.

FIFTEEN
THE KNIGHTS OF MALTA

Since there is so much confusion about Joyner's ties to the Knights of Malta, I feel the need to clarify some things before continuing. Much of the confusion comes in differentiating between the different groups that go by the same, or similar names.

First, let me emphatically state that Joyner is not now, nor has he *ever* been, part of the *Catholic* Knights of Malta! The Catholic order goes by the name, The Sovereign Military Order of the Knights of Malta, or the acronym SMOM. It is the *only* Catholic order and the *only* order by that specific name. It is headquartered in Rome, *not* in Malta.

In addition to the Catholic SMOM, there is an alliance of four mutually recognized, *non-Catholic* orders in Europe. The Alliance members have signed a series of agreements of cooperation with the Catholic SMOM and are recognized as *legitimate* orders. One of these four alliance members is the Most Venerable Order of the Hospital of Saint John of Jerusalem which is often shortened to the Venerable Order of Saint John, or the acronym VOSJ. This one is known as the British Order and Queen Elizabeth II is the head. *This* order is headquartered in Malta. Although the British Order is considered Protestant, the Queen's participation in the order requires her obedience to the Pope.

The other three alliance members are the Johanniter Order, the Dutch Order, and the Swedish Order.[1] Joyner is *not* a part of *any* of

---

1. "Structure and Organization of the Order of Malta." 1998.

these *recognized* orders. What he *is* part of, is one of the many self-styled, *unrecognized* orders.

The Catholic order, along with the Alliance of the four recognized Protestant orders, do not take kindly to others calling themselves Knights of Malta. To prevent people from being taken advantage of by imposters, the Alliance has formed a false orders committee headed by historian Guy Stair Sainty. He is considered to be *the* authority on the history of the recognized orders. Mr. Guy Stair Sainty has stated unequivocally that anyone belonging to an order outside the *officially* recognized alliance of four orders detailed above is part of an unrecognized, self-styled order. Therefore, the group that Rick Joyner belongs to is an unrecognized, self-styled order.[2]

Joyner's group goes by the name Knights Hospitallers of the Sovereign Order of St John of Jerusalem, Knights of Malta—The Ecumenical Order. The Prince Grand Master is Nicholas F.S. Papanicolaou. Incidentally, Papanicolaou is also a board member of Joyner's highly Dominionist Oak Initiative.

I find it more than a little intriguing that, according to his order's website, Papanicolaou holds senior rank in the Swedish Order of the Amaranth.[3] This is a fraternal organization composed of Master Masons and their duly qualified female relatives.[4] Evidently, Joyner has no problem with allowing a Master Mason on the board of his Oak Initiative, nor does he have a problem submitting to one as his Prince Grand Master, despite having said the following.

> As a Christian, I am deeply alarmed by everything I have
> studied about the Masons. I do not know how any Christian
> can make the basic vow required for entry to the Masons. I
> have not, nor would I ever be a part of any secret society, or
> one that has secret rituals. —Rick Joyner[5]

Oddly enough, Papanicolaou was previously the Grand Master of a *different* self-styled group but was disassociated for undisclosed reasons. Their website states that it was for "grave reasons already explained in

2. Sainty, Guy Stair. 1991.
3. Swedish Order of the Amaranth. 2012.
4. Op. Cit.
5. Joyner, Rick. "Knights of Malta: Is The OSJ Connected to the Masons?"

detail to him by correspondence, after due warnings and requests for his resignation."[6] The name of the group he was disassociated from is called the Sovereign Hospitaller Order of St. John of Jerusalem Knights of Malta. They list Papanicolaou as being *their* Prince Grand Master from 2006 until he was disassociated in 2011.

Then, suddenly another group appears on the scene calling themselves The Knights Hospitallers of the Sovereign Order of St John of Jerusalem, Knights of Malta—The Ecumenical Order. This group lists Papanicolaou as being *their* Prince Grand Master from 2006 to the present. Now, how on earth could he have been Prince Grand Master of both groups? He couldn't and quite frankly, he wasn't.

I love a good mystery and the fact that both groups shared an almost identical list of past Grand Masters provided me with one. As it turns out, this mystery had a very simple explanation. Papanicolaou formed his *own* group once he was ousted and took on the history of the group he was ousted from.

Papanicolaou's new group (of which Joyner is a part), is *not* a recognized order– but then the group Papanicolaou was ousted from was not a recognized order either. Neither group has observer status in the UN. like recognized Knights of Malta groups, nor are they considered a sovereign subject of international law. So where *did* they come from and why are they calling themselves the Knights of Malta? Well here is where it gets *really* interesting.

Both the order that Papanicolaou was ousted from and the order he now heads as Prince Grand Master are continuations of *another* order that originated with a man named Charles Pichel. However, don't go looking for Pichel's name in either group's list of Past Grand Masters. They have conveniently written him out of their history. Now, why do you suppose they would want to go and do a thing like that? Well, let's take a closer look at Pichel and see why they might not want to make that connection known.

Pichel was con man if ever there was one. He was not only convicted of trafficking narcotics, but he was also convicted of selling memberships and collecting dues for various bogus organizations. He headed a false Knights of Malta group headquartered in Shickshinny NY, which earned his group the irreverent nickname, the Shickshinny Knights.

---

6. "Past Grand Masters." 2013.

Pichel was an advisor to Hitler's aid Ernst Hanfstaengl, and many of his leaders were anti-Semites who worked with the quasi-Nazi Liberty Lobby.[7]

The Shickshinny Knights were, among other things, an intelligence front. It "became an extreme cabal of right-wing military and intelligence men plus a gaggle of Russian nobles who had lost their lands (and possibly their minds) after the Russian Revolution of 1917." [8] Pichel called his order, the Sovereign Order of St John of Jerusalem, Knights of Malta and claimed they were part of the *real* Knights of Malta via the Russian line of succession. Of course, they were nothing of the sort. Allow me to explain.

In 1911, a semi-masonic organization which emerged from the Orange Lodges registered themselves as a corporation in the State of New Jersey under the name, "Knights of Malta." One year later the group was already defunct. Pichel needed a believable history for his bogus group, so naturally, he invented one. He claimed his order was a continuation of the Orange Lodge group, and he stole their history. He then embellished it, "by mimicking the foundation of a Paris group, complete with its Russian Hereditary Commanders."[9]

The truth is, Pichel's group, the Sovereign Order of St John of Jerusalem, Knights of Malta, was not *actually* incorporated until August 18, 1956 in Dover Delaware by three women![10] Pichel, in all likelihood, bought it as an empty shell corporation because it was not until June 30, 1960 that he and his colleagues were added as Officers of the Corporation. So, if we are to believe Pichel's bogus history of his order being active in America since the turn of the century, we will *also* have to believe that three women ran the Knights of Malta in America for four years as its chief officers (*ahem).[11]

Rick Joyner's Knights of Malta group, headed by Papanicolaou descended from the Pichel Order. Let me explain how. Roberto Paterno Castello, who had been the Grand Master of the Pichel Order from 1979–1992, left to become Grand Master of his *own* Order. Frendo

---

7. Bellant, Russ. Old Nazis, the New Right, and the Republican Party. 1991.

8. Levenda, Peter. "Sukarno's Gold." The Hitler Legacy. 2013.

9. Sovereign Order of St John of Jerusalem, Knights of Malta 1956.

10. Registration # 0503716 4100.

11. Sovereign Order of St John of Jerusalem, Knights of Malta 1956.

Cumbo was a Grand Prior in Castello's order and in the mid to late 1990's left to form his own order appointing *himself* Grand Master. It was from *this* order that Papanicolaou was disassociated. Undeterred, however, he has now started his own self-styled group presumably copying the history from the group he left. See chart below.

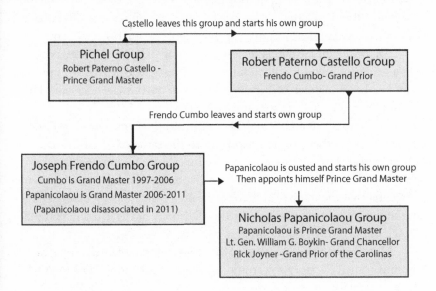

Now, not only is Papanicolaou the head of his own self-styled order, but he is also co-founder of World Public Forum's, "Dialogue of Civilizations." Participants of this forum "strive to establish **a new order** based on mutual respect and opinion exchange across national borders."[12] Papanicolaou formed the World Public Forum in partnership with one of President Vladimir Putin's closest political allies, Vladimir Yakunin. This is deeply alarming. Papanicolaou is not only tied to a political ally of Vladimir Putin but also with Joyner, who has openly called for a military Coup in America. Then, to make matters worse, both Papanicolaou and Joyner are tied with General Jerry Boykin, former undersecretary of defense, implicated in torture and illegal covert operations.[13] The same Jerry Boykin who has been touring American churches trying to raise

---

12. World Public Forum. "Dialogue of Civilizations for Successful Global Changes"
13. Gore, Al. The Assault on Reason. 2007

up an end time army and bring in a worldwide theocratic government. Yikes, what a mix!

Many of Papanicolaou's self-styled order are aligned in one way or another with Joyner. The groups Grand Chancellor, General Gerry Boykin, is a board member of Joyner's Oak Initiative. Jorge Parrott, an order chaplain, is the head of MorningStar Missions. Members William NeSmith, Randal Cutter and Randal White, are all pastors of church's directly aligned under MorningStar, and there are others—lots of others.

Papanicolaou's group is made up of many priories. A priory is simply a group of men or women under religious vows, headed by a prior. The head commander of a priory is known as the Grand Prior. The Grand Prior for the Carolinas is Rick Joyner.

In 2011, the Knights and Dames under Joyner's Carolina Priory invited all the other priories belonging to the same self-styled group to a Solemn International Investiture. An investiture is a process by which persons admitted to the order as probationary candidates, take their vows, receive their robes and are officially received as members. This particular investiture was held in the Ballroom of the Heritage Grand Hotel, in Fort Mill, South Carolina.

MorningStar purchased the 501 room Heritage Hotel, along with the unfinished 21 story tower and 52 acres of adjoining land in 2004. This site was the former home of Jim Bakker's Heritage USA and PTL Ministries. Renovations have been extensive and donations ongoing. Heritage Grand Hotel is advertised as a conference center, retreat and a location for weddings—in other words, it's a business.

The investiture was followed by dinner and a ball, followed by drinks and fellowship. The Gala was a formal event complete with tuxedos, evening gowns, a cigar tent and of course, a cash bar for cocktails. The cost of the three-day event for meals and a standard room was 399.00 payable to Heritage International Ministries—of course.

Remember these are, as Rick insists, Christians who have risked their very life for the Gospel—those of impeccable moral character ready to defend the faith at all costs.[14] If that is so, then why do they feel the need to dress in shiny satin robes, play with swords, smoke cigars, drink cocktails and prance about conferring titles of honor on one another? Is that how they honor Christ—by honoring themselves?

---

14. Joyner, Rick. "Why I joined the Knights of Malta."

> But when you do a charitable deed, do not let your left hand
> know what your right hand is doing, 4 "that your charitable
> deed may be in secret; and your Father who sees in secret will
> Himself reward you openly. —Mat 6:3–4

Do these titles make them more spiritual, more committed? Do they believe their charitable deed somehow make God indebted to them? These are mere titles of honor that exalt *men* and give occasion to pride—they have *nothing* to do with God. Regardless, titles and accolades are paramount to this group. Nicholas Papanicolaou, who incorrectly styles himself as Baron Nicholas Papanicolaou, *purchased* the Scottish feudal barony of Finlaystone Maxwell.[15] Why would he want to purchase a title? Well, I can think of several reasons, but none of them are good.

Speaking of titles of honor, I wish to deviate slightly and address the matter of academic dishonesty among this group. Just so there is no misunderstanding I want to state at the outset that I am all for one pursuing higher education. However, I *am* very much against diploma mills who exchange a worthless vanity degree, for money.

How do you suppose Rick Joyner, with only a Grade 12 equivalency diploma, obtained a Ph.D. in such short order? I am not trying to infer that he lacks intelligence, as that is certainly not the case, however, he most definitely has not *earned* a doctorate degree.

A bachelor's degree takes four years to complete, and a Master's Degree generally takes two to three years. Both these degrees *must* be completed before a Ph.D. is undertaken. Generally, a Ph.D. will take 2–6 years to complete—not always, but that is a good general rule. That means that to obtain a *real* (earned and accredited) Ph.D., recognized by the *academic* community, you would need to complete a minimum of eight years of post-secondary education.

For some reason, many want the academic honor and prestige of having a Ph.D., but they don't want the academic work. So, they turn to diploma mills. This is rampant among charismatic pastors, and if you take the time to investigate, you will find that the vast majority of big name ministers who claim to have a Ph.D. have purchased and not earned their degrees.

Rick Joyner's doctoral degree, along with that of his Missions

---

15. Turcopilier, 2012

Director Jorge Parrott, came from the North Carolina College of Theology. The college *claims* to be accredited but so what? I could crawl into my oven and call myself a biscuit, but it wouldn't make it so. They *claim* accreditation by the International Accrediting Association and Transworld Accrediting Association International. In all honesty, they might as well be accredited by Phantom Bigfoot and the Loch Ness Monster. Neither of these accreditation agencies is recognized by the U.S. Department of Education as a bona fide crediting agency! Furthermore, both these "accrediting" agencies are well known for issuing "accreditation" to diploma mills.

The Accrediting Commission International, Inc., of Beebe, Arkansas is run by a non-Trinitarian Pentecostal preacher by the name of Dr. John Scheel, holder of another diploma mill doctorate. "Dr. Scheel got his PhD. from Toledo Bible College and Seminary, which had to be re-branded when it was run out of Ohio by the authorities. A.C.I. is also a rebranding of the International Accrediting Commission (IAC) which was run out of Missouri after a sting operation. [16]

However, aside from being accredited by bogus agencies, here is where it gets ridiculous. The Doctoral program for the North Carolina College of Theology requires only a G.E.D. (Grade 12 equivalency). As a Master's Candidate in English and a holder of two earned Bachelor Degrees, I know full well that *no* accredited school will *ever* let someone enter a doctoral program with a G.E.D. You need to have the preliminary degrees *and* a very high grade point average—period! Not so at the North Carolina College of Theology. No, all you need there is experience—well, experience *and* money, let's not forget the money!

I don't understand why Joyner would get hooked up with a diploma mill, but I guess if you are running a so-called University it's hard to attract paying students when professors only have a G.E.D.

Not only is Joyner's own degree false, but he is issuing bogus degrees through his University. His degrees are granted through the same degree mill that his own bogus doctoral degree came from. In fact, it states right on MorningStar's website that their bachelor's degrees are awarded by the North Carolina College of Theology. Oh, and get this—you can obtain a bachelor's degree after just one year. That's right, why slave away for four years for a *real* degree when you can go to MorningStar

---

16. Holford, 2011

University and be granted a fake degree from a diploma mill after just one year. All you need is one short year—and money, don't forget the money.

I am in no way trying to demean those who have not obtained a degree, nor am I insinuating that those who *have* a degree are more qualified to be ministers of the Gospel than those who do not. What I *am* saying is that claiming you have attained a certain level of educational accomplishment when clearly you have not, is unconscionable and fraudulent.

Now, getting back to our main topic, let's take a look at some of the charities Papanicolaou's order claims to raise money for. Most are headed by members of the order themselves.

Papanicolaou's group, The Knights Hospitallers of the Sovereign Order of St John of Jerusalem, Knights of Malta—The Ecumenical Order, is registered by Papanicolaou as a 501C3 (tax exempt religious organization) in Texas, under the name Hospitallers. The address for the group is listed as 2104 Underwood Rd La Porte, Texas.[17] Also registered at this same address is a 501C3 organization registered as New Life Christian Church. This church is headed by Archbishop Gregory Holly who coincidentally enough is the Grand Prelate (USA) for Papanicolaou's group. However, there's more. Gregory Holly runs another 501C3 tax-exempt organization registered to the same address called Independent Christian Churches International. On the organization's website, Holly claims to have ordained 10,300 ministers worldwide.[18] According to Holly, the organization's mission is to "provide relationship, accreditation, and strategically relevant information for Ministers and Business leaders across all Christian faith through its Mission and Marketplace Initiatives." In case we had any doubt about what he is talking about, he further states that these initiatives are for the release of the Kingdom Mandate of God's rule and order. He then assures us that this fellowship is "founded upon the Apostles leadership of the uninterrupted transmission of spiritual authority from the Apostles of the New Testament Church to the present day."[19] This belief is called apostolic succession— the belief that the apostles passed on their authority in succession to others who passed it on to others and so on. It is not found in Scripture

17. The Hospitallers, 501C3 Nonprofit, La Porte, TX — 272088495
18. Holley, Gregory. President: Biography.
19. Holley, Gregory. About Us: Statement of Vision and Mission.

169

and is considered heresy. What this "charity" is doing is ordaining ministers and training them in the Dominionist agenda—an agenda whose ultimate aim is the installation of theocratic rule in America and beyond.

We are not finished yet, though. There is still *another* 501c3 registered to this location. This one is called, "Moms Against Hunger" and is reportedly run by Gregory Holly's wife, Gayla. Both of them are active in the group and, not surprisingly, both these charities, Moms against Hunger and Independent Christian Churches International, are charities that Papanicolaou's group supports.

However, there are other charities that the group supports which tie directly back to members of the group itself as well. One is a 501c3 tax-exempt religious charity called Generations of Virtue. This organization is dedicated to promoting sexual wholeness and integrity. According to their website, one of their mandates is to teach families how to transform culture. While this is indeed a worthy cause, their website seems to be more geared toward selling books, purity rings and collecting donations than anything else. This is run by Kay and Julie Hiramine who are also members under Papanicolaou. The contact address for Generations of Virtue is P.O. Box 62253 Colorado Springs, CO 80962, but again, that is not the only 501c3 that shares the same address. Humanitarian International Services Group, (now Sustainable Communities Worldwide) is also listed under this address and is likewise headed by Kay and Julie Hiramine.

Now, let's push through and look at two more charities that Papanicolaou's self-styled group raises money for.

Hydrating Humanity is run by MorningStar's Matt Peterson. Peterson was there when I was part of MorningStar, and he is, by his own admission, a former CIA agent. He now heads MorningStar Fellowship in Winston-Salem, North Carolina and is the founder of Zao water. Oddly enough, there is a website registered to MorningStar Ministries called Zaowater.com. On their website it states that;

> ZAO provides wells, springs & hygiene training to transform communities by providing safe water, education, and hope for people in developing nations. Zao is the spring, wells and hygiene training arm for MorningStar Ministries and is now part of MorningStar Missions.

Zao is *not* registered as a 501c3 tax exempt charity, at least not under its own name. The director is listed as Jorge Parrott, and the executive assistant is listed as his wife, Anna Parrott. Again, both Jorge and Anna Parrott are involved in Papanicolaou's Knights of Malta group. However, it does not appear that the Knights of Malta supports Zao water but rather Hydrating Humanity, a 501c3 charity that seems to serve the same function and have the same goals as Zao water. The director is listed as Matt Peterson and Pat Selvey is listed as the international director. At any rate, this charity ties back to MorningStar.

Okay, take a deep breath and grab a piece of chocolate to power your way through the last one. You might even want to go get yourself a coffee—you will need to be awake for this.

Let's take a look at General Boykin's, Kingdom Warriors an organization that urges Christians to become warriors in God's Kingdom. Kingdom Warriors has been active on the internet since 2008, a year after Boykin retired from the military. The first contact information listed for the organization is 439 Westwood Shopping Center PMB #134 Fayetteville, NC 28314. This address tracks to a UPS store run by army veteran Debbie Millburn just outside the Fort Brag Military Base. However, the number to reach the organization begins with a 303 area code which is Colorado. Later contact information has the organization listed at 373 Inverness Parkway, Suite 100, Englewood, Colorado. Interestingly enough, this is a 15,383 square foot office—(that is 1429 square meters for my Canadian and European readers). That is a whole lot of space for an organization which consists of speaking engagements, selling books and soliciting donations. Of course, no office would be complete without six drive-in docks for shipping and receiving. Oh, and look, it is conveniently located within access to I-25, E-470, and C-470, all major highways—not to mention the Denver International Airport. Why does someone whose sole ministry is speaking, need that much office space? Does he bowl in there? I don't have concrete evidence of anything but I am sure you'll agree that it's very odd.

As of this printing, Boykin has no mission statement on his organization's website. He openly solicits donations but fails to tell potential donors what the money is used being for. I presume he is being given an honorarium for speaking engagements. I am also sure he pedals his books at these events as well. His expenses *must* be covered, so what *exactly* is the public donating toward?

GuideStar is an information service specializing in reporting on U.S. nonprofit companies. On their website, you can see a copy of Boykin's Kingdom Warrior's 990 form filed with the Internal Revenue Service for years 2011–2013. On form 990, Part III (1) they state that "the organization is dedicated to assisting military personnel with spiritual guidance and support. To spread the New Testament and the teachings of Jesus Christ."[20] However, in Part III, (4) he states that the "prime activity was the identification of qualified speakers and[also]sponsoring faith-based seminars and various seminars at churches throughout the nation. This was to "encourage prayer for our nation, the United States of America."[21]

Now, I know that I don't need to point this out to you, especially after that cup of coffee you just had, but these two statements do not match! Furthermore, if you look into what he *actually* spoke about at these speaking engagements you will soon find that it doesn't line up with *either statement*!

On April 10, 2008, Boykin spoke at Epicenter, a conference in Israel hosted by Joel C. Rosenberg. The message was called appropriately enough, "Inside the Revolution." His message was about the mission of Islam and how to stop Islamic terrorism. In fact, if you investigate, you will find *all* of his messages are about the threat of Islam and raising up a Christian army to fight it.

> Some of these people we just need to fight and kill. It is really no different than when the Israelites crossed the Jordan River, and the Lord said kill em, kill em all, don't even leave their animals to corrupt you in the future. There are some that we are going to meet on the battlefield, and we are gonna have to kill em. But that's not the ultimate solution the ultimate solution is the Gospel of Christ.
> —General Boykin[22]

So, Boykin wants to take the Gospel to the Muslims, and as Christians we certainly want *everyone* to know and follow Christ. However, if

---

20. Direct link: http://www.guidestar.org/FinDocuments/2013/208/234/2013-208232-0ad0e11e-9.pdf
21. Op. Cit.
22. Inside The Revolution by Lt. General Jerry Boykin. YouTube. 2011.

that doesn't work, Boykin says we just need to kill em. Now, we already know that Boykin does not want to take the *real* Gospel to the Muslims. He wants to take them the Dominionist Gospel, and that is something very different.

When asked by an interviewer how Boykin sees his role in regards to the Gospel today and with regards to our republic, Boykin stated the following:

> I took an oath in December of 1970 to support and defend the Constitution of the United States against all enemies foreign and domestic, I believe that the 36 and a half years that I spent in uniform was nothing but preparation for the real battle that we are in today and I believe that my role is to raise up an army you know, a godly army and a righteous army to fight the spiritual battle- you know our weapons are not carnal and uh I believe that what God has prepared me to do and has now called me to do is to raise up an army of Godly men and women that understand the concept of spiritual warfare and are willing to get in the battle.[23]

So, according to Boykin, he has been given a divine mission to raise up an army but the weapons of his warfare are not carnal—or so he *claims*. This is a perfect example of the double speak Dominionists engage in to mask their agenda. If he states that "some of 'em we just need to kill" then how can he be talking about *spiritual* weapons? In a speech he gave on behalf of the Family Research Council to the Wall-builders' Pro-Family Legislators Conference, he stated that:

> The Lord is a warrior and in Revelation 19 it says when he comes back, he's coming back as what? A warrior. A mighty warrior leading a mighty army, riding a white horse with a blood-stained white robe. I believe that blood on that robe is the blood of his enemies 'cause he's coming back as a warrior carrying a sword. And I believe now - I've checked this out - I believe that sword he'll be carrying when he comes back is an AR-15. —General Jerry Boykin

---

23. Op. Cit.

Now I want you to think about this: where did the Second Amendment come from? ... From the Founding Fathers, it's in the Constitution. Well, yeah, I know that. But where did the whole concept come from? It came from Jesus when he said to his disciples 'now, if you don't have a sword, sell your cloak and buy one.'

I know, everybody says that was a metaphor. It was not a metaphor! He was saying in building my kingdom, you're going to have to fight at times. You won't build my kingdom with a sword, but you're going to have to defend yourself. And that was the beginning of the Second Amendment, that's where the whole thing came from.... And the sword today is an AR-15, so if you don't have one, go get one. You're supposed to have one. It's Biblical.

—General Jerry Boykin[24]

As a hardcore Dominionist, Boykin is recruiting *warriors* to fight and establish God's Kingdom on earth through armed sectarian violence. As a Dominionist, Boykin's words are neither rhetoric nor are they mere saber rattling! He actually *believes* that his mandate as a believer, is to gain control over the governments of this world, including the government of the United States. *This* is why he and other Dominionists cast the war on terror in terms of a holy war. Rest assured, God is not American, and *our* enemies are not *His* enemies.

Do you *really* think God is angrier at the Muslims than He is at America who has flooded the earth with violence and pornography and killed more than 57 million unborn children? Really? Look, I *believe* the Bible, I believe that Jesus is *the* Way *the* Truth and *the* Light and that no man comes to the Father except through *Him*. However, He gives the same opportunity for salvation to *all*. He does not love the Muslim less. We are to pray for and love our Muslim neighbors and, as far as it depends on us, live in peace with *all* men. We are *commanded* by Scripture to overcome evil with good. We have not done that, we have instead tried to overcome evil with evil and in the end have become monsters ourselves.

---

24. Hafiz, Yasmine. General 'Jerry' Boykin Says Gun-Toting Jesus Will Lead 'Mighty Army' During Second Coming. The Huffington Post.

The Dominionists would have us believe that we are still living in the Old Testament, waging wars against the enemies of God like Israel of old. However, Christians need to imitate Christ who suffered an agonizing and humiliating death out of love for His enemies.

> Blessed are the peacemakers for they shall be called the sons of God. —Mat 5:9 ESV

> But love your enemies, and do good, and lend, expecting nothing in return, and your reward will be great, and you will be sons of the Most High, for he is kind to the ungrateful and the evil. —Luke 6:35 ESV

The problem with believing that God is using the church to set up God's Kingdom on earth is that the focus shifts from winning souls to gaining the political power and might needed to gain power. The church gains a crusader mentality bent on bloodshed and conquest, and the military industrial complex is glorified as an extension of justice.

Alarmingly, recruiting soldiers to set up Dominionist rule is the *real* purpose of Boykin's 501c3 charity. Of course, Boykin is certainly not the *only* one calling forth an army to defeat the enemies of God. Joyner has openly called for a military coup in America.

> I mean, there's no way our Republic can last much longer. It may not last through Obama's second term. There are a lot of people that feel, you know, it can't. There are forces right now seeking to undermine and to destroy the Republic. There's almost a glib and almost a joyful disregard of the constitution, and a belittling of the Constitution. We can't make it without that—that's our foundation, our moorings. We're heading for serious tyranny.

> I think we've been used in some wonderful and powerful ways by God, we've been one of the most generous nations in history, we've done so much good—and that's why I appeal to the Lord—don't let us be totally destroyed. Please, raise up those who will save us. And as I start telling friends from a long time that no election's going to get the right person in there that can restore us because the system is so broken, so

undermined right now—the whole system. I believe our only
hope is a military takeover: martial law. —Rick Joyner[25]

We cannot continue to dismiss Dominionism as the radical views of
a few Christian extremists. I think many who have neither experienced
this nor sat under Dominionist teaching might be tempted to shrug it
off. After all, it sounds ludicrous and conspiratorial. Well, hello! It *is*
ludicrous and conspiratorial—but it's also real. Even the secular media
is standing up and taking notice now while many Christians continue to
slumber and deny its danger. It is a cancer, and it has metastasized into
the military, the Republican Party and the church at large. I beg you to
wake up!

A pastor speaking at the Spiritual Warfare Conference held at
Joyner's MorningStar church claimed that Jesus was not going to come
back until God could see that the church was a mature, overcoming
bride operating at the same level as Jesus. Then, Christ will return and
Christians "will work with Jesus to rule and reign." Later, Wyatt said that
"we are to rule, reign, govern, expand, advance and establish the government of God on the earth" since "this is about world domination." Not
surprisingly, he called on followers to "infiltrate" the seven mountains
of influence, especially the mountain of government, to attain "prepara-
tory dominion."[26] *This* is what this group of would-be-knights is working
toward—a total take-over.

However, I am certain they could support one another's Dominionist charities and pal around together drinking cocktails and smok-
ing cigars without forming their own order, playing adult dress-up and
knighting each other with swords. So, what gives? Certainly, Joyner,
even though his group is unrecognized, *wants* to be associated with the
real Knights of Malta, but why? Is it for recognition or prestige? Is it so
people can feel a sense of legitimacy in giving? Does it act as a front for
other activities like money laundering? I honestly don't know.

In a litigation case between the (real) Soverign Military Order of
Malta and Papanicolaou's self-styled Florida Priory, the district court
wrote that, although it understood that the parties presented themselves
as Christian charities, it "struggle[d] with the parties' characterizing

25. Mantyla, Kyle. Right Wing Watch. 1 Oct. 2013. Web.
26. Tashman, Brian. Right Wing Watch. 14 Oct. 2011. Web.

themselves in that manner."[27] The district court attributed this confusion to the "unimpressive" amount of money each group raised for charitable purposes, which led the court to believe that the members of both organizations were "more interested in dressing up in costumes, conferring titles on each other and playing in a 'weird world of princes and knights' than in performing charitable acts."[28]

If this is true, that the amount of money raised for charities by both Papanicolaou's self-styled Ecumenical Order and by the Catholic SMOM order is unimpressive, then what *is* the purpose? The Catholic order does have considerable clout. After all, they have their own passports and have been given observer status in the United Nations. However, Papanicolaou's group has no such privilege. If the amount this group has raised for charity is unimpressive, as the Florida Court determined, then what *are* they doing? Does this group have some other purpose? Having descended from a group that was well known as an intelligent front, are they too being used for this purpose?

---

27. Sovereign Military Hospitaller, 816 F. Supp. 2d at 1294 n.2.
28. Id. (quoting the judge's comments in the trial transcript, D.E. 144, 131:19–20).

SIXTEEN
CIA

I never meant to write this chapter. I really didn't. It demanded to be written. I avoided it, I wrote around it, and eventually I just set the entire book aside. I would pick it up a year or so later, and the whole frustrating process would begin again. This happened more times than I care to admit. Those who knew the book was in progress kept asking me why it wasn't finished. I didn't know why! There was something missing, something that I wanted to say—that I *needed* to say.

It was a strong hunch that went back to my early days at Morning-Star. However, a hunch is just a hunch unless there is something tangible to hang it on. I was driven to investigate one rabbit trail after another, frustrated with myself for seemingly wasting time. However, those rabbit trails ended up building a foundation of knowledge that was necessary to understanding what came next.

I cried the night I found out Paul Cain was a CIA operative. In fact, that night is indelibly imprinted on my mind. It validated me on some level and released me from my relentless pursuit. I knew it was over at that point—I had found what I had always known was there but could never prove. It was one of those cries that make you feel like your tears are washing things away—washing years away, releasing the weight of what you've been carrying for far too long.

You see, I had always felt something more nefarious was happening at MorningStar—something I couldn't see with my eyes but could none-the-less perceive. I felt like somehow I was involved in a bigger agenda—an agenda I *knew* I was in the middle of but knew nothing about. I felt tampered with, like the very core of my being was being changed, altered, and manipulated. Certainly, being a Christian involves change and regeneration, but this was vastly different than that. I felt, near the end of my time there, that I was being systematically brainwashed. I could never seem to shake that feeling. I had a degree in Psychology from a Canadian University. I had studied brainwashing both in school and out but obviously having studied it did not protect me from it.

Several things didn't sit well with me. The constant repetition of music in both word and beat, the frenzied worship, the constant repetition of themes of domination and warfare, and the effectiveness of their thought stopping techniques. They always used the same techniques it seemed. Leadership seemed *too* effective in shutting down logical thought or questions—*way* too effective. At one point, I even wondered if MorningStar was part of some larger experiment but would quickly castigate myself for such irrational thoughts. However, those pesky thoughts and observations would always come back around. *Something* was not right.

Perhaps it was the presence of former CIA agent, Matt Peterson in the leadership at MorningStar that first piqued my interest in the possibility of CIA involvement at MorningStar. This former agent was intelligent, well-groomed and attractive. He was also kind and gentle-spirited, something sorely missing in the other leaders. He stuck out like a boulder on a beach at MorningStar. His being there seemed strange to me—it still does.

I remember a conversation with someone at MorningStar in which I intimated that perhaps Matt had never quit the CIA and was still on their payroll. They looked at me puzzled, brows pulled together, mouth ajar. I never mentioned it to anyone again, but still, there was that gnawing feeling inside that things were not as they seemed—not at *all* as they seemed. After all, MorningStar was a fledgling ministry at that time. The church was not large by any stretch of the imagination, so *why* would someone quit their job with the CIA to become part of MorningStar?

It was a curious thing to me was how well connected Joyner was— *too* well connected. The people that marched through his little church were the who's who of the charismatic world at that time. It was not just them though, it was the *other* people he was connected to— like Reggie White the best defense in NFL history, and American Country music and bluegrass singer, Ricky Skaggs. Suzy Wills (now Yaraei), the woman who led worship at MorningStar had been a backup singer for both Reba McIntyre's and Wynonna Judd. How did Joyner just appear out of nowhere and suddenly *know* all these people—people like Dexter Yaeger. His Amway empire embraced a million people and distributed more than two *billion* in sales annually—an output that the Charlotte Observer claimed exceeded the gross national product of thirty-nine nations.[1]

Somehow Joyner, who by his own admission was never part of Amway, was given a breathtaking property on Lancaster Highway in Pineville North Carolina by none other than Dexter Yaeger himself. The property contained the old Governor's Mansion and a 15,000 square foot building they called "the cabin." At that time Joyner had his offices in the mansion. Incidentally, Joyner later allowed Jim Bakker to take up residence in the so-called "cabin" after his exit from prison. If you hear Bakker talk about living in "a cabin" after his exit from prison, this is the cabin that he is referring to. I think we can all agree that 15,000 square feet is a bit more than "a cabin."

Yaeger was, and presumably still is, a major contributor toward Dominionist causes. In fact, the organization of the modern Dominionist movement is largely attributed to Richard DeVos, head of Amway and Bill Bright of Campus Crusade for Christ.[2] So, in light of this, it makes perfect sense that Yeager, a major contributor to Dominionist causes would feel inspired to give to Joyner. After all, Joyner would, in time, become a force to be reckoned with within the politically-minded, Dominionist circles. But how did Yeager *know* how essential Joyner would become to the Dominionist agenda? In fact, how did he even *know* Joyner in the first place?

In a 2015 article, Joyner claimed he had been friends with Dexter Yeager for 30 years, and yet I remember him plainly stating that he had never been a part of Amway and was against multi-level marketing—especially in the church. So how did they meet? Incidentally, that would date the start of their friendship to somewhere around 1985, a mere one year after MorningStar Ministries was founded. How does a man with a bankrupt company and a fledgling ministry just happen to meet and befriend Dexter Yeager?

---

1. Morrill, Jim, and Nancy Stancill. "Amway the Yager Way." 1995.
2. DogEmperor. "Dominionism's Parallel Economy: Corporate Sponsors." 2007.

When I got to MorningStar twelve years later in 1997, the ministry was *still* very small, and the school was in its infancy. In fact, the school was still meeting in the same warehouse space used for the church. Joyner was really not that well known, and yet many of the people around or connected to him *were*. That is what troubled me—the connections. None of it made sense.

I want to take you through a narrative of Joyner's time in Berlin. It is taken word for word from the audio of MorningStar Cassette tape. Some of the things I am about to point out to you may not make *immediate* sense but please allow me to build a foundational understanding so you can later draw your own conclusion.

> I was in Berlin with a man who is considered one of the foremost authorities on Nazi Germany, Colonel Eugene Byrd, And, Colonel Byrd had just taken myself and Paul Cain and a friend of ours on the most incredible tour of Berlin that day … And, you know we went to Hitler's bunker, and we went all over the place, and he just gave us a personal tour....
>
> And, uh, we were eating dinner (with Colonel Byrd), and I was saying, and we're talking all this stuff, and I said, 'You ever heard of these Knights of Malta?' And he said, 'Well, I am one.' And he pulls out his credentials … And he said, 'As matter of fact, this one knight, who is called a Knight Commander, has recommended you to be knighted, and he's looking for you now.' I talked to him … They had been reading our journals, and stuff like that and head of the order had been baptized in the Holy Spirit and wanted to see them become a spiritual force just like they had been a natural force. Colonel Byrd tells me this one guy, he was an Austrian Baron. He said, 'He is looking for you. He's already recommended you to be knighted.' —Audio by Rick Joyner Ministries, no date on tape [emphasis mine][3]

The Austrian Baron that Joyner is referring to here is Baron Newman Bailey Peyton Jr. Colonel Byrd tells Joyner that Baron Peyton is looking for him because he wants to knight him. So, *who* is Baron

---

3. Originally taken from Trouble in Prophet Land. Havestnet.org

Newman Bailey Peyton? Well, I will tell you who he isn't, and that is an Austrian Baron! In fact, according to the US Census, he was born in Houston Texas in 1932 and his Father Newman B. Peyton Sr. was born in Keatchie Louisiana in 1910. His father was neither wealthy nor Austrian. However, Newman Peyton Jr. did *very* well financially and was known to have amassed considerable wealth.

So, if he was not *born* a Baron, was he lying? I doubt it—but he was obviously very economical with the truth. One can certainly purchase a Baronship if one has too much cash laying around. However, the Baronship will not be worth the paper it is written on. Austrian nobility was officially abolished in 1919. The title retains no privileges except perhaps to open doors—or impress the easily impressed.

However, there is another possibility. He *may* have been given the honorary title by his good friend Kurt Waldheim, former president of Austria (and former Nazi war criminal). One thing is certain, he was not born into nobility. He is an American, and that is *very* easily proven.

Aside from the Baronship issue, Newman Peyton Jr. is a very curious fellow. He was head of the Full Gospel Business Men's Association International for Central and South America, and he seemed to be able to meet with Heads of State all over the world with incredible ease—*too* much ease, if you know what I mean. In fact, it was Peyton who arranged with Nicaraguan President Daniel Ortega to have Jimmy Swaggart speak in Revolution Square in Managua Nicaragua in February 1988.[4] That alone was a *massively* impressive feat—*especially* considering the volatile political situation in Nicaragua at that time.

The list of Heads of State in Central and South America that Peyton personally met with during that period in history is staggering—and all at a time when the political climate in Central America was searing hot and extremely volatile. If we couple the fact that he had unfettered access to some of the most important depots in the Western Hemisphere and the fact that he just *happened* to be in Guyana on the eve of the Jonestown Massacre we have the stuff that conspiracy theories are made of. He reportedly converted Forbes Burnham, the president of Guyana and Lionel Luckhoo, Jim Jones' Guyanese lawyer. He was also reportedly in touch with Jim Jones through the Full Gospel Businessman's Association when Jones was still in Ukiah California.[5]

4. Diamond, Sara. "Notes." Spiritual Warfare. 1989. 247. Print.
5. Full Gospel Business Men's Voice: 1981–1982, Volumes 29–30.

Does that seem strange to anyone else but me? Now, what if I told you that there is more than ample evidence to indicate that Jonestown was a CIA mind control experiment that went terribly wrong.[6] It is a known fact that the Guyanese army uncovered enough mind control medication at Jonestown to keep a population of 200,000 drugged for over a year. Now, what if I added the fact that many of the heads of State that Peyton met with were known CIA assets? The odds of all that being a coincidence are astronomical, especially when you realize that Peyton was *also* present when the infamous CIA asset Efraim Rios Montt was "converted".[7]

Rios Montt went on to win the distinction of being the only Central American dictator to ever be convicted of genocide. He was responsible for widespread human rights abuses, torture, assassinations, disappearances, and the massacre of tens of thousands of Guatemalans by death squads. Call me crazy, but I somehow doubt he was *converted.*[8]

Now, let's go back to our narrative. According to Joyner's testimony, (some of which will follow), this same Newton Peyton had just come from the office of Kurt Waldheim, President of Austria. Joyner informs us that Peyton has, in the past, met with Indira Gandhi, Prime Minister of India. I presume Joyner is wanting to impress us with the fact that such an important person would be looking to knight him. He continues by informing his audience that Peyton is also friends with Arab Heads of States including Saddam Hussein. In fact, ultimately it is Peyton who will get Paul Cain an audience with the Sadaam.

If you do not find this very intriguing you must be far less curious than I am. After all, one does not just flit around the world meeting with Heads of States to "witness" to them. A good ole Texas boy, even an obscenely wealthy one like Newman Bailey Peyton Jr., can't just call up a dictator and ask them to go for coffee with him. That is just not how the world works. Think about it—Peyton seems to be magically present at all the political hot spots at just the right time and is either given immediate audience with, or becomes friends with, the heads of those countries. What are the odds?

I think the most likely explanation is that he worked for the CIA. Which brings us around to how Newman Peyton knew Rick Joyner and

6. Meiers, Michael. Was Jonestown a CIA Medical Experiment?

7. Judge, John. Jonestown: A Review by John Judge. Spike News, 6 Feb. 2014.

8. Balmer, Randall Herbert, 2004. 466. Print.

why he was looking to Knight him. Rick was there with Paul Cain. Paul Cain is not, nor has he ever been a part of the Knights of Malta, but he most definitely *was* a member of the CIA.

Cain was a Former Senior Diplomatic Advisor for the Washington Federal News Service and an advisor to the American Central Intelligence Agency. He was employed by the Defense Intelligence Agency in the paranormal division. Yes, you read that correctly. He was part of the *paranormal* division.

In 1985 Cain joined the controversial Stargate program as a remote viewer. The Stargate Project was initiated by the Defense Intelligence Agency in part to investigate whether remote viewing could be used militarily. For those perhaps unfamiliar with these terms, remote viewing involves the ability to see, or get impressions about, a distant, unseen "target." The CIA supposedly defunded the project in 1995 claiming that success with remote reviewing was not statistically significant, and they could therefore no longer justify its funding. This was shown to be a lie when a 1977 internal CIA investigation into the phenomenon showed that remote viewing *had* proven useful.[9]

Remote viewing is also known as astral travel, and it is an occult practice. Cain did not just work in the Stargate Program he also used his psychic powers to help the FBI's National Center for Intelligence and Counter-Terrorism. While this is admirable, the ends do not justify the means.

When I was in this movement, I remember hearing that Paul Cain's presence blew out power circuits and caused power surges. According to David Pytches, author of the book, *Some Said it Thundered*, Cain caused an expensive video camera to short circuit and the following night the phone system was blown out during a conference in Anaheim California.[10]

For now, however, let's push on with Rick's narrative

> "I'm sitting in the lobby (Nuremberg, Germany) with Bobby Conner and a few other people there and this guy comes walking in the lobby of the hotel who was an interesting looking guy. And Reed, who was Paul Cain's assistant, was

---

9. Mandelbaum, W. Adam. The Psychic Battlefield. 2000. Print.
10. Pytches, David. Some Said It Thundered. 1990. 52. Print.

standing behind me. And he said, 'Hey, there's Newman
Peyton.' And this guy was Baron Newman Peyton, who
Colonel Byrd had told me was looking for me. I said, 'Reed,
do you know that man.' He said, 'Oh, yeah, we met him years
ago.' And he came over, walked over to me, and said he had
been looking to meet with me. And I stopped him right away.
I said, 'Bobby, give me a readout on this guy.' And this guy's
going, 'What's a readout?' " —Rick Joyner[11]

Okay, let me interject here for a moment. First of all, a *read-out*
amounts to nothing more than a psychic reading. At MorningStar, this
was commonly referred to as *reading someone's mail*. It was divination, plain
and simple. I learned to do this myself with a high degree of accuracy
during my time at MorningStar and have subsequently repented with
tears. I was convinced at that time that these so called *revelations* came
from the Lord. However never once did I hear someone call someone
to repentance or discern someone's sin. For example, Reed, Paul Cain's
assistant in the narrative above is the same man with whom he later
confessed to having a long time homosexual affair. Why were none of
these men able to discern that? Using a more recent example, why could
Rick Joyner and the other so-called Apostles of the New Reformation
not discern that Todd Bentley, one of their own, had an alcohol problem
was having an extramarital affair with his nanny at the time they commissioned him? Why couldn't they read *that* mail?

Getting back to our narrative, Joyner is sitting in the lobby of the
hotel with Bobby Connors, Paul Cain's assistant, and a few other people.
As we will soon find out, Paul Cain is not there as he is at the office of
Kurt Waldheim, the President of Austria. Waldheim was president of
Austria from 1986 to 1992 so that gives us the time frame that the narra-
tive occurred. This will become important later on.

"And Bobby goes, 'Sir, when you came in I just saw
something, I saw that you had just come from the office of a
man named Kurt Waldheim.' And his eyes got real big 'cause
he had just come from his (Kurt Waldheim) office. And then
he (Bobby Conner) said, 'I saw you, or I saw him opening

---

11. Originally taken from Trouble in Prophet Land. Havestnet.org

this briefcase and giving you something out of it.' And Bobby described the briefcase. And his eyes got real big then. He said, 'This is incredible!' He (Baron Peyton) said, 'That is the only briefcase like that in the world. I had it custom made for Kurt Waldheim.' And it was a weird thing Bobby had described." —Morning Star Ministries, Rick Joyner audio, no date given[12]

So we learn here that Newman Bailey Peyton Jr. has just come from the office of the President of Austria. Bobby Connor describes to Peyton (through a psychic reading), a particular briefcase.

Bobby told him a little bit more about the papers and everything and it really got his attention. He was captured from then on ... And he was a prophetic man. He was the one who prophesied to Indira Gandhi that if she did not give her heart to the Lord, she would be dead in one week ... Five days later she was assassinated. And he is a friend with head of number of the Muslim nations, as well as other countries, and he's been a prophetic voice to them, but he had never seen the gift operate like this in such a specific way about details like that, so he was just capture. —Rick Joyner.[13]

So here we learn that not only is Newman Peyton friends with the Heads of State of a number of Muslim nations, but he has also had contact with Indira Gandhi, the Prime Minister of India. Joyner claims that Peyton warned her that if she did not give her heart to the Lord, she would die within the week.

Now, let's think this through. Why would Newman Peyton have been given an audience with the president of India or Muslim Heads of State unless he was on *official* business? How possible is it that a Muslim leader would give a little known Texan born businessman the time of day? How did he even know *how* to contact Prime Minister Indira Gandhi? Think about it! It really makes no sense that he was acting on his own accord. Did he just call her up? How did he get through to

12. Originally taken from: Trouble in Prophet Land. Harvestnet.org
13. Op. Cit.

187

her? How did he have the number? What was the conversation—"Hello Prime Minister Gandhi, um, I am a businessman from Texas, and I just wanted to let you know that if you don't get saved, you are going to die this week." I can assure you, there is much more to the story.

Indira Gandhi was assassinated in 1984, and it *has* been claimed that the CIA orchestrated the Sikh uprising that led to her assassination by two Sikh bodyguards. So, is it not far more *likely* that Newman Peyton was a CIA operative and was passing her a "do or die" message?

As we are about to see in the narrative that follows, this same Newman Peyton gets Paul Cain an audience with Saddam Hussein. We can already logically surmise that Peyton was a US operative, and we also know, by his own admission, that Paul Cain was also a CIA operative. In light of that information, Joyner's narrative below seems quite ludicrous.

> This worked out strategically in a way you wouldn't believe. It was important, but this was the guy who was key to getting Paul Cain an audience with Saddam Hussein. You may have heard us talk about that. And Paul went. Saddam Hussein, some of his guys had been in a meeting, had seen the prophetic gift operate, and they were utterly convinced that Paul is a true prophet. Saddam became convinced, and he wanted to meet with Paul. Okay! It all worked out. Well, Newman was the guy who worked this out. And right after he sent the fax to start this process all this fear came on him, 'What have I done … this could really mess up world events and things like that.' He didn't know Paul Cain that well … And right after that, the Lord had told Bobby Conner to fax Newman Peyton and just write this that Paul Cain is my man, he's okay, don't worry about it or something like that.[14]

So Joyner is claiming here that Saddam Hussein and some of his guys were at a Paul Cain meeting. Think about that! Saddam was a Sunni Muslim, and his elite guard were almost exclusively Sunni Arabs. Are we supposed to believe that Cain was holding meetings there in Iraq, and Saddam and the guys just sauntered down to hear him speak? I think we are safe to assume that didn't happen.

---

14. Quoting Rick Joyner. Originally in Trouble in Prophet Land. Harvestnet.org

I want to point out something else in this narrative that is at odds with common sense. Joyner claims it was Saddam that wanted to meet with Paul Cain, not the other way around. So why then was Newman Baily Peyton so nervous about setting up the meeting? Wouldn't he have been doing Saddam a favor if that was the case? Stranger yet is the fact that Paul Cain would later claim he was sent to Iraq at the behest of President Clinton![15] In fact, Cain has acted as Presidential Consultant and Special Envoy for *three* presidents. Why would he have needed Newman Peyton to set up the meeting?

Additionally, why would a US President choose to send Paul Cain? Well, here is my educated guess. Since Paul Cain was part of the government's paranormal Stargate Program, perhaps he was there to *read* Saddam Hussein. I can assure you however that Clinton did not send him there to *witness* to Hussein! In fact, it is well known the Hussein *himself* was a CIA asset.

I find so much of this narrative downright odd. Why was Newman Peyton looking to Knight Rick Joyner? How did he even know him? There are far too many questions, but for now, let's push on and finish the narrative.

> So, Newman sends this fax to make this connection between Paul and Saddam, to work out this thing. And he's sitting there going, 'Oh, no, what have I done?' Can't get the fax back. Another fax comes in, 'Don't worry, Paul Cain's okay.' You know, I mean, it's exactly on time. They still have the little strips of paper. He sent one out. One minute later, one comes in, this is it. So, these things happen strategically. Anyway, we went on, and a bunch of us got knighted by these Knights of Malta. Okay, I did first. And I wasn't even going to do it. I thought it was a great honor and all. But, I just don't join things like that ... Anyway, Paul Cain called me from Austria. And said, you know, 'Just tuned in on it.' And said, 'The Lord is going to give you some credentials like Paul's credentials where his Roman citizenship really was used at times' And he said, 'You're really supposed to do this thing.'
>
> So, I did and then later some of the other guys, we even

---

15. Giberti, R. Scott. Paul Cain: A Prophet in the Hall of Kings. 2011. Print.

got Bobby Connor knighted and Steve and Leonard. Anyway, we had a big time. Bobby, we dubbed Sir Bubba, and Mahesh (Chavda) became Sir Loin. We seriously polluted the Blue Blood of Europe. I mean it was bad. Ricky Skaggs, you know, country (singer). Aw man, it was a blast. We had a great time, though. Anyway, we got knighted by this thing. It's a real, this somehow is real important to the Lord. He's kept this order in existence, I think like He has Israel. It has an end times purpose and destiny ... They went on, made me a knight commander which gave me authority to Knight others and then they made me something else, where I have authority over all the knights supposedly in the U.S.

—Audio Tape, Rick Joyner Ministries, no date on tape[16]

So, where does all this leave Rick Joyner? Well, generally where there is smoke, there is fire, but I honestly don't know. I can *surmise* based on an abundance of circumstantial evidence, but I certainly can't conclude. I *do* know that what I witnessed and what I experienced while at MorningStar Ministries, begs for that kind of explanation. I personally believe that MorningStar is part of a much bigger agenda and is connected to some powerful people who are diligently working toward a New World Order. I think that fact is inarguable. I also believe that Joyner has done more than any ministry before him to pave the way for a unified religion.

---

16. Quoting Rick Joyner. Originally in Trouble in Prophet Land. Harvestnet.org

SEVENTEEN
RITUALS

About a year ago, while cleaning out some old boxes of books, I happened to stumble upon a notebook I'd kept during my sojourn at MorningStar. In the years after MorningStar the color had drained from my memories and in time some of them were forgotten altogether. As I flipped through the pages of the notebook, the color flooded back into those gray recollections and engulfed me in waves of raw emotion. Overwhelmed, I considered closing the notebook or tossing it in the trash, but then my eyes fell on my handwriting from the eve of the new millennium, December 31, 1999.

It was hard to believe that I had scrawled these notes so many years earlier, in a notebook I had balanced on my knees while I listened intently. So much had happened in my life since that night, yet these notes were still frozen in time. Now, here they were before me as a testament to my former apostasy—affirming that I was there, that I *heard* this, that I *experienced* this, that I *believed* this! Looking at the notebook, the hidden meanings embedded in the words were so palpable, so undeniably evident. How could I have been so blind? How could we *all* have been so blind?

The meetings referred to in these particular notes took place at a three-day conference held in Wilkesboro, North Carolina. They were held in a long abandoned honky-tonk beer joint called Jubilee Junction. The ministry had rented the run down former bar for their Wilkesboro

Church and conducted conferences and weekly services there. These were some of the last meetings I attended at MorningStar.

On the evening of December 29, 1999, I hastily scribbled the following notes taken word for word from Rick Joyner.

> In the second temple, the Glory was greater than in the first—it was built out of burnt stones. Unless you have been burned you don't qualify. —Rick Joyner[1]

Certainly, these words were not new to me that night. I had heard this same thing repeated over and over again in these circles. It didn't make it true—it only made it *seem* true. This lie about the burnt stones is very prevalent at MorningStar and really in the Dominionist movement at large. It may seem innocuous, but then many lies in this movement do. It is actually of monumental importance, as I will soon show you.

First, let's look at the verse they use to substantiate this claim.

> And he spoke before his brethren and the army of Samaria, and said, "What are these feeble Jews doing? Will they fortify themselves? Will they offer sacrifices? Will they complete it in a day? Will they revive the stones from the heaps of rubbish —*stones* that are burned? —Neh 4:2

Now, let me give you some background on this particular verse so we don't isolate it from its context. Nehemiah was a cupbearer to King Artaxerxes, the King of Persia. King Artaxerxes would have been Queen Esther's stepson, for what it's worth. Persia had control of Judah at that time, and Nehemiah asked the king for permission to return to the Kingdom of Judah to rebuild the broken wall around Jerusalem. The king consented to grant Nehemiah's request, and he was sent as the Governor of Judah to Jerusalem with the express assignment of rebuilding the broken wall. The wall, *not* the temple.

Because there were hostile groups that had filled the void left by the Jews 70-year exile in Babylon, Nehemiah had to endure opposition from enemies on all sides. Now remember, the *entire* walled city had been burned by the Babylonians during the siege of Jerusalem so there is no

---

1. From the personal notes of M. McCumber Dec. 29,1999

way of knowing the exact origin of the stones referred to in the Scripture above. However, I think it would be *reasonable* to assume that they were from the ruins of the former wall itself.

God did *not* use burnt stones to rebuild the second temple. The very idea that Nehemiah used *these* burned stones (the ones referenced in Neh 4:2), in the construction of second *Temple* shows how Biblically illiterate this movement really is. The second temple had already been rebuilt 72 years *prior* to Nehemiah's arrival![2]

The second temple was rebuilt by Zerubbabel, not Nehemiah! Zerubbabel had been assisted by a group of Jewish exiles from Babylon, who had been allowed to return to Judah by decree of Cyrus, the Great, of Persia.

I know, you are saying to yourself so what, maybe Zerubbabel used burnt stones. He couldn't have! First of all, the Jews would *never* have reused burnt stones, symbolic of their judgment by fire, to rebuild their holy temple. The whole of the city including Solomon's Temple had been burned and pillaged by the Babylonians as a judgment from God for their disobedience.

Secondly, the Israelites were given a hefty grant from the Zerubbabel which included money for freshly quarried stones. Why would they have used burnt stones when money had been generously provided for fresh ones?[3]

Thirdly, the charred heaps of ruins from the destruction of Solomon's Temple had been carted off *prior* to the foundation of the second temple being laid.[4] These stones would have been considered defiled to the Jews, and as such, would have been discarded outside the city. In all likelihood, they were cast into the Kidron valley on the eastern side of Jerusalem.

Nehemiah rebuilt the wall around the city—and only the city. Common sense tell us that he would have built it out of the remains of the former wall! The old wall had been burned in the Babylonian siege as well so it is inevitable that the debris held burnt stones!

Now, lest I weary you, let me tell you *why* this matters. If you do

---

2. Second Temple completed 516 BCE Nehemiah sent to rebuild wall around the city in 444 BCE, 72 years after the completion of the Temple

3. Ezra Chapter 2, Haggai 2:3; Zechariah 4:10; *Easton, Matthew George (1897). "Temple, the Second". Easton's Bible*

4. Ezra Chapter 2

a Bible word search on the term "burnt stones", you will find that it is mentioned only one other place in Scripture. Burned stones were used to build the tower of Babel.

The word "Babel" is ultimately derived from the Akkadian word meaning "gate of the god." A similar Hebrew word is "balal" which means "confusion." It is an interesting play on words.[5] The original Akkadian word, "gate of the god," encapsulates quite nicely the religious purpose of the temple tower. It was, after all, a tower built with the express purpose of becoming a gateway or portal to the Heavens.

The Tower of Babel was a self-glorifying effort that symbolized pride and rebellion. As such, it was an affront to God. While the Jewish temple was built to glorify and provide a habitation for the one *true* God, the Tower of Babel was created for the glorification of *man* and the habitation of demons. While the rocks for the Lord's temple were hewn from natural stone, the material used to build the tower of Babel were man-made bricks baked in fire to become as stones.

> And they said one to another, Go to, let us make brick, and burn them thoroughly. And they had brick for stone, and slime had they for mortar. —Gen 11:3 KJV

Now, let's look at some additional verses concerning the tower of Babel before examining a quote by Bob Jones that will *prove* to you that this movement knows full well whose temple they are *really* building

> Now the whole earth had one language and one speech. And it came to pass, as they journeyed from the east, that they found a plain in the land of Shinar, and they dwelt there. Then they said to one another, "Come, let us make bricks and bake [them] thoroughly." They had brick for stone, and they had asphalt for mortar. And they said, "Come, let us build ourselves a city, and a tower whose top [is] in the heavens; let us make a name for ourselves, lest we be scattered abroad over the face of the whole earth. —Gen 11:1–4

Although Bible scholars and historians do not know for *sure* that

---

5. Youngblood, R. F. Nelson's New Illustrated Bible Dictionary, 1995. 147. Print.

the tower of Babel was round, it has *always* been depicted as such. On the other hand, we *know* for a fact that Lord's Temple *was not* round. Neither Solomon's nor the later rebuilt temple was round. Additionally, we are aware from Scripture that the Third Temple (described in Ezekiel 40–47) will *not* be round either. Therefore, the following quote from Bob Jones leaves no doubt as to *whose* temple he is referring to.

> These people the Lord is getting ready to use ... **these burnt stones** that are being burned into the body of Christ are getting ready to be built into the temple of living stones.
>
> So, get ready for a temple to be built now that no flood, no storm can blow down 'cause it will be a **round temple**. It'll be literally like an elevator right into the Heavens to where people can go and come literally at will to begin a relationship in the Heavenly realm. —Bob Jones[6]

It is said that the Tower of Babel was pitched with bitumen to make it waterproof as its builders were fearful that God might decide to send another flood. However, the Jewish historian Josephus in his book, *The Antiquities of the Jews*, mentions storms of wind that came and overthrew the tower.

In light of this, it is fascinating that Jones mentions that the temple the *Lord* is building, is a *round* temple. A round temple reaching to the Heavens that floods and storms will not knock down! I think it's pretty evident which *Lord* he is talking about.

Nimrod, the great-grandson of Noah, was the founder of the first pagan world empire at Babel (Babylon).[7] Ancient Babylon was located on the plain of Shinar by the River Euphrates in what is today, modern Turkey. Inarguably, the tower of Babel, as a symbol, is synonymous with the New World Order and the Beast system. It is the fountainhead of evil and *all* pagan gods, and occult doctrine can be traced back to it. Babel was a forerunner, if you will, of the coming New World Order and the Beast system of the Anti-Christ.

Of course, the mystery religion created in Babylon was nothing more than the inversion of the Biblical story of Adam and Eve. In the

---

6. Jones, Bob. "To the 3rd Heaven." Also YouTube A New Sword of the Spirit.
7. Genesis 10:8–12; Genesis 11:1–9

mystery religion, the serpent was worshiped as God for opening their eyes and showing them the knowledge that a lesser vengeful God had tried to keep from them in the garden. In this Luciferian version, the snake becomes the savior of mankind. He tells Eve that if she would just eat from the tree of the Knowledge of Good and Evil, she would gain the necessary gnosis (knowledge) to become a God herself. This gnosis (knowledge) would bring illumination which would provide a pathway to Godhood.

In the inverted version, the *real* God is seen as a hateful, vengeful God called the Demiurge, and Lucifer is the one who brings salvation through knowledge. In this version, Lucifer is Lord of the universe, and his power has only temporarily been usurped by a lesser God (the Demiurge).[8]

When Nimrod was killed by the sons of Noah in 2167 B.C., his wife, who, believe it or not, was also his mother, promoted the idea that he had ascended and became a god so she could maintain control of the Kingdom after his death. When she subsequently became pregnant with her son Horus, also known as Tammuz, she claimed that she had been visited by the Nimrod's spirit who had left her pregnant. She subsequently claimed that Horus was the reincarnation of Nimrod (God made flesh) and thus the perverted unholy trinity was formed.

Semiramis and her son Horus were worshiped as the Madonna and child, and Nimrod, as the Father God. After Babel was destroyed by God and the languages confused, worship of this unholy trinity spread into the surrounding regions where they took on different names.[9] Nimrod became known as the sun god, and Semiramis became referred to as the lesser light, the moon goddess and also the Queen of Heaven.

> The Tower of Babel was actually the worship of Satan in the form of fire, the sun, and the serpent. However, Satan worship could not be done openly because of the many who still believed in the true God of Noah. So a mystery religion began at Babel where Satan could be worshiped in secret."
> —Alexander Hislop[10]

---

8. Fairly, Mark. Know Your Enemy
9. Op. Cit.
10. Hysop, Alexander The Two Babylons 1959

For interest's sake, I have included some of the names that this unholy trinity was known by after the fall of Babel. This is in no way an exhaustive list and is in no particular order.

> After Nimrod was killed by the sons of Noah, tradition says they cut his body into many pieces and distributed it throughout the kingdom. Semiramis gathered up these pieces but was unable to find her lover's male organ. It is from this Babylonian tradition that phallic worship began. Obelisks were erected to remember the sacred penis of the sun god Nimrod (later called Baal). The illegitimate son of Semiramis, Tammuz, became the son of god, (Baal/Nimrod) in the flesh.[11]

As an aside, one of the most famous obelisks in the world is the Washington Monument in Washington D.C. Each side is directly aligned with North, South, East, and West and measures 666 inches each. The height of the obelisk from base to the tip at the top is 6666 inches. I could say *much* more about this, but in the interest of staying on track, I would ask that you do your own investigation into how and why obelisks are used today if you are so inclined

Now, we are going to shift gears a bit here, but I promise it will all tie together. I am sure you have heard the word *Shekinah* used as a synonym for the Glory of God or His presence. I never paid much attention to its use until I read an article somewhere and decided to investigate it for myself. Interestingly enough, the word Shekinah is not in the Bible—not in the Greek nor the Hebrew.

Shekinah comes from the Hebrew word *shä·kan'* [H7931 in the Concordance]. It is a verb that means to dwell, abide, or inhabit. However, that is not where the word Shekinah comes from—like I said, there *is* no Hebrew word *Shekinah*. The word Shekinah originated from the Kabbalah. The Kabbalah teaches that God has a female side called Shekinah. She is also known as the consort or Bride of God—or the Divine Feminine.

The Kabbalah teaches that when God (male) copulates with Shekinah (female), the glory of their pairing is released. I apologize for having

---

11. Fairly, Mark. Know Your Enemy

to be graphic, but I want people to understand—this is literally the ejaculate. This, sadly enough, is where the idea of Shekinah being the Glory of God comes from—*not* the Bible, but the Kabbalah! This is utterly blasphemous and against what Scripture teaches!

This Shekinah concept seeped into the soil of Judaism at large, and over time she became known as the Queen of the Sabbath or the Sabbath Bride. However, she is none other than Semiramis of the Ancient Babylonians or Sophia of the Greek Gnostics, or Ashera of the Canaanites, Diana of the Ephesians, Queen of Heaven to the Catholics and Muslims, Mother Nature to the Pantheists, or Heavenly Mother to the Mormons.

If you know anything about Todd Bentley who touched off the Florida Outpouring, then you will know about the controversy his female angel, Emma, caused. Well, Emma is actually *Eema*, another name for Shekinah.[12] Bob Jones was the one who introduced Todd Bentley to his infamous angel, and it is *Eema* that helped birth the entire Prophetic Movement.[13] The alarm bells should be deafening at this point. It is also Eema, aka Shekinah, Queen of the Sabbath that the Jews welcome in at sundown every Friday night by the lighting of the Sabbath candles(Shabbat in Hebrew).

It may seem like I have wandered from my topic somewhat, but this foundational understanding is critical to understanding what comes next. Joyner stated that evening that the year 2000 was a Sabbatical year and that going forward, the ministry would rest every seven years. He also stressed that we *all* must enter the Sabbath rest.

I am going to do my best to explain all this but first, we need to take a look at a quote from Joyner's book, *There were Two Trees in the Garden.*

> The Tree of Knowledge of Good and Evil is a powerful biblical model of the Law. As the Apostle Paul declared "The power of sin is the law" (I Corinthians 15:56). This is because it is through the Law that we must derive our knowledge of good and evil. We may wonder how this knowledge brings death until we see the fruit. —Rick Joyner

---

11. This is readily verifiable by a host of books and websites—do a google search with Shekinah and Eema in the same sentence.
13. Ray, S.E., n.d., * these facts can also be validated through a host of readily available resources.

Whoa, hold on for a minute! Did Joyner just say that God's Holy Law, the law passed down from God Himself to Moses on Mt. Sinai, was the fruit of the forbidden tree? Yes, that is *exactly* what he just said! Seriously, why would anyone entertain the idea that God's Holy Law is the fruit of the forbidden tree, the mere knowledge of which, brings death? That is some messed up doctrine!

> Therefore the law [is] holy, and the commandment holy and just and good. —Rom 7:12

Now, let's take a look at the Scripture Joyner has misapplied.

> The sting of death [is] sin, and the strength of sin [is] the law. —1 Cor 15:56

Was Paul telling us that the law was sin? No, he most certainly was not! He was telling us that the strength of sin is in the Law *because* the Law *shows* us what sin *is* through it! As Paul stated in Romans, how could we possibly know we were sinners apart from the Law?

> What shall we say then? [Is] the law sin? Certainly not! On the contrary, I would not have known sin except through the law. For I would not have known covetousness unless the law had said, "You shall not covet. —Rom 7:7

Joyner's assertion that it is the *knowledge of the Law* that brings sin and death is asinine. Knowledge of sin does *not* equal guilt of sin!

Now, my purpose for including that quote from Joyner's book was not actually to refute it (although I felt I must for the sake of clarity). I added it to show how self-refuting this would be *if indeed* he was talking about keeping the Sabbath as part of the Law. How could he be saying that God's Law was evil on one hand, but then advocating that we keep it by observing the Sabbath, on the other?

I think it is fairly obvious that he is *not* talking about the Biblically defined Sabbath. As is usual, he has substituted a Biblical term to mean something *entirely* different. This will become clearer as we continue.

For Adam to enter fellowship, he had to enter the Sabbath

rest. In fact, he could not even have fellowship with God without entering this Sabbath rest. —Rick Joyner

Now, first of all, there *was* no Sabbath in the Garden of Eden! In fact, there was no real labor of *any* kind until *after* Adam and Eve sinned by partaking of the fruit from the Tree of the Knowledge of Good and Evil as recorded in Genesis 3:9. Why then, would Adam have needed a Sabbath to rest from his labors? Why would he have needed to enter the Sabbath to have fellowship with God? He had continual and perfect fellowship with God before the fall.

Additionally, The Ten Commandments had not been given, as there was no need for them. There *was* no sin! There wasn't even *knowledge of sin* in the Garden before the fall. Adam had only *one* commandment—he was not to eat the fruit of the Tree of the Knowledge of Good and Evil.[14]

In light of this, and keeping in mind that that Joyner uses double speak as a form of coded communication, he *must* have been using the word *"Sabbath"* to mean something entirely different. There is no other conclusion. Otherwise, the emphasis on Sabbath keeping would be curious indeed in a fellowship that places so little emphasis on holiness in general.

So what *did* Joyner mean by the word *Sabbath* and why was he insisting that Adam had to enter into it to have fellowship with God? He obviously didn't get this idea from Scripture, so where did he get it? Well, perhaps I am flogging a dead horse, but I don't want anyone to miss this. The following is a word for word quote from that evening.

> Abide in the Sabbath rest of the Lord. This will become an increasing emphasis in the teaching and a reality as the Lord enters His temple, the church. Our growing intimacy with Him will bring a peace that will actually calm the storm of the rising sea of humanity. The intensity of the times will overwhelm any pseudo peace. We must be one with the "Lord of the Sabbath." —Rick Joyner[15]

So, Joyner is stating here that abiding in the Sabbath rest of the

---

14. Genesis 2:17
15. Joyner, Rick. War and Glory

Lord will become *more* of an emphasis as the Lord enters his Temple, the church. First of all, let me quickly correct this false teaching. We who are truly born of Him *are* his Church. His *true* Church, his *remnant,* are those who are born of Him and have His Spirit residing within them.

> Or do you not know that your body is the temple of the Holy Spirit [who is] in you, whom you have from God, and you are not your own? —1 Cor 6:19

In light of this scripture, the statement from Joyner that our entering the Sabbath will increase in importance as the Lord enters His temple makes no sense. Sure, it *sounds* Christian, but it's not! As Christians, we *already* have the Lord dwelling within us. We do not look for some future indwelling; He *already* dwells within us. However, it *does* make sense if we keep in mind that Joyner believes that Christ (the Christ Spirit/Christ Principle/Christ Consciousness) is coming *in* his church and not for them. Of course, this is *another* Christ and another Gospel.

Now why do you suppose Joyner ties the entering of the Sabbath rest with the act of the *Lord* (it) entering (possessing) the temple (our body)? The Kabbalah teaches that the Sabbath is the gateway to Gan Eden or the Garden of Eden. In other words, in order to return to the garden, we must enter the Sabbath. The Kabbalah is Gnostic Luciferianism, and as I have earlier stated, the Sabbath is synonymous with Shekinah. Shekinah is synonymous for Eema, Asherah, Isis, Ishtar, Semiramis or a host of other names. They are *all* names of the *same* demon spirit and remember, *all* occult doctrine and *all* false gods and goddesses can be traced back to Nimrod and Mystery Babylon!

Basically, what Joyner was advocating is a type of alchemical sex magic in which Corporate Adam (masculine) enters into Shekinah/Sabbath (female) resulting in the Shekinah Glory (demonic entity) *possessing* the temple (Corporate Adam/ so-called body of Christ, but not the real Church). I know this is a lot to take in especially if this has never been revealed to you before.

The first time that I really got a revelation of this, I felt physically sick to my stomach. It all makes perfect sense to me *now,* the bridal mysticism, the simulated sex acts that I had seen mimicked by people taken by this spirit of "it" in *worship* services. The moans of ecstasy, the groans, the gyrating hips—*this* was what it was all about!

I remember seeing Julie Joyner at the front of the MorningStar church when it was still in the warehouse on Presley Road in Charlotte. She was on the platform moaning in ecstasy while being *touched* by *"it"*. With this revelation, I understood what "it" was all about—this is what they meant when they talked about—letting "it" take control. *This* is what has entered and split our churches! This movement talks about *it* bringing unity—it's a lie! *It* only brings unity among those who have already submitted to *it*, and even then it's a false unity that will ultimately bring death!

As I push on with the notes from the Dec. 30, 1999 meeting, I pray that the occult nature of this movement will become clearer and clearer to you. Next in the meeting, we had Bob Jones warn us that there would be things happening in the body of Christ that many would find sacrilegious.

> Many things are gonna happen in the body of Christ this year that many will think are sacrilegious, but this will be the year that we sack religion. As we sack religion the Lord will change the way we think, understand. —Bob Jones[16]

Now, let's take a closer look at what the word sacrilegious really means and then we can evaluate whether or not this is something we really want or need in the body of Christ.

> **Sacriledge:** Desecration, profanation, misuse, or theft of something regarded as sacred.[17]
>
> The thesaurus lists the following words as meaning the same as (synonym for) sacrilege:[18]
>
> Desecration, mockery, profanation, offense, violation, heresy, impiety, profanity, blasphemy, irreverence, curse, and sin.

So, this is Bob Jones' idea of what we need to see in the body of Christ? Does he actually want the sacred profaned, violated, blasphemed, cursed and mocked? Yes he does, because this is precisely what

16. Taken from M. McCumber's personal notes Dec 30, 1999
17. "Sacrilege." Collins English Dictionary –Complete and Unabridged, 12th ed.
18. "Sacrilege." Collins Thesaurus of the English Language

he and others from this movement have done. Talk about self-fulfilled prophecy!

According to my notes, Jones promised us that night that we were going to the next level—that we would have Scripture fulfilled in us that night.

> We are ready to transfer to the next level- he is going to fulfill Scripture in us tonight. —Bob Jones[19]

I know I keep repeating this, but this concept is critical to understand if we are to avoid deception. Their false Christ is coming *in* the church; our Christ is coming *for* the church. Their false Christ will possess their temples (bodies) and elevate them through gnosis to Godhood where *they* will reign on earth. *Our* Christ is coming *for* His remnant church (those who have accepted his shed blood for the propitiation of their sin, and who do His will). Our Christ will rule and reign for eternity. This will be very significant to keep in mind as I further outline what took place in these meetings.

Now, the next thing I need to highlight from my notes that evening is the emphasis put on Psalm 24.

> Psalm 24—we need to get hold of this transitory Psalm. We have felt a transition in the body since 1948 we are about to see a birthing. There is a sound coming to the body of Christ. He can do in a day what historically has taken 10 years. —Rick Joyner[20]

It is important to actually *look* at the Psalm referenced above. Pay careful attention to the fact that Joyner is associating this particular Psalm with transition and birthing. Now, since the second half of this Psalm is the part that is stressed in my notes, let's begin there.

> Lift up your heads, O you gates!
> And be lifted up, you everlasting doors!
> And the King of glory shall come in.

---

19. Op. Cit.
20. Op. Cit.

Who is this King of glory?
The LORD strong and mighty,
The LORD mighty in battle.
Lift up your heads, O you gates!
Lift up, you everlasting doors!
And the King of glory shall come in.
Who is this King of glory?
The LORD of hosts,
He is the King of glory. Selah.
—Ps 24: 7–10

I think you will agree that this Psalm has *nothing* whatsoever to do with either transition *or* birthing. In fact, this Psalm was written by King David when the Ark of the Covenant (which was God's pledge of His Presence among his people) was being brought to the place prepared for it. When the Ark was stolen, the Glory departed Israel (I Samuel 4), so here we have David bringing the Ark back to its rightful place.

Now, keep in mind that the temple they are building—is *round* and made of *burnt* stones. This is *not* His true Church, His remnant church— but the unified harlot church. So *that* is the temple that they want their *Lord* to fill. This is precisely why Joyner was stressing a Psalm about the Lord filling his temple and associating it with transition and birthing! He did this because it would be the act of *his* Lord filling the temple that would lead to transition and birthing.

Not surprisingly, Jones also stressed the importance of Psalm 24, that evening.

> The Governments of the world are about to see *who* is the
> King of Glory. —Bob Jones[21]

Now, I pray that I'm able to illustrate to you through the words of Bob Jones, the occult nature of the apostasy inherent in this move- ment. What I am about to say next is *critical*. These are the words that I scrawled in black ink in my little book that evening so many years ago. I had *no* idea what it meant then. I do now.

---

21. Taken from M. McCumber's personal notes from Dec 30, 1999

God is speaking of three things—transfiguration,
translocation, and transfer. The mountain of transfiguration
will bring trans- location and they are being transferred from
death to life. —Bob Jones[22]

It is critical to understand *exactly* what Jones is talking about here because he has intentionally veiled it. As I have explained in previous chapters, it is common in these circles to have one spiritually-sounding meaning given on the top layer while hiding a more nefarious one known only to higher initiates, underneath. Let's dissect what he is saying carefully and examine it piece by piece.

Transfiguration means a change that glorifies or exalts.

Trans-location literally means, across-location. It refers
to a chromosomal change from one position to another.
We need to really understand this in order to figure out
what is *really* being said. If you have ever wondered why
this movement uses the term DNA so much, this is why.
It stands for **D**ivine **N**ature **A**ctivation. They believe their
divine nature (divine spark) is *activated* when the Christ Spirit/
Christ Consciousness, or whatever else they choose to call
"it," comes to possesses their temple (bodies). They believe
it changes them on a cellular level, and they become gods.
To them, Jesus was just a pattern to follow, he was *a* Christ
but not *the* Christ. In other words, he was just another initiate
who attained Christhood through following the path of
enlightment through gnosis.

Gnostic sects and keepers of the secret doctrine have spoken of humankind evolving into a God-like being since the beginning of time. The Kabballah calls this being the Adam Kadmon or the "God-Man." The name "Adam" refers to the entire human race, and the term "Kadmon" refers to completion. Thus, Adam Kadmon speaks of a return to our beginning, with all the knowledge, wisdom, and enlightenment of the first Adam. Those who embrace this doctrine firmly believe we can

22. Op. Cit.

return to the Garden of Eden by becoming the Adam Kadmon, creating Heaven on Earth.

Adherents of these occult beliefs claim it is the inactivated part of our DNA that is preventing us from becoming God. They insist we have the divinity and enlightenment of the Adam Kadmon encoded into our DNA and believe that as we activate this Divine Nature (the Christ Spirit), we will corporately return to the Garden, ushering in Heaven on earth. This is also what the New Age teaches.

Now, I pray that you understand this because what Jones was encapsulating is the heart of what this movement teaches minus all the Christian doublespeak. At the center of this movement is a solid core of Satanic Luciferian doctrine that exists in every esoteric religion. It is not Christianity!

Jones was telling us there would come a change in us—the Christ Spirit would indwell us. This spirit that would then glorify or exalt *us* causing the divine nature in our DNA to be activated. This activation of our previously dormant DNA would result in us being *transferred* from death to life since we would have achieved eternal life as gods.

We already know that the Christ spirit they are referring to is none other than Lucifer. Let's look at a quote by David Spangler, one of the founding fathers of the New Age Movement.

> Christ is the same force as Lucifer ... Lucifer prepares man
> for the experience of Christhood. (He is) the great initiator ...
> Lucifer works within each of us to bring us to wholeness,
> and as we move into a New Age ... each of us in some way is
> brought to that point which I term the Luciferic Initiation ...
> for it is an invitation into the New Age—David Spangler.[23]

Rest assured friends, there is indeed a light and illumination that is actually darkness!

> Take heed therefore that the light which is in thee be not
> darkness. —Luk 11:35

> Woe to those who call evil good, and good evil; Who put
> darkness for light, and light for darkness; Who put bitter for
> sweet, and sweet for bitter!— Isa 5:20

23. Spangler, David, 1981 44–45

If you take New Age philosophy, Eastern Mysticism, Theosophy, Gnosticism, Rosicrucianism, Kabbalism and all other occult doctrine, and boil it down to its most basic and fundamental element, you will get precisely what Jones encapsulated above—transfiguration, translocation, and transfer. *All* occult doctrine comes from the same source and is, in its most succinct form, the embodiment of what the serpent promised Eve in the Garden of Eden. He promised her that her eyes would be opened (attainment of gnosis), that she would not die (attainment of immortality) and that she would be like God (attainment of divinity).

This is precisely why Joyner stated that Psalm 24 is a Psalm of transition and birthing. He believes that when the Christ Spirit (who we have unmasked as Lucifer) indwells us, it activates our divine nature, changes our DNA, and makes us god.

However, important as this point is, I am going to have to leave it and shift gears slightly. I need to show you that what took place on the New Year's Eve of this three-day conference was nothing less than a ritual. In my notes from December 30, 1999, there was a great deal of emphasis placed on bells.

I am just going to be perfectly honest and tell you upfront that there is some confusion as to who actually spoke the words about the bells. It is one of the details that has faded and it is not clearly delineated in my notes. I *believe* it was Bob Jones, but can't be certain as he and Rick Joyner were bouncing a running commentary back and forth between them several times throughout the evening. At any rate, *these* are the notes.

> Factories have been working for months to meet the demand for bells that will be heard tomorrow evening.
>
> Bells were used to sound a death toll. They believed if you rang the bell it would scare the spirits away long enough [for the person] to get to Heaven.
>
> Bells were used as a Proclamation, on priest's robes, and on horses of war. They would also ring to declare the birth of a king.[24]

Joyner and Jones went on to explain that the following evening we

---

24. Taken from the personal notes of M. McCumber Dec 30, 1999

would each be given a bell to ring. This was to signal the death knell to yesterday and declare the captives had been set free. This brings us to the evening of December 31, 1999, the New Years Eve of the New Millennium.

Rick introduced Jim Bakker, who was the principal speaker for the evening. Bakker began by stating that II Chronicles 5:12–14 was the word for the hour. This particular passage takes place after the building of Solomon's temple. In this passage, the Lord is taking possession of the Temple by filling it with a cloud of His Presence. The Lord covers himself with a cloud as the people would not have been able to bear the Glory of the Lord in their natural bodies. By highlighting these verses, Bakker, like Joyner before him, was placing emphasis on the *Lord* filling his temple.

Tell me, what purpose could have possibly been served in highlighting a Scripture that talks about God taking possession of His temple? As you know, when Christ dwells in us, we literally *become* the temple of the Holy Spirit. He takes up residence within us, and we are restored to God through faith in and acceptance of the shed blood of His Son Jesus Christ as the sacrifice for our sins.

> Or do you not know that your body is the temple of the Holy Spirit [who is] in you, whom you have from God, and you are not your own? —1 Cor 6:19

> But we have this treasure in earthen vessels, that the excellence of the power may be of God and not of us. —2 Cor 4:7

Nothing even *remotely* close to an altar call was given over this three-day conference. In fact, in all my time at MorningStar I never *once* saw an altar call—not for salvation *or* repentance. There *were* calls to the altar for *ministry*, but not anything remotely close to what a Christian would term an altar call. Since Bakker is *presumably* speaking to a Christian audience, who exactly did he plan to invite in to take control of the temple? Why the emphasis on the Lord filling or *possessing* His temple?

Bakker also insisted that religion was going to be shaken that year which, of course, went hand in hand with the statements Jones had made earlier about this being the year they would sack religion.

After Bakker had spoken, Jones added something interesting.

At midnight tonight the Son will be revealed, and the vision will be for the Son." —Bob Jones[25]

Just before midnight, we were instructed to ring the tiny bells that had been provided. I innocently thought we were ringing in the New Year. I was wrong. I firmly believe we were involved in a mass ritual to invoke the Christ Spirit—Lucifer. Allow me to explain.

Joyner emphasized, and stressed the importance of, Adam entering the Sabbath while Bob Jones spoke about the King of Glory coming in. The goal here was to role play Adam's coming transformation to Godhood, which they believe would occur when the Shekinah returns to the temple, activating the inactive part of our DNA. They believe that Christ will indwell his church and will reign on earth as the "Corporate Christ" or "Christ Spirit," through his church (Adam Kadmon).

It will be this mystical alchemical union that will result in the transfiguration; a change that glorifies and exalts man to godhood. This glorifying change will occur with the translocation; our divine nature will be activated, and our human DNA will be modified. Without this translocation, we cannot "evolve" into Godhood. Once this has been fully accomplished, we will be transferred from death to life and will ourselves be god. We will be the New Breed, the God-Men, the Manifest Sons of God, Joel's Army, the Man-Child Company. You can *call* it whatever you will—God calls it blasphemy.

If you are wondering where the bells fit in, consider this. It is a well-known fact that the ringing of a bell in occult circles is done to summon an entity (demon). This entire three-day conference was a mass ritual, and we were the unwitting participants. With the bells, we were literally summoning the Christ spirit (Anti-Christ) to take possession of the temple (the corporate Adam).

While I realize that this is a lot to digest for anyone not familiar with their documented connections, I would ask that you do your own research. The more you are willing to dig, the more obvious it will become.

I find it interesting that I participated in this ritual but had no idea

---

25. Op. Cit.

of its significance. I was uncomfortable and knew something had happened, but, unfortunately, I didn't have sufficient knowledge at that time to process it, and my discernment had been dulled by years of false doctrine. Between the time of my participation in these meetings and finding the notebook, I had studied an inordinate amount about correct doctrine versus false, Christian- sounding Kabbalism, Gnosticism and even Luciferianism. It was only in sitting down and writing out these notes that I was finally able to fully process what had happened.

How many other meetings did I participate in where similar rituals took place? It's hard to tell. Unfortunately, I didn't begin to take notes in these meetings until the end of my sojourn there.

I drifted in and out of meetings for the first part of the year 2000, trying to cut ties but always being lured back by some unseen hand. I was researching the ministry intensely by this time and knew in my heart that what I was involved in was very evil, but I didn't know where to turn. Literally, every person I knew was in this movement—it was all I knew at this point. When my job in Charlotte ended, I landed a job in the Wilkesboro area and moved in the spring of that year to the mountains. On Easter of that year, I attended my last MorningStar meeting. It was the Sunday morning service held at Jubilee Junction. I do not recall much, other than a young lady prophesying nonsense over me. What I *do* recall is the resolve that washed over me and the promise I made to God as my foot touched the threshold of the door on my way out. As I left the building that day and climbed into my little red Ford, *I* quietly prayed. *I promise You God, I will never have anything to do with MorningStar again. I will cut all ties and will not step a toe across the threshold of one of their meetings for as long as I live.* It is a promise that I've kept.

Driving home from the meeting that afternoon, there was the most brilliantly colored rainbow off in the direction of my house. Maybe in my broken and confused state I *needed* that rainbow. Even though years later He would teach me the truth about *signs*, maybe He just met me where I was at that day. I was, after all, so *desperately* reaching out to Him. It might even have been a coincidence—I don't know. What I *do* know is that seeing it brought me peace, made me smile through my tears, and reminded me that I still belonged to Him. I felt at that moment that my decision was right. I knew that leaving behind everything and everyone in my world would be difficult, but I also felt sure that He would be with me.

It is the oddest feeling—being alone, yet somehow, *not* alone. My closest family member was over 700 miles away and literally everyone I knew at that time was in this movement. I was confused and *knew* that MorningStar was wrong, but didn't *understand* the *nature* of what I had been involved with or *why* it was wrong—not entirely anyway.

I found a church that was preaching the Word and found it to be a wonderful refuge and source of healing. Unfortunately, this church would years later, descend into the same Dominionism (minus the Gnostic Mysticism and strange manifestations). So, nine years after leaving MorningStar, I was faced with leaving *another* church and going through the painful process of separation once again. However, it was in dealing with the false doctrine in *this* church that my freedom came.

One day, as I talked things over with my friend Donna, I confessed that I felt I was being deceived, again. I expected her to tell me that I was being ridiculous. She didn't. Instead, she said that perhaps I had better listen to that little voice. That night as I was lying in bed, I prayed and asked God to reveal to me any areas of deception in my life. I told Him that I wanted the Truth at *any* cost, *even if it wrecked my whole world*—and it did.

A few days later, as I was sitting on the spare bed in my office, a feeling of horror rose up as the Truth washed over me. Even as a writer, I am at a complete loss to explain precisely what happened. It was as if my mind was on fast-forward, remembering the words I had heard in Sunday School as a child, remembering Scriptures I had memorized, remembering old sermons of foundational teachings—comparing them to what I had been taught at MorningStar and what was being taught now at *this* church. It was a sudden knowing, an immediate understanding—a flash of insight—an epiphany. I was on the wrong side! I was following an inverted Gospel—a Luciferian Gospel! I was deceived—still!

Sure, I had left MorningStar with all its mind-bending weirdness, but I was *still* walking in error because I had never *actually* understood the nature of the lie. Oh, I understood what was wrong on the surface, but

I had never really looked beneath, *way* beneath. Now, alone in my office on the second floor of a historic house in Statesville, North Carolina. Now, with the light of the afternoon sun flooding my room and the fluttering leaves brushing soundlessly at my oversized window. *Now*, I understood. I *really* understood. I was following an inverted Gospel—Lucifer's Gospel!

This touched off months of crying and repentance as I spent every spare moment searching the Scriptures. Finally, I felt as if the Lord said, *enough*—stop asking for forgiveness. You see, I was forgiven the moment I asked, and no amount of tears and confessing was going to make me any freer or any more forgiven. Oh, I *knew* the work wasn't over—the study, the searching for answers. In fact, I knew *that* part was just beginning. But the repenting, the tears, the brokenness over my own apostasy—over what I had believed and what I had done. *That* was over. I knew it was time to get up from the dust, wash off the ashes, take off my sackcloth, and learn to live again. And that is what I've done my friend—that is *exactly* what I've done.

BIBLIOGRAPHY

Angebert, Jean, Michel. *The Occult and the Third Reich: The Mystical Origins of Nazism and the Search for the Holy Grail.* 1st ed. London: McGraw-Hill, 1975. 178. Print.

Arnott, John, Speaking at Holy Trinity in Brompton England, February 14, 1995. As quoted in, Unbiblical Doctrines, Teachings, and Phenomena of the Third Wave Counterfeit Revival Movement Compiled by Sandy Simpson, 1997. *Deception in the Church.* Web. 01 March 2013.

Bailey, Alice. *The Rays and the Initiations.* New York: Lucis Press, 1972. 754–55. Print.

Bailey, Alice, and Wendy Boyd. "The Great Invocation, The Sword of God." Lucis Trust. Lucis Trust, 2010. Web. 07 Aug. 2016.

Balmer, Randall Herbert. *Encyclopedia of Evangelicalism.* Rev. and Expanded ed. Waco: Baylor UP, 2004. 466. Print.

Baynes, Norman H. *The Speeches of Adolf Hitler, April 1922 – August 1939.* London: Oxford University Press. Print.

Bearden, Michelle. "The Holy Ghost Bartender." *The Tampa Tribune,* June 28, 1999. Print.

The Beatles. *Here Comes the Sun.* Abbey Road EMI Electrola. 1979.

Bellant, Russ. *Old Nazis, the New Right, and the Republican Party.* Boston: South End, 1991. 45. Print.

Bentley, Todd. "Stirring Up the Spirit of Wisdom and Revelation." *Elijah List.* Steve Shultz, 10 Nov. 2003.

Bickle, Mike. *Growing in the Prophetic.* Creation House; New edition, 1996. 14. Print.

Brother Greg. "What on Earth? - Toronto 'Drinking Song." *Sermon Index* [web forum post] 2006. Web. 25 Oct. 2014.

Buren, Elizabeth Van. The Secret of the Illuminati. Sudbury: Spearman, 1982. Print.

Cain, Paul. The New Breed. [As quoted by *Let Us Reason Ministries*]. 2009 Web. 7 Jan 2014. http://letusreason.org/Latrain55.htm

"Catch the Fire: History." *Catch the Fire.* N.d., Web. This information is adapted from an article by Daina Doucet which appeared in *Spread the Fire*, January/February 1995, Volume 1. Issue 1. Copyright 1995 by the Toronto Airport Vineyard. Revised version Copyright 1996 by the Toronto Airport Christian Fellowship.

Creme, Benjamin. "The Gospel Story and the Path of Initiation." The Gospel Story and the Path of Initiation. Share International, n.d. Web. 07 Aug. 2016.

Creme, Benjamin. "The Requirements for Initiation." Share International, n.d. Web. 07 Aug. 2016.

Crow, Jeremy. "What Is a Luciferian and Who Is Lucifer." Luciferianism. Greater Church of Lucifer, n.d. Web

Cumby, Constance. *The Hidden Dangers of the Rainbow: The New Age Movement and Our Coming Age of Barbarism.* Revised ed. Portland: Huntington House, 1983. Print.

Cumby, Constance. *A Planned Deception the Staging of a New Age Messiah.* Stevens Pointe: Pointe Publications, 1986. Print.

Dean, Robert, Jr. "The Vineyard and the Kansas City Prophets." *World View Weekend: News.* Vol. IV, No. 2. Mar-Apr 1991. 2011. Web. 05 Oct. 2014.

Dean, Robert, Jr. WorldView Weekend. Rep. Brandon Howse, 21 July 2011. Web. Originally written and published in 1991

Deer, Jack. "Joel's Army," *Vineyard International Ministries.* 1990. Print. Transcript.

Diamond, Sara. "Notes." *Spiritual Warfare: The Politics of the Christian Right.* Boston: South End, 1989. 247. Print.

DogEmperor. "Dominionism's Parallel Economy: Corporate Sponsors." *Talk to Action.* 27 Aug. 2007. Web. 23 June 2015.

DogEmperor. "Joel's Army" and Omnicide in the Name of God. *Daily Kos.* 21 May. 2008 [Online forum comment]. Web. 3 June. 2014.

DPA. "Former Governor of Spandau Prison Dies in Berlin." *Expatria News – German News.* Expatria, 7 Nov. 2005. Web. 15 Aug. 2014.

Earl, Terri Lee. "Footnotes for Prophetic Mandate - Levels of Integrity Truthfulness and Responsibility" *Harvest Net.* Originally published July 1999. Web. 9 Feb. 2015.

Earl, Terri Lee. "Rick Joyner and Charisma Magazine." *Harvest Net.* Harvest Net, n.d. Web. http://harvestnet.org/lookback/joynerincharisma.htm. This is an addendum to what is commonly known as the Open Rebuke to Rick Joyner and Morningstar at http://www.harvestnet.org/lookback/godmanDec97.htm as well as its ancillary article, Trouble in Prophet Land.

Fairly, Mark. Know Your Enemy: The New World Order From a Christian Perspective. N.p.: The Fuel Project, 2011. DVD.

Farah, J. "WND Author, CBN Expose Hitler's Hatred of Christians." *WND Faith.* WND, 27 Apr. 2013. Web. 19 Dec. 2014.

Flood, Charles Bracelen. *Hitler: The Path to Power.* Boston, Mass: Houghton Mifflin Company. 1989. 261–262. Print.

Franklin, Anna. *Midsummer: Magical Celebrations of the Summer Solstice.* St. Paul: Llewellyn Publications, 2002. Print.

Full Gospel Business Men's Voice: 1981–1982, Volumes 29–30. Print.

Giberti, R. Scott. *Paul Cain--A Prophet in the Hall of Kings: Between Iraq (eh-rok) and a Hard Place*. Lakewood: First Stone, LLC, 2011. Print.

"God's Bartender in Good Spirits" *Mail & Guardian* March 16, 2012. Web. 10 June. 2015

Gore, Al. *The Assault on Reason*. New York: Penguin, 2007. Print.

"Grace Communion International" Is the Sabbath Required for Christians Today? GCI.org, n.d. Web. 08 Aug. 2016.

Grady, Lee J. "Morningstar Ministries Backs out of Prophetic Retreat Center Plan." *Charisma Magazine*. Charisma Magazine, 10 Dec. 2000. Web. 10 Dec. [no longer available at http://www.charismanews.com].

Grady, Lee J. "Prophetic Minister Paul Cain Issues Public Apology for Immoral Lifestyle." *Charisma Magazine*. Charisma Magazine, 28 Feb. 2005. Web. 17 Apr. 2013.

Gruen, Ernie, *Documentation of the Aberrant Practices and Teachings of the Kansas City Prophets* exact date unknown. [Documentation provided to the author by Ernie Gruen].

Hachmeister, Lutz, and Michael Kloft. "The Man Behind Hitler (Transcript) Diary Entry for October 16, 1928." *American Experience*. PBS. Web. 23 Apr. 2015.

Hafiz, Yasmine. "General 'Jerry' Boykin Says Gun-Toting Jesus Will Lead 'Mighty Army' During Second Coming." *The Huffington Post*. 20 Feb. 2014. Web. 26 May 2015.

Hamilton, J. Taylor & Kenneth G. Hamilton. *The History of the Moravian Church*. Bethlehem, PA: Moravian Church in America. 1967.30. Print.

Harnon, Cedric. "God's Lightning Rod." *Charisma Magazine* 1 Apr. 2001. Print.

Hattemer-Higgins, Ida. "Hitler's Bodyguard." *Salon*. Salon, 21 Feb. 2005. Web. 8 Mar. 2013.

Heindel, M. *The Rosicrucian Mysteries an Elementary Exposition of their Secret Teachings*. University of Michigan Library. 1916. Print.

Herrou Aragon, Jose Maria. The Forbidden Religion. Raleigh: Lulu, 2011. Print.

Hitler, Adolf, *Mein Kampf*, Ralph Mannheim, ed., New York: Mariner Books. 1999. 161. Print.

Hitler, Adolph. *My New Order*. New York: Reynal & Hitchcock. 1941. 147. Print.

Hitler, Adolph. Quoted by Hermann Rauschning, Hitler ma'a dit [Hitler Speaks] p.147, translated in *The Occult and the Third Reich*, Jean & Michel Angebert, p.178.

"Hitler's Escape." *Mystery Quest*. New York, NY: A&E History Channel. 2009. [Television series episode].

Holford, David. "North Carolina College of Theology." *David's Daily Diversions*. 30 July 2011. Web. 19 May 2015.

Holley, Gregory. "About Us: Statement of Vision and Mission." *Independent Christian Churches International*. Web. 23 May 2015.

Holley, Gregory. "President: Biography" *Independent Christian Churches International*. Web. 23 May 2015.

"The Hospitallers - 501C3 Nonprofit - La Porte, TX - 272088495." *Tax Exempt World*. Web. 22 May 2015.

Howland, C.L. *A Brief Story of Our Church: A Historical Outline of the Origin and Growth of the Free Methodist Church of North America*. Free Methodist Publication House; Winona Lake. 1953. Print.

Hislop, The Two Babylons, 2nd American ed.(Neptune, New Jersey: Loizeaux Brothers, 1959)

"Inside The Revolution by Lt. General Jerry Boykin." *YouTube*. 11 Apr. 2011. Web. 26 May 2015. https://www.youtube.com/watch?v=tVmnGlmD5is.

Jennings, Hargrave. *The Rosicrucians, Their Rites and Mysteries*. New York: Arno, 1976. Print.

Jones, Bob. Kansas City Fellowship, 1988 Print. Transcript.

Jones, Bob. "To the 3rd Heaven." {Bob Jones} To the 3rd Heaven. The Quickened Word, n.d. Web. 09 Aug. 2016.

Jones, Bob. *"Visions and Revelations: Prophetic History of the Kansas City Fellowship."* 1988. Audio Cassette.

Jones, Bob. Vineyard Prophecy Conference 1989 as cited in "The New Order" Jewel van der Merwe, 7. 1991. Print.

Joyner, Rick. "Advertisement for Conference." *MorningStar Prophetic Bulletin* (1994). Print.

Joyner, Rick. "A Prophetic History Part III." *The MorningStar Journal* 18.3. 2008. Print.

Joyner, Rick. "The History and Future of the Present Revival, Part 8." *MorningStar Ministries*. 1 Jan. 2008. Web. 20 Apr. 2015. http://www.morningstarministries .org/resources/special-bulletins/2008/history-and-future-present-revival-part -8#.VTRy82yUDIU.

Joyner, Rick. "The History of Moravian Falls, North Carolina Part II." *Prophetic Perspectives*. MorningStar TV. 2012. Television.

Joyner, Rick. "Joel's Army." *The Harvest*. New Kensington, PA: Whitaker House, 1993. Print

Joyner, Rick. "Knights of Malta: Is The OSJ Connected to the Masons?" *MorningStar: Questions and Answers. MorningStar Publications and Ministries*, 26 June 2007. Web. 2 May 2015.

Joyner, Rick. "Report from the Round Table by Rick Joyner Prophetic Bulletin #15." *MorningStar Publications and Ministries*, 1 Jan. 1996. Web. 21 Apr. 2015.

Joyner, Rick. "Rick Joyner with Dutch Sheets: The True Soldiers of the Cross are Mobilizing. The Church is about to be Clothed with a Beauty that is Beyond this World!" *Elijah List*. Steve Shultz, 2007. Web. 9 Nov. 2014.

Joyner, Rick "The Spiritual Significance of the Japanese Earthquake." *Prophetic Perspectives*. MorningStar TV. 2011.

Joyner, Rick. "Taking the Land-We Are Establishing Our Eternal Place and Position Here On Earth." *Elijah List*. Steve Shultz, 29 Nov. 2005. Web. 19 Mar. 2015.

Joyner, R. *There Were Two Trees in the Garden*. Springdale, PA: Whitaker House. 1986. Print.

Joyner, Rick. "War and Glory." MorningStar Journal 4.2 (1994): 56–65. Print.

Joyner, Rick. "The Warrior Nation: A New Trumpet Sound." *MorningStar Prophetic Bulletin* 2006–1.49 2006. *MorningStar Ministries*. Web. 19 Mar. 2015.

Joyner, Rick. "Why I Joined the Knights of Malta." Questions and Answers: Knights of Malta. MorningStar Ministries, 26 June 2007. Web

Joyner, Rick. "Words for the Coming Times." New Year's Eve. MorningStar Ministries Charlotte NC. 31 Dec. 1997. Cassette Tape.

Judge, John. "Jonestown: A Review by John Judge." Jonestown. *Spike News*, 6 Feb. 2014. Web. 9 July 2015.

Kandell, Jonathan. "Kurt Waldheim Dies at 88; Ex-UN Chief Hid Nazi Past." *The New York Times Europe.* The New York Times, 1 June 2007. Web. 3 Nov. 2014.

Keeler, Bob. "Waldheim Knighthood Upsets Jews." Tribune Digital-SunSentinel. *SunSentinel*, 28 July 1994. Web. 22 Sept. 2014.

Klee, E. Persilscheine und falsche pässe: wie die kirchen den nazis halfen ("whitewash certificates and false passports. Frankfurt am Main: Fischer-Taschenbuch-Verlag. 1991. Print.

"Knights Hospitaller." *Knights Hospitallers: Mimic Orders. New World Encyclopedia.* Web. 6 May 2015.

Lachman, Gary. *Politics and the Occult: The left, the right, and the radically unseen.* Quest Books; 1st Quest Ed. 2008. Print.

Lachman, Gary. "Why Mrs. Blake Cried by Marsha Keith Schuchard: The Lineaments of Gratified Desire." *The Independent.* Independent Digital News and Media, 12 Mar. 2006. Web. 5 Sept. 2014.

"Latter Rain and Manifest Sons of God." *Way of Life Literature.* Way of Life Literature, 8 Mar. 2012. Web. 14 May 2014. www.wayoflife.org/index_files/latter_rain_and_manifest_sons_of_god.html.

"A Leading Figure in the New Apostolic Reformation." *NPR.* NPR, 3 Oct. 2011. Web. 21 July 2014. http://www.npr.org/2011/10/03/140946482/apostolic-leader-weighs-religions-role-in-politics.

Leslie, Sarah. "Dominionism and the Rise of Christian Imperialism." *Discernment Ministries.* Discernment Ministries, n.d. Web. 15 May 2013. http://www.discernment-ministries.org/ChristianImperialism.htm.

Levenda, Peter. "Sukarno's Gold." *The Hitler Legacy: The Nazi Cult in Diaspora: How It Was Organized, How It Was Funded, and Why It Remains a Threat to Global Security in the Age of Terrorism.* Lake Worth: Ibis, 2013. 273. Print.

"Luciferianism – What Is It?" Compelling Truth. Got Questions Ministries, n.d. Web.

Mackey, A, G., and Haywood, H. L. *Encyclopedia of Freemasonry Volume I.* Kessinger Publishing, LLC. 2010. Print.

Mandelbaum, W. Adam. *The Psychic Battlefield: A History of the Military-occult Complex.* New York: St. Martin's, 2000. Print.

Mantyla, Kyle. "Joyner: 'Our Only Hope Is A Military Takeover'" *Right Wing Watch*, 1 Oct. 2013. Web. 27 May 2015.

Martin, Walter, Jill Martin Rische, and Kurt Van Gorden. *The Kingdom of the Occult*. Nashville, TN: Thomas Nelson, 2008. Print.

McCumber, Mishel. "Adrift In the River of God." *Deception Bytes*. N.d., Web. 9 Feb. 2015.

McCumber, Mishel. "The Hidden Agenda of the Order of the Mustard Seed." *Deception Bytes*. N.d., Web. 9 Feb. 2015.

McCumber, Mishel. "Spiritual Drunkenness." *Deception Bytes*. N.d., Web. 25 Oct. 2014.

Meiers, Michael. Was Jonestown a CIA Medical Experiment?: A Review of the Evidence. Lewiston, NY: E. Mellen, 1988. Print.

MorningStar Ministries. 15 Jan. 2001. Ministry support team membership advertisement letter. (delivered February 28, 2001. Page 3, 3rd full paragraph).

Morrill, Jim, and Nancy Stancill. "Amway the Yager Way." NewsLibrary. The Charlotte Observer, 19 Mar. 1995. Web. 23 Sept. 2014. http://www.amquix.info/tosp/YAGER1.htm.

"Nazi War Criminals Released 1966." *Unused Material Media URN: 89973*. British Pathe. Film ID: 3215.05, Spandau, Germany, n.d. *Nazi War Criminals Released 1966*. Web. 14 May 2015.

"The Origins in Revival." A Brief History of Harmony Community Church 1885–2008. *Harmony Community Church 2013*. N.d., Web 30 Oct. 2013.

Panek, Joseph. "A Seeker's Thoughts." The Sword. N.p., 18 Nov. 2008. Web. 07 Aug. 2016.

"Past Grand Masters." *Knights Hospitallers of the Sovereign Order of St. John of Jerusalem-Knights of Malta the Ecumenical Order*. Knights Hospitallers of the Sovereign Order of St. John of Jerusalem-Knights of Malta the Ecumenical Order, 1 Jan. 2013. Web. 21 Apr. 2015. http://shosj.org/web/past_grand_masters.html.

Parrott, Jorge. "Mission Base Update April 1, 2013." *Missions MorningStar*. MorningStar Ministries, 3 Dec. 2012. Web. 15 Apr. 2015. http://missionsbase.eaglemissions.org/2012/12/03/moravian-falls-december-1-2012.

Philp, Rowan. "God's Bartender in Good Spirits." *Mail & Guardian*. Mail & Guardian, 16 Mar. 2012. Web. 6 June 2014.

Piccolo, B.J. July 2008. Vol. 1. The Grail Newsletters. Web. http://www.brianjohnpiccolo.com/The-Grail-Newsletters/2008-July-The-Grail-Vol-1.pdf.

Poloma, Margaret, "Toronto Blessing" *M. Hartford Institute for Religion Research* February 1998. Web. 03 Jan. 2015

Poloma, Margaret M. 1996a. "By Their Fruits: A Sociological Assessment of the Toronto Blessing." Paper presented at the *Society for Pentecostal Studies Annual Meeting*. Toronto.

Poloma, Margaret M. 1996b. "The 'Toronto Blessing' in Postmodern Society: Manifestations Metaphor and Myth." Paper presented at *The Globalization of Pentecostalism Conference*. San Jose, Costa Rica. June.

"Prophetic History of the Moravian Falls Land and Mountain View Retreat Center." The History of Moravian Falls. *MorningStar Ministries*. N.d., Web. 19 July 2015. http://missionsbase.eaglemissions.org/

Prophetic History of the Moravian Falls Land and Mountain View Retreat Center."
MorningStar Ministries Missions Base. MorningStar Ministries. 2008. Web. 8
Apr. 2015. http://missionsbase.eaglemissions.org/history-moravian-falls.

"A Prophetic History Part III." *Triune Last Days*. N.p., N.d., Web. 9 Feb. 2015
http://www.triunelastdays.org/articles-2/a-prophetic-history-part-iii.

Pytches, David. *Some Said It Thundered*. London: Hodder & Stoughton, 1990. 52. Print.

Rauschning, Hermann. *Hitler Speaks*. London: Thornton Butterworth, 1939. Print.

Ray, S. E. "Todd Bentley, Fresh Fire Ministries and Lakeland Revival." *Deception in the
Church*. Deception in the Church, n.d. Web. 25 Mar. 2014. http://www
.deceptioninthechurch.com.

Reckhart, G. "The Tragic Car Wreck and Branham's Tomb Stone." Branham's Car and
His Occult Tomb Stone. *Jesus Messiah Network of Websites*, n.d. Web. 20 Apr. 2014.
http://jesus-messiah.com/branham/car-tomb.html.

Rimius, H. *A Candid Narrative of the Rise and Progress of the Herrnhuters, Commonly Called
Moravians, or, Unitas Fratrum; with a Short Account of their Doctrines, Drawn from
their own Writings*. London: Linde, A., Stationer to his Majesty and to his Royal
Highness the Prince of Wales, in Catherine-Street in the Strand. 1753(a). Print.

Rimius, H. *The history of the Moravians: from their first settlement at Herrnhaag in the Country
of Budingen, down to the present time; with a view chiefly to their political Intrigues*. London.
1754(b). Print.

Rimius, H. *A Second Solemn Call on Mr. Zinzendorf: Otherwise Call'd Count Zinzendorf, &c.
the Author and Advocate of the Sect of Herrnhuters, Commonly Known by the Name of
Moravians to Answer All and Every Charge Brought Against Them, With Some Remarks
Concerning a Pamphlet, Intitled, An Essay Toward the Personal Character of Count
Zinzendorf*. London: Linde, A., bookseller to her Royal Highness the Princess of
Wales, in Catherine-Street in the Strand. 1757. Print.

Rimius, H. (1754). *A Solemn Call On Count Zinzendorf: The Author, And Advocate Of
The Sect Of Herrnhuters, Commonly Called Moravians, to answer every charge brought
against them in the Candid Narrative with some further Observation on the Spirit of that
Sect*. London: Linde, A., Stationer to his Majesty and to his Royal Highness the
Prince of Wales; and bookseller to her Royal Highness the Princess of Wales, in
Catherine-Street in the Strand. 1754(a). Print.

Rimius, H. *A supplement to the author's A candid narrative of the rise and progress of the
Herrnhuters, commonly call'd Moravians or Unitas Fratrum, in which, among other things,
the political scheme and artful proceedings of their patriarch are disclosed, and a number of
authentic documents produced, to sow in what light the sect has been considered by foreign
powers and learned universities*. London; A. Linde, bookseller to her Royal Highness
the Princess of Wales, in Catherine-Street in the Strand. 1753(b). Print.

Rosenberg, Paul. "America's Own Taliban." Al Jazeera. *Al Jazeera*. 28 July 2011. Web.
13 June 2015.

Rosio, Bob. Hitler & the New Age, Huntington House, 1993. 137–144. Print.

Row, A. *Masonic Biography and Dictionary: Comprising the History of Ancient Masonry*.
Philadelphia: J.B. Lippincott & Co. 2008. Print

"Sacrilege." Collins English Dictionary – Complete and Unabridged, 12th Edition

2014. 1991, 1994, 1998, 2000, 2003, 2006, 2007, 2009, 2011, 2014. HarperCollins Publishers 10 Aug. 2016

"Sacrilege." Collins Thesaurus of the English Language – Complete and Unabridged 2nd Edition. 1995, 2002. HarperCollins Publishers 10 Aug. 2016

Sainty, Guy Stair. *The Orders of Saint John: The History, Structure, Membership and Modern Role of the Five Hospitaller Orders of Saint John of Jerusalem.* New York: American Society of the Most Venerable Order of the Hospital of Saint John in Jerusalem for the Benefit of Saint John Ophthalmic Hospital in Jerusalem, 1991. Print.

Schuchard, Marsha, Keith. "Why Mrs. Blake Cried Swedenborg Blake And The Sexual Basis Of Spiritual Vision." *MSU- Esoteric.* Michigan State University, 2006. Web. 4 Jan. 2014. http://www.esoteric.msu.edu/VolumeII/BlakeFull.html.

Selby, S. A. The Axmann Conspiracy: The Nazi Plan for a Fourth Reich and How the U.S. Army Defeated it. New York, NY: Berkley Books. 2012. Print.

"Seven Mountains." *Herescope.* Discernment Research Group, 24 June 2010. Web. 7 Feb. 2014. http://herescope.blogspot.ca.

Shantz, Douglas H. *An Introduction to German Pietism: Protestant Renewal at the Dawn of Modern Europe.* Baltimore: Johns Hopkins UP, 2013. Print.

Slayford-Wey, Lian. The History and Significance of the God: Emma-O. *Hellium.* 2009. Web. 26 August 2015.

Sovereign Military Hospitaller, 816 F. Supp. 2d at 1294 n.2. United States Court of Appeals, Eleventh Circuit. SOVEREIGN MILITARY HOSPITALLER ORDER OF SAINT JOHN OF JERUSALEM OF RHODES AND OF MALTA, Plaintiff–Counter Defendant–Appellant, v. The FLORIDA PRIORY OF the KNIGHTS HOSPITALLERS OF the SOVEREIGN ORDER OF SAINT JOHN OF JERUSALEM, KNIGHTS OF MALTA, The ECUMENICAL ORDER, Defendant–Counter Claimant–Appellee. No. 11–15101. Decided: December 18, 2012. Web. 08 October 2014

"Sovereign Order of St John of Jerusalem, Knights of Malta 1956." *Sovereign Order of St John of Jerusalem, Knights of Malta Research Webpages.* Web. 22 May 2015.

Spangler, David. Reflections on the Christ. Moray: Findhorn, 1981. Print.

Spelman, F. "Albert Speer Talks of Spandau, His Atonement—and Hitler's Strange Affection for Him." *People Magazine,* 12 April 1976. Vol. 5. No. 14. Print.

Spencer, D., Myers, G., Steven. *Social Psychology* (3rd Canadian ed.). Toronto: McGraw-Hill Ryerson. 2006. Print.

"Structure and Organization of the Order of Malta." *Museum of the Order of Malta,* 1 Jan. 1998. Web. 21 Apr. 2015.

Sturgeon, Brian. *Holiness Movement in Eastern Ontario and Western Quebec and the Sturgeon Family.* 1 May 2008. Untitled entry [Weblog post] Web. 17 April 2014. http://www.bytown.net/holiness.htm.

"Swedish Order of the Amaranth." *Knights Hospitallers of the Sovereign Order of St. John of Jerusalem-Knights of Malta the Ecumenical Order.* 1 Jan. 2012. Web. 21 Apr. 2015. http://theknightshospitallers.org/swedish-order-amaranth.

Synan, Vinson. *The Holiness–Pentecostal Tradition: Charismatic Movements in the Twentieth*

Century. Grand Rapids, Michigan: William B. Eerdmans Publishing Company, 1997. Print.

Tashman, Brian. "Dominionism at MorningStar Ministries." *Right Wing Watch.* 14 Oct. 2011. Web. 27 May 2015.

Turcopilier. "Papanicolaou and the So-called "Ecumenical Order" Lose in the Court of Appeals." Chivalry and Honor. Blogspot, 21 Sept. 2012. Web.

Van Der Merwe, Travers & Jewel. *Strange Fire: The Rise of Gnosticism in the Church.* Conscience Press 1995. Print.

"Wachovia." William S. Powell, ed. Encyclopedia of North Carolina. *University of North Carolina Press:* Chapel Hill, NC 2006. Print.

Wagner, C. P. May 2007 letter, posted at http://www.erwm.com/ApostolicLetter.htm. As found at apprising.org/2011/09/04/documenting-dominionism. Web. 04 Aug. 2015.

Wanagas, Ewald A. *The Revival & Outpouring of the Holy Spirit: Things I Have Seen and Heard,* North Battleford: Sharon Children's Homes and Schools. 2000. Print.

Wilder, Forrest. "Rick Perry's Army of God." *The Texas Observer.* The Texas Observer, 03 Aug. 2011. Web. 21 Sept. 2014.

"William Branham: Healing and Heresy." Africa Center for Apologetics Research. *Africa Center for Apologetics Research,* 2008. Web. 21 Sept. 2014..

Woer, Samael Wor. *The Major Mysteries: The Gnostic Jesus and the Path of Initiation* Glorian Publishing; 2 ed. 2013. Print.

"World Public Forum – Dialogue of Civilizations for Successful Global Changes (About)." *World Public Forum.* Web. 21 Apr. 2015. http://wpfdc.org/about-us/about.

Youngblood, Ronald F. *Nelson's New Illustrated Bible Dictionary.* Nashville: T. Nelson, 1995. 147. Print.

Yurica, Katherine. "Infiltrating the U.S. Military: Gen. Boykin's Kingdom Warriors." *Yurica Report: News Intelligence Analysis.* 12 Oct. 2004. Web. 26 May 2015.

ABOUT THE AUTHOR

Mishel McCumber is a writer, researcher and artist, who spent close to twenty years deeply indoctrinated in the Dominionist Movement. After an extended period of study and detoxification, she made it her mission to educate others on the dangers of apostate faith and instill in them a desire for sound biblical doctrine.

She holds a BA in Psychology, a BA in Media Arts, and is currently finishing an MA in English. She makes her home in the United States but is temporarily residing in Canada with two ridiculously spoiled rescue cats.